Liquid Jade

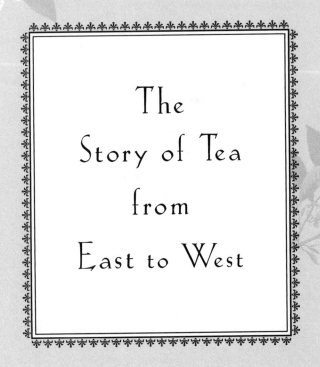

The Story of Tea from East to West

ST. MARTIN'S PRESS
New York

Liquid Jade

Beatrice
Hohenegger

To all the children on all the tea plantations
in the hope for a better future,
and to my own Sofie and Martin

www.stmartins.com

Design by Kathryn Parise

LIBRARY OF CONGRESS CATALOGING-IN-PUBLICATION DATA

Hohenegger, Beatrice.
    Liquid jade : the story of tea from east to west / Beatrice Hohenegger. — 1st ed.
    p. cm.
    Includes bibliographical references and index.
    ISBN-13: 978-0-312-33328-7
    ISBN-10: 0-312-33328-5
    1. Tea—History.   2. Tea—Social aspects.   3. Tea trade—history.   I. Title.
GT2905.H65 2006
394.1'2—dc22

                                                    2006017724

First Edition: December 2006

10   9   8   7   6   5   4   3   2   1

Contents

Acknowledgments

Delving into the profound and multidimensional subject of tea, I have come in contact with many people around the world (see Notes for individual names and acknowledgments where appropriate)—academics and independent scholars; technicians and experts in the different tea specialties; growers and inspectors; museum curators and art collectors; tea masters and tea aficionados; tasters, brokers, and nutritional scientists; social activists and laborers; and librarians willing to go on a quest for rare and precious books for me—all ready to give their time, to share information, to point me in the right direction. A profound and heartfelt thank-you to all. The human connection with you is as important as the help I received. The knowledge and expertise is yours; any mistakes that might have occurred in the transfer are only mine.

Thank you to Diane Reverand, my editor, for believing in this first-time author and for her guidance—Diane helped me see what I didn't want to see, and I am a better writer for it. I'm also grateful to assistant editor Regina Scarpa for her warm presence and unfailing efficiency. Thank you to Henry Dunow for being not only a great agent but a great human being—forthright, caring, and with an excellent sense of what really matters in the world. I am indebted to my

LAEWG friends, who insisted I should write a book in the first place when I thought such a thing was an utter impossibility, and who patiently read parts of my manuscript and made invaluable suggestions. Thank you to my brother and graphic designer, Alberto Hohenegger, for his ongoing expert advice and hands-on help during the fascinating and challenging process of image selection for the book—I did test his patience repeatedly, and yet we are still on speaking terms.

And a very special and affectionate thank-you to Lenny Isenberg for making it possible for me to work on this project and also for being the kind of man who passes the tea cozy test (the one by Scottish comedian Billy Connolly: "Never trust a man who, when left alone in a room with a tea cozy, doesn't try it on").

$\mathcal{P}reface$

What drew me to tea initially was opium. I researched the dark chapter of British colonial trade affairs that forged a sinister link between the two commodities. This led me to look into tea's existence and significance during the time before the British arrived on the scene, which opened up a fascinating door into the wisdom and the refined sensibilities of Chinese and Japanese thought. From those ancient cultures I learned how tea was used as a medicinal brew in the hills and jungles of Southeast Asia, how it played a central role in the development of Taoist and Zen spirituality, how it stimulated the literary and visual arts, to this day admired and imitated throughout the world. I tried to convey this atmosphere of early tea lore and culture in Part 1 of the book. (Please note that I used the old Wade-Giles system of romanization of Chinese names, rather than the more modern pinyin, in order to be more consistent with historical sources. Please refer to the table in Appendix B for more information.)

After the Western traders arrived on the Eastern shores, tea underwent a profound transformation. The sacred beverage, the elixir of immortality, was reduced to a commodity. The more I researched historical events, the more the story of tea became the story of the traumatic encounter and clash of cultures between East and West

(Part 2). Yet, within this large story I began to see many individual stories and tales around tea—the introduction of the beverage to Europe, the surprising connections to other commodities, tea's role as casus belli in the New World and as major product of the British empire in colonial India, with all its tragic consequences. Tales of conflict and adventure, of treachery and greed, and sometimes of romance and humor. In my research I began to fish these tales from the sea of history as though they were pearls of dazzling but disquieting beauty. Then came the work of polishing them and stringing them into a storytelling sequence.

Part 3 is a small, and certainly not comprehensive, collection of diverse and informative topics around tea. Some are of historical interest—for example, the discovery of the tea plant, or the etymology of the word *tea*. Others relate curious beginnings, such as how the tea bag and iced tea were born. Some provide basic factual information around the beverage—types of tea, the importance of water, caffeine content. Yet others explain misnomers—*high tea*—or describe lesser-known areas in the tea world—the profession of the tea taster. The last chapter of this section comes back full circle to the very beginnings of tea as a remedy, exploring how Western science is devoting increasing attention to the ancient Chinese claims of the many health benefits of tea.

The last part of the book (Part 4) is somewhat different in tone from the rest. Here, I explore contemporary issues and circumstances around today's tea trade. This was not my initial intent, but researching the past brought urgent and unavoidable questions about the present. What is the state of things in the world of tea today? In what practical ways can we in the West begin to address the social inequities initiated by colonialism and perpetuated in today's trade practices? And what is the condition of the earth, of a soil dried out and deadened by decades of chemical agriculture in the large tea plantations? I researched the principles of sustainability, fair trade, and organic agriculture as possible, and perhaps even imperative, answers to these questions; our planet is running out of options. I only sketched out what I see as the main themes around these issues. In a world where one-sixth of the global population lives on less than a dollar a day and our ecosystems are breaking down before our eyes, these are questions that lie close to my heart and certainly merit further attention.

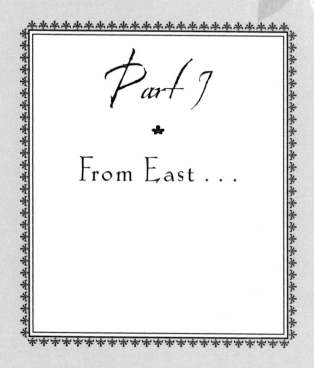

Part 1

❧

From East . . .

Behind the Veils of Legend and Myth

On the peaks of Mount Ling,
a wondrous thing is gathered:
It is tea.
Every valley and hill is luxuriously covered
with this wealth of the Earth,
blessed with the sweet spirit of Heaven.
In the month of the harvest moon,
the farmers get little rest.
Couples at the same task, searching and picking.
Take water from the flowing river Min,
drawn from its pure currents.
Select vessels and choose ceramics
produced from Eastern Ou.
Emulate the example of Duke Liu:
Serve tea with a gourd ladle;
In only this way can one begin to perfect
thick froth, afloat with the 'splendor of the brew:'
Lustrous like piling snow,
resplendent like the spring florescence.

—Tu Yü, *Ode to Tea*, fourth century C.E.

Tea is not only the most consumed beverage on the face of the Earth; aside from water, it is also one of the oldest known to humankind. Its beginnings date back to a time before history, behind the veils of legend and myth.

The ancient Chinese healers believed that the spirit and essence of the Great Mother Goddess flowed from the center of the Earth into plants and minerals. They collected and experimented with herbs and stones thought to contain varying degrees of "soul substance," which was beneficial for health and longevity. The plants and stones that stored up the greatest amount of soul substance were the ones with "good color." Jade, for example, was considered very powerful on account of its brilliant shades of green. The good color may be what attracted the healers also to the luscious, evergreen tea plant and might explain why, in China, tea as a beverage came to be known as the "froth of the liquid jade," in honor of the much revered magical stone.

One such healer was Shen Nung, the second of China's three San Huang, the mythical emperors and forefathers of Chinese civilization. The word *shen* refers to a benevolent spirit and is associated with the positive, enlightened aspect of reality. According to the legend, Shen Nung was born in the twenty-eighth century B.C.E. (Before Common Era) to a beautiful young princess who was possessed by a heavenly dragon. Shen Nung had the head and horns of a bull and the body of a man; he spoke after three days and walked after seven. With the invention of the plow he gave his people the gift of agriculture, for which he earned the title of Divine Husbandman. He also studied herbs and developed many herbal remedies. Some say Shen Nung had a transparent stomach, which he used as a research laboratory: he would taste leaves, fruits, berries, and roots of all sorts, observing the effects and thus determining the toxicity or usefulness of each plant. It is said that one day during his experiments he was poisoned seventy-two times. For his invaluable contributions in the field of herbal remedies, he was elevated to the status of patron saint of Chinese apothecaries. The story of how he discovered tea has become a touchstone of tea lore around the world.

During one of his expeditions the emperor was traveling through a hilly region of the south of China. It was late in the afternoon. The emperor was tired and ordered his party to stop for a break. His aides

The Bohea range was a renowned tea-growing region in southeast China. The word *Bohea* is a corruption of the Chinese Woo-e or Wu-i (Wu-i shan is a different spelling of the same name).

Woo-e-shan, or Bohea Hills, Fo-Kien, by Thomas Allom, engraving, England, c. 1840s. Reprinted from Wright, *The Chinese Empire: Historical and Descriptive,* 1843.

were setting up camp and boiling some water in a kettle—the emperor had taught his people that only boiled water was safe—when a sudden wind blew down from the hills. Some dried leaves from a nearby bush whirled up in the air and fell into the boiling water. Ever the curious herbalist, the emperor decided to try the concoction. He liked the refreshing and slightly bitter flavor and felt cheerful and energetic that evening. His experience taught him that there was much soul substance in those leaves, so he collected some and took them home to experiment. They were, of course, the leaves from a tea bush. Thus humanity is said to have received the delightful gift of tea. The year was 2732 B.C.E.

This curiously exact date, for such an ancient story, provides only the illusion of historical precision and is most likely the result of the Chinese habit of adjusting tales and dates to correspond to the didactic goal of the moment. Though it is generally accepted that in the beginning tea was used as a health remedy, not a leisure drink, the search for its verifiable first uses and true origins is challenging at best. The *Pen Ts'ao ching*, one of the earliest and most important medical books in China, in which tea is mentioned, was attributed to Shen Nung and therefore held as proof of the existence of tea very early on. But it was written much later, during the later-Han period (25–220 C.E.), by unknown authors, and tea appears to have been added three more centuries after that. Yet, aside from historical discrepancies, the *Pen Ts'ao ching* does contain interesting information about tea, including insightful commentaries such as: "Tea is better than wine for it leadeth not to intoxication, neither does it cause a man to say foolish things, and repent thereof in his sober moments. It is better than water for it does not carry disease; neither does it act like a poison, as does water when the wells contain foul and rotten matter."

According to French ethnobotanist Georges Métailié, it is not the *Pen Ts'ao ching* but the *History of Huayang* by Ch'ang Ch'ü that contains the oldest reference to tea. Here we find out that tea was part of a tribute offered to the Chou emperor Wu as early as the eleventh century B.C.E. Several other possible references to tea make their appearance around the beginning of our Common Era (C.E.). But because many different languages were spoken in China, and written Chinese is different from the spoken one, misunderstandings were unavoidable, and what was translated as "tea" may have meant something entirely different. The Han scholar and philosopher Yang Hsiung (53 B.C.E.–18 C.E.) was the first who examined the different languages and wrote a dictionary—the *Fang-yen*—in which he also mentioned that tea was first used by the inhabitants of the Szechwan and Yunnan Provinces of China. These are the southern and western regions in which tea first made the transition from a wild herb to an agricultural crop, most likely during Han times (206 B.C.E.–220 C.E.). Over time, tea cultivation also spread to other parts of China. By the third and fourth centuries C.E. credible references to tea occur relatively often. The noted physician Hua T'o is reported to have said that drinking tea makes one think better, and the *Erh-ya* dictionary gives a definition of tea as a "beverage made from the leaves by boiling." In the *Shih-shuo*, a fourth-century text, we read that the emperor Hui-ti loved tea and would offer it to his friends but "they, finding it too bitter, generally declined, feigning some indisposition." By the fifth century C.E. tea had become an article of trade as a medicinal beverage and an item of common use in China, although it was prepared mostly as a boiled concoction, often mixed with other ingredients.

Yet, though few will question that the practice of drinking tea was popularized in China, and that it was China that turned tea into the world-renowned and revered beverage it is today, the actual origin and birthplace of the tea plant itself is disputed by conflicting mythologies: China or India? According to a different legend of later-Han times, the Chinese scholar Kan-lu went to India to study Buddhism and from there brought back seven tea plants and planted them on Mount Meng-ting in Szechwan; hence, tea's origin would be India. Indeed, indigenous peoples of northeastern India may have been familiar with tea for centuries, perhaps millennia—a fact that will become of crucial importance in the story of tea, as we'll see later. Age-old, indigenous ways of making tea, not only as a beverage but as a food—pickled, with oil, salt, garlic, sesame, or mixed with fish or animal fats—are still in use today in those geographic areas. Jungle-dwelling hunter-gatherers may have passed on tea seeds and practices to neighboring Chinese populations at the beginning of agricultural civilization. But, as no written history is available, this explanation remains only a possibility. Either way, the point is moot, says William Ukers in his encyclopedic 1935 treatise *All About Tea*, because the existence of the tea plant predates national boundaries by thousands of years. From a purely botanical perspective, Mother Nature's primeval tea plantations are to be found in the hilly regions of northeastern India, southern China (Szechwan and Yunnan Provinces),

The Tao of Tea

Attain the climax of emptiness,
preserve the utmost quiet:
as myriad things act in concert,
I thereby observe the return.
Things flourish,
then each returns to its root.
Returning to the root is called stillness:
stillness is called return to Life,
return to Life is called the constant;
knowing the constant is called enlightenment.
Acts at random, in ignorance of the constant, bode ill.
Knowing the constant gives perspective;
this perspective is impartial.
Impartiality is the highest nobility;
The highest nobility is divine,
and the divine is the Way.
This Way is everlasting,
not endangered by physical death.

—Lao-tzu, *Tao-te ching*, sixth century B.C.E.

Though the beginnings of tea were medicinal, in the ancient Chinese herbalists' and healers' search for soul substance lay the seeds of Taoist thought, which would elevate tea from simple remedy to nothing less than sacred beverage and elixir of immortality.

Taoism flourished during the Warring States Period (480–221 B.C.E.), a time of great tumult in China. For more than two centuries, warlords assembled armies and new weaponry and invaded neighbor-

Lonely Temple in the Mountains, hanging scroll, ink on paper, China, Ming dynasty. Freer Gallery of Art, Smithsonian Institution, Washington, D.C. Gift of Charles Lang Freer.

ing states, fighting one another bitterly and endlessly to increase political and military control. Ultimately, the state of Ch'in emerged victorious over all other states, establishing the first unified Chinese empire in 221 B.C.E. Taoist thought developed in part as a reaction against the unstable and destructive atmosphere of the times. Disenchanted with the way of the world, followers of the Tao, the Path, found refuge in mysticism and personal and spiritual growth. They sought harmony with nature and the universe, living according to the principle of *wu-wei*—yielding to the stream of life rather than working against it. The great return to the Root, to the primeval stillness and the unity of all things, was pursued through living with mindfulness and simplicity. Many centuries later in 1906, Kakuzo Okakura, the author of *The Book of Tea*, would recognize these beliefs in Japanese tea practices and say that "Teaism is Taoism in disguise."

The concept of the immortal soul was a natural extension of Taoist views. Finding anything that could help reach immortality was a central pursuit of Taoist alchemy. And because Taoists believed that it was impossible for a soul to reach immortality if the body was not healthy, physical well-being became an essential element of spirituality. The ancient Taoist notion of integrating mind, body, and spirit for good health is one of the main foundations of Chinese medicine to this day. When the first healers discovered tea, they marveled at the multitude of benefits this magical plant appeared to offer. It kept them alert, it healed their wounds, it was an invaluable food complement, and it was a beverage safer than water. Tea was so universally good, for the body's energy and vitality and also for the spirit, that Taoist alchemists believed they had found the answer to their search. Tea became their ingredient for eternal life.

Taoist monks became the first tea-plantation owners of sorts. They started cultivating tea around the perimeter of their monasteries, which were often built at an altitude ideal for the tea bush to grow. Along with other herbs the monks grew and gathered, they dispensed tea as a remedy to nearby villagers and treated people too poor to afford a doctor's visit. Taoist monasteries were social and cultural centers, and communities grew around them, similar to the way villages developed around castles and churches in the West. Over time, tea became the daily beverage in the monasteries and acquired a revered status in the population at large. From this perspective, Taoist monks can be seen as the first propagators of the values of tea, in the realms of both health and spirituality.

According to an old Taoist story, even Lao-tzu, the father of Taoism and alleged author of the widely read *Tao-te ching*, is seen with a cup of tea in his hand before departing this world. When Lao-tzu was a very old man, he saw that his wisdom was ignored by the people and started walking away toward the west. When he arrived at the Han Pass, he found one of his disciples, Yin Hsi, waiting for him. Yin Hsi told Lao-tzu that he had been waiting for a long time. He offered his master a cup of tea and persuaded him to stop for a while and write down his teachings, which became the *Tao-te ching*.

In addition to the profound insight imparted by this sacred book, the meeting at the Han Pass is also credited as the origin of one of the friendliest and most common gestures in Chinese households: the offering of a cup of tea to a guest as a sign of hospitality. This is a Taoist act, complete in its simplicity.

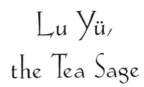

Lu Yü, the Tea Sage

Tea may be the oldest, as it is surely the most constantly congenial, reminder of the West's debt to the East.

—Francis Ross Carpenter, introduction to *The Classic of Tea— Origins and Rituals*, by Lu Yü

Tea and Taoism are linked in more ways than one. Dragon Cloud, a Taoist monastery, plays a central role in tea lore as the adoptive home of Lu Yü, the Tea Sage.

In 733 C.E. in the Hupeh Province of central China, a boy was born and abandoned along the banks of a river. Chi Ch'an, the abbot of Dragon Cloud Monastery, happened to be walking along that same river on that day and heard the newborn's wails. He followed the sound and gently picked up the boy from his little basket and carried him to the monastery. Chi Ch'an decided to adopt the boy and named him Lu Yü, a name that promised good fortune according to the Taoist classic *I Ching*, the Book of Changes. And good fortune according to delivered, for Lu Yü was to become a revered figure in all of China.

Lu grew up in the monastery but was not inclined to make monastic practices a life choice, although he was thirsty for secular knowledge and eager to learn what he could. Noticing the lack of interest in spiritual affairs, or maybe to teach him a lesson in humility, Chi Ch'an put Lu to work tending a herd of cattle. This was a demeaning task, but it didn't stop Lu from studying. Some images of Lu Yü show him sitting on the back of an ox practicing calligraphy. Lu's additional occupation while living in the monastery was that of growing, processing, and preparing tea. He became so skilled at these practices that his adoptive father claimed no one could make tea as well as his son and would drink no other tea but the one prepared by Lu Yü.

As he grew older, Lu Yü felt constricted by life in the monastery and went on the road with a group of traveling performers. After years of this wandering and adventurous life, Lu felt the need to settle and chose Chekiang Province, southeast of his native Hupeh, to do so. While there, he began work on what would become his lifetime achievement: the *Ch'a-ching,* or *The Classic of Tea.* At the time, drinking tea was a common occurrence in Chinese households and monasteries as well as a social occasion for the cultural and political elite. Tea was cultivated and traded throughout China, but the knowledge around growing, manufacturing, and the various uses and rituals of tea was scattered and passed on by oral tradition. Lu Yü changed that. For twenty years he patiently collected and codified information concerning everything there was to know about tea. Whether he was motivated by sheer passion for the subject or, as some speculate, prompted by tea growers and merchants in an effort to boost sales, we don't know. What we do know is that the *Ch'a-ching,* published in 780 C.E. became the world's first authoritative and comprehensive treatise on tea. Its popularity made Lu Yü a celebrity, admired by rich and poor, and it elevated tea to unprecedented levels of cultural prominence all across China.

Divided into three volumes and ten parts, the *Ch'a-ching* describes the origins of tea; the plucking and processing methods; the varieties of tea and the equipage necessary for drinking it; issues around the quality of water; different tea-drinking habits; stories concerning tea; and even instructions on how to copy the book on "four or six rolls of white silk." Some of the objects and elements described in the

Ch'a-ching were commonly adopted and later imported to Japan and incorporated into the Japanese tea ceremony. Lu Yü also discouraged certain practices, such as the age-old use of tea as a soup, in which other ingredients were added to the tea leaves, and the concoction was boiled for a long time. Although not disinclined to adding salt to tea water—a common habit in his time—Lu Yü didn't favor tea soup mixes and didn't mince words in commenting on them: "To brew tea with spring onions, ginger, jujube, quince, dogwood berries, peppermint and the like, all thrown in for show and boiled to a hundred

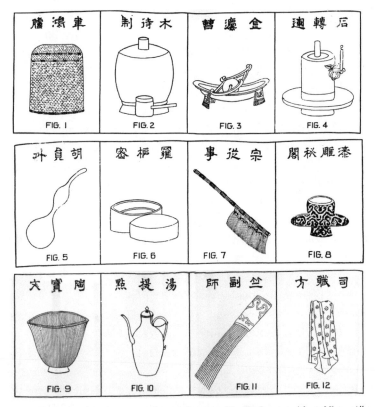

Utensils used in the preparation of tea in the time of Lu Yü. Reprinted from Ukers, *All About Tea*, 1935.

boilings until the froth boils away—this is simply ditch and gutter slop, but it is nonetheless a common and ceaseless custom."

In T'ang China (618–907 C.E.), the use of tea was already widespread, so widespread that the government had recognized the income potential and levied a tax on tea as a trading commodity. The notoriety of the *Ch'a-ching* contributed to an even further expansion of tea, from what had so far been limited to the medicinal realm to society at large. As a social beverage, tea became an object of cultural expression and the initiator of a fashion craze, which lasted well into the Sung dynasty (960–1280 C.E.), albeit with different types of tea. T'ang tea was cake tea, made of tea leaves that were processed and compressed into different round or square shapes. From these cakes, pieces were broken off and boiled in a water cauldron, and then the tea was poured into bowls. Sung tea aficionados were more favorably predisposed toward powdered tea, made of finely ground tea leaves, and whipped with bamboo whisks and hot water in the individual bowls. Powdered tea, bamboo whisks, and tea bowls would later become the essential elements of ceremonial *matcha* tea in Japan. Either way, drinking tea became not only a harmonious accompaniment to the flourishing of the visual and literary arts within the splendors of T'ang and Sung cultures, but also an art form in and of itself. Poets composed odes to the wonders of tea. Tea parties and various forms of ceremonies were held at the imperial court and in aristocratic salons. The appreciation of tea utensils as artistic objects became an integral component of a tea party. For the common folk, tea stalls appeared at street corners and in marketplaces, where a traveler or an errand boy could stop for a moment of rest and buy a bowl of tea. Tea had a special place in people's lives, and tea affairs prospered.

But the *Ch'a-ching's* success was not just a result of its practical instructions or its social role in fashionable circles. Steeped in Taoist and Confucian thought, the book had succeeded in associating the art of tea with the Taoist value of living life in the present moment— "always sip tea as if tea were life itself"—and the Confucian emphasis on the harmony of ritual. Lu Yü believed that the ritualized act of drinking tea was an act of consciousness and a celebration of life. He saw the moment of tea as an opportunity to recenter the self, away from everyday pressures, and the ritual of tea as a means to create beauty and peace, essential elements of life. This was true for the warrior and the peasant, the merchant and the king. In his own way, Lu had come back to the spiritual beginnings he had rejected, seeing tea drinking as an earthly joy as well as a path to higher realms.

Aside from his spiritual growth, another event brought Lu close to his adoptive father again. At the height of his career, Lu Yü was summoned to the imperial court one day without being given a reason. The emperor had heard that Dragon Cloud's abbot, Chi Ch'an, had given up drinking tea since he could not enjoy the one prepared by his son. The emperor simply could not believe that Lu's tea could be so far superior to anything else. He therefore invited the abbot to court and offered him a bowl of tea prepared by his most expert court lady. Chi Ch'an tasted it politely and quietly put the bowl down. Now the emperor had Lu, who was waiting in another room, prepare a second bowl of tea, without telling him for whom it was intended. He was sure the abbot would not be able to tell the difference. But Chi Ch'an was ecstatic. This, finally, was a good bowl of tea! "Not even my son could do better than this!" he exclaimed. The emperor was amazed and humbled. Calling Lu to the presence of the "unknown guest," he was nonetheless happy to have created the opportunity for their long-overdue reunion.

Lu Yü spent the last years of his life in seclusion, writing other books, including one on water—a very important factor in the quality of tea—all of which are now unfortunately lost. He died in 804 a national icon and a cultural hero. Among the stories he reported in the third part of the *Ch'a-ching*, one stands out as an allegory on the power of tea. During the reign of Emperor Yüan-ti of the Ch'in dynasty, an old woman went to market every day and sold tea from her kettle. All day long customers stopped by her stall to get their tea, and all day long she filled their cups from her kettle. And yet, no matter how many cups she filled, the kettle remained mysteriously full. At the end of the day, the old woman distributed the money she had received for her tea to poor people she met along the road. But some of the market people grew suspicious, or perhaps jealous, of her behavior and notified the authorities, who promptly had her incarcerated. That same evening the old woman flew out the window of the jail on the kettle from which she sold her tea.

The *Ch'a-ching* is still in print today—twelve hundred years after its first publication—not only in China but throughout the world.

I Care Not a Jot for Immortal Life, but Only for the Taste of Tea

> The effect of tea is cooling and as a beverage it is most suitable. It is especially fitting for persons of self-restraint and inner worth.
>
> —Lu Yü, *The Classic of Tea—Origins and Rituals*
> (Carpenter translation)

The T'ang period was the height of Chinese tea culture. If Lu Yü was tea's chronicler, Lu T'ung (775–835 C.E.) was its poet. His poem "Writing Thanks to Censor Meng for Sending New Tea" is as much a testament to the glory of T'ang tea as Lu Yü's book is. The verses about the seven bowls of tea are some of the most quoted in tea history. Chinese tea lovers know them by heart. The reference to the seventh, and last, bowl of tea is still a topic of debate among scholars: Did he, or did he not, drink it? According to British scholar John Blofeld, whose translation is often quoted, Lu T'ung does drink the tea: "This seventh is the utmost I can drink, A light breeze issues from my armpits." Art historian Steven D. Owyoung, an expert of tea culture in ancient China whose translation is quoted here, thinks otherwise. Owyoung sees Lu T'ung as having drunk six cups of tea, re-

Landscape, A Man Resting Under Pines, Two Boys Preparing Tea, album leaf, ink and color on silk, China, Ming or Ch'ing dynasty. Freer Gallery of Art, Smithsonian Institution, Washington, D.C. Gift of Charles Lang Freer.

sulting in six sensations, but unable to drink the seventh cup because the only feeling left is that of having grown wings from under his arms, wings that send him flying in the air on a gentle wind. For Owyoung, the poetic image of the flight of a winged being is in keeping with the Taoist notion that drinking tea imbues immortality. Taoist immortals of antiquity are often portrayed as feathered men in art and poetry of the Western Han dynasty (206 B.C.E.–8 C.E.).

Lu T'ung did live a secluded life according to Taoist principles and loved tea so much that a line in one of his poems, perhaps written in jest, reads: "I care not a jot for immortal life, but only for the taste of tea." Ironically, he met a tragic and unexpected end. On a rare visit to Emperor Wen Tsung's court, Lu T'ung was caught in a brutal clash between the emperor's loyalists and regiment guards suspected of sedition. Two thousand civilians and six hundred soldiers were slaughtered. Lu T'ung, the poet and tea lover, was beheaded, and his head was exposed in public.

Writing Thanks to Censor Meng for Sending New Tea
by Lu T'ung

The sun is as high as a ten-foot measure and five; I am deep asleep.
The general bangs at the gate loud enough to scare the Duke of Chou!
He announces that the Censor sends a letter; the white silk cover is triple
    stamped.
Breaking the vermillion seals, I imagine the Censor himself inspecting
    these three hundred moon-shaped tea cakes.
He heard that within the tea mountain a path was cut at the new year,
    sending insects rising excitedly on the spring wind.
As the emperor waits to taste Yang-hsien tea, the one hundred plants
    dare not bloom.
Benevolent breezes intimately embrace pearly tea sprouts, the early
    spring coaxing out buds of golden yellow.
Picked fresh, fired till fragrant, then packed and sealed: tea's essence and
    goodness is preserved.
Such venerable tea is meant for kings and nobles; how did it reach the
    hut of this mountain hermit?
The brushwood gate is closed against vulgar visitors; all alone, I don my
    gauze cap, brewing and tasting the tea.
Clouds of green yielding; unceasingly, the wind blows; radiantly white,
    floating tea froth congeals against the bowl.
The first bowl moistens my lips and throat.
The second bowl banishes my loneliness and melancholy.

The third bowl penetrates my withered entrails, finding nothing except a
literary core five thousand scrolls.

The fourth bowl raises a light perspiration, casting life's inequities out
through my pores.

The fifth bowl purifies my flesh and bones.

The sixth bowl makes me one with the immortal, feathered spirits.

The seventh bowl I need not drink, feeling only a pure wind rushing beneath my wings.

Where are the immortal isles of Mount P'eng-lai? I, Master Jade Stream,
wish instead to ride this pure wind back

To the tea mountain where other immortals gather to oversee the land,
protecting the pure, high places from wind and rain.

Yet, how can I bear knowing the bitter fate of the one hundred, the ten
thousand, the hundred thousand peasants toiling beneath the tum-
bled tea cliffs!

I have but to ask the Censor about them; whether they can ever regain
some peace.

Gloved Virgins at Dawn

Among the kind of teas, the bitter still exceeds the sweet,
But among them all, these tastes can both be found;
We know not indeed for whom they may be sweet or bitter;
We've picked till the ends of our pearly fingers are quite marred.

—A stanza from the Chinese tea pluckers' song
"A Ballad on Picking Tea in the Gardens in Springtime," 1859

While poets sang the praises of tea, emperors were served nothing but the best: tribute tea, especially plucked and prepared for the Son of Heaven, the ruler of the Middle Kingdom. The tribute system had its ancient beginnings during the Warring States Period (480–221 B.C.E.), before China was even unified, as a diplomatic exchange of gifts among rival states. In dynastic China, the practice consolidated in one direction, and Chinese provinces were required to send a yearly shipment of each region's best product to the imperial court. Thus, the emperor developed a habit for the choicest silks, first-rate horses, fine porcelain, and, of course, the best tea. In T'ang times, tribute tea came from Hangchow in Chekiang Province and later from Fukien and Szechwan Provinces, particularly around the famed Mount Meng-ting where, according to legend, Kan-lu planted the seven tea bushes he had brought back from India.

Imperial tea plucking took place only for a short period, generally during the spring season. Because purity was an essential factor, imperial tea plantations were set up with strictly codified harvesting and production rules. The tea pluckers were mostly young girls—whence the legend that only virgins, and therefore pure, were chosen for the job. By some accounts, they were required to wear gloves so as not to contaminate the leaves with their own perspiration. Even without gloves, they were expected to keep their fingernails at a specific length in order to be able to snip off only the youngest and most delicate

A tea picker, engraving, England, c. 1850s. Reprinted from Fortune, *A Residence Among the Chinese*, 1857.

leaves from the top of the bush without touching them with their fingers. For three weeks before the harvest, the girls were not allowed to eat any garlic, onion, or spices, nor any foods with strong odors, such as fish or even some vegetables, to avoid compromising the delicate scent of the tea leaves with their breath. For the same reason, they were also expected to bathe every morning before going to work. Some of the rarest tribute teas were best if plucked when still damp with morning dew, which required the young pluckers to start their work at dawn and pluck the moist and tender shoots swiftly before sunrise.

Imperial officials were then put in charge of supervising the tea processing in its minutest details. Both T'ang and Sung tribute teas were still the compressed type of tea, which was shaped into a variety of forms—cakes, wafers, balls, or bricks being the most popular. Sung tribute teas were often scented with essential oils, spices, or other aromatics. Art historian Steven D. Owyoung, an expert in the art and culture of tea in ancient China, mentions that one of these, favored for its somewhat peppery fragrance, was "dragon brain." In spite of the disquieting name, dragon brain in reality was nothing more than an unusual type of camphorlike substance imported from Borneo, very popular in Sung times for tea and other beverages. Special transportation systems were also devised so that imperial tea chests would never have to touch the ground during the voyage between the plantation and the court pantry. Sometimes, even the water from special wells would be shipped to the emperor to ensure the best combination between the type of tea and the taste of water. Such was the complex and delicate balance at work behind the emperor's tea. The following passage by Sung historian Chou Mi (1232–1308 C.E.) may give an idea of how precious tribute tea was:

> In the first ten days of mid Spring, the Canal Bureau of Fukien sends as tribute the first wax tea which is named the "new tea for examination from North Garden." All of the tea is in the shape of squares in small measures. The imperial household is offered only one-hundred measures; they are kept in soft pouches of yellow silk gauze, wrapped in broad, green bamboo leaves, and lined in,

Special transportation systems were devised for the choicest teas (left), so that the tea box would never have to touch the ground even when the porter took a rest. Other teas were carried in the traditional manner (right), and the boxes regularly placed on the ground during breaks.

Tea coolies, two engravings, England, c. 1850s. Reprinted from Fortune, *A Journey to the Tea Countries of China*, 1852.

again, yellow silk gauze. The tea, which is sealed in vermillion by officials, is enclosed by a red lacquered casket with a gilt lock. It is further kept in a satchel woven of fine bamboo and silk, and thus protected by these many means. The tea is made with the tenderest leaf-buds whose shapes resemble bird tongues. One measure of tea requires 400,000 leaves. Yet, this is barely enough to make a few cups to sip. Sometimes, one or two measures are given to the outer imperial residences, their distribution determined by family lineage. The dispersal of these gifts is a favor and considered a wonderful present. . . . Outsiders rarely know of this, so the nearest thing is this description.

Other rare teas destined for the emperor's palate were the ones that came from the tall tea trees growing in the wild. Here, monkeys—not virgins—allegedly performed the plucking job. The version passed down in tea lore concerning monkey-picked tea is that only monkeys could scramble up trees, often thirty or forty feet tall. Once the monkeys were perched up there, the people below provoked them by throwing stones at them. In retaliation, the monkeys tore off tree branches and threw them back at the people. That being exactly the point, the people then gathered the branches and walked home. A more credible story, if any monkeys were involved in tea picking at all, is that they were trained to pick tea leaves by being rewarded with desirable foods. In time, the term *monkey-picked tea* came to be applied to rare teas from specific regions.

Celestial emperors were generally far removed from day-to-day reality and had no awareness of the scores of young girls employed in tea plucking, let alone of monkeys. Nor did they ever bother about the details of preparing the official court beverage. Such an activity was left to concubines and was often a source of great jealousy and competition among the ladies in their effort to obtain the ruler's favor. Emperors did not know or care that the farmers suffered considerable hardship under the tribute system, which—from the farmers' perspective—amounted to yet another ill-disguised form of taxation. Even less were emperors aware of the blackened hands or perennially sore fingers of the tens of thousands of young tea pluckers, who never even dreamt of tasting imperial tea. Only one Sung emperor, Hui-tsung (1082–1135 C.E.), showed any interest in the details of tea production and wrote a treatise on it, the *Ta-kuan ch'a-lun*. He is said to have often brewed his own tea and served it to his guests and concubines—and of the latter he had a great deal. Contrary to the fashion of the day, he favored unscented teas, particularly the rare white tea grown in the wild, and counseled against dragon brain, or camphor, in tea. He was ahead of his time, as it was not until the Ming era (1368–1644 C.E.) that loose-leaf, unscented teas became popular.

Hui-tsung was an unusual emperor in more ways than one. He found himself ruler of the Middle Kingdom against his wishes. As the eleventh in line for the throne, he never thought he would become emperor. He was an accomplished calligrapher, poet, and painter; some of his works are exhibited at the Metropolitan Museum of Art in New York and the Museum of Fine Arts in Boston. He founded an art academy that became the center of Sung arts and was also a sophisticated art collector. Clearly, he put art before politics. As a result, Hui-tsung so disregarded the management of his empire that he soon found it taken over by northern nomadic tribes from Manchuria, thus triggering the end of the Northern Sung dynasty in 1127 C.E. He was imprisoned and exiled to the north, where he died eight years later. Had he been exiled to an imperial tea plantation instead, he would perhaps have been the one emperor to brew and serve tea to the tea pluckers, while discussing the merits of white tea.

Tea Bricks, Ox Blood, Horses, and Cash

Tartar-tea . . . When required for use, a piece of the brick is broken off, pulverised, and boiled in the kettle, until the water assumes a reddish hue. Some salt is then thrown in, and effervescence commences. When the liquid has become almost black, milk is added, and the beverage, the grand luxury of the Tartars, is then transferred to the tea-pot. Samdadchiemba was a perfect enthusiast of this tea. For our part, we drank it in default of something better.

—Evariste Régis Huc, *Travels in Tartary, Thibet, and China,* *1844–1846*

The nomadic tribes of the north and of the western steppes may have been China's invaders, but they were also great tea addicts. And for good reason. Their daily meals consisted mostly of sheep and mutton meat, horse or camel milk, and butter. A cold climate and a nomadic life guiding herds to better pastures were not conducive to planting vegetable gardens. Tea was an ideal addition to such diets, which were rich in protein but dangerously poor in vitamins and essential minerals. Not only did tea provide the necessary supplements, but it also functioned as a valuable digestive aid, breaking down the large amounts and varieties of animal fats. And a cup of tea was also a wonderful way to warm up on a cold night.

China's traders had identified the nomads' need. Ever since tea had become a major commodity, long camel caravans, loaded with hundreds of pounds of the precious leaf, had made the long trek to the northern, western, and southwestern border areas. Over the centuries, tea had become a staple food for Manchu, Mongols, Tibetans, and other border populations. Yet the nomads, too, had identified one of China's needs: horses. These were plentiful and well taken care of among all the nomadic horse-worshipping tribes. And so the tea-for-horses barter was born: the nomads got vitamins and the Chinese a cavalry, which substantially amplified their military power. A horse was worth anywhere from twenty to fifty kilograms of tea (45 to 110 pounds). This trade became of such national importance that, during the T'ang dynasty, China stepped up tea production to an industrial level, mainly in the regions of Szechwan and Yunnan. Sometimes even the increased production was not sufficient. The government then had to prohibit the sale of tea within its own borders—but only to the lower-class citizens, as high-ranking officials could not be left without tea—in order to have enough tea in stock to provide the necessary amount of horses to the military. The control of the tea supply was also used as a political tool: the withdrawal of it to maintain control over belligerent border tribes, the distribution of it to forge alliances. In Sung China, the trade had reached such proportions that a Tea and Horse Bureau was established to administer its affairs on a national level. The bureau was an influential institution, a sort of Ministry of Foreign Affairs, and it maintained control of the exchange up to the Ming era.

Along with the horse trade, tea came to play an even more ubiquitous role in China and central Asia. It not only *made* money, it *was* money. Just like the Mayans used cocoa beans and the Arab traders coffee beans as a form of currency, so the Chinese used tea, albeit not on a per-leaf basis. Ever since the early T'ang production of tea cakes, popular during Lu Yü's time, the concept of compressing tea leaves had been refined and perfected, both for reasons of durability and ease of transportation. China's tea money was brick tea, produced in a similar way as the tea cakes. The leaves were dried in the sun, then pounded and broken up, steamed and pressed together. According to at least one source, sometimes ox blood and yak dung were used as binding agents, and soot was added to give the brick a darker, more appealing hue. The leaf mass was then pressed into rectangular molds of varying sizes, and the resulting bricks were left to dry for several weeks. Tea bricks had different inscriptions and decorations, which identified the region of origin. The value of the brick increased the farther away from its region of origin it was carried. Tea brick money was used along with paper money, which was also invented by the Chinese and used as common currency in Sung China. Yet tea bricks were certainly more solid than paper money, known as "flying money" because of its lightness. The "lightness" referred not only to the actual weight but also to the lack of real value, especially when an

For the manufacturing of caper tea, dry tea leaves were sprinkled with water to make them soft and pliable, then placed in canvas bags and trod upon and twisted and turned. As the leaves were compressed and lost volume, the bag was continually tightened, until the end product was a firm, compressed ball of tea leaves, which was then dried again to maintain the shape.

Method of making caper tea, by Mr. Scarth, engraving, England, c. 1850s. Reprinted from Fortune, *A Residence Among the Chinese*, 1857.

excess issue of paper money caused inflation during later-Sung times. Tea bricks are still used, if not as money, then as an article of trade in barter economies in the more remote parts of central Asia.

While the finer tea made its way to the northwest and later into Russia, a coarser type of brick tea, which included lower grade leaves, twigs, and stalks as well as leftover tea dust, was produced for the Tibetans. For transport, four bricks at a time would be packed in bamboo wrappings and stacked up to form a load of three hundred pounds or more. But, contrary to the tea bricks crossing the northern plains on the backs of camels, these loads were destined for the backs of men. Only men were small and nimble enough to negotiate narrow and treacherous mountain roads, or brave enough to cross rope bridges over raging waters, wearing straw sandals and enduring freezing temperatures. For centuries, the livelihood of villages in southwest China depended on these transports. Young boys and old men climbed up the eastern slopes of the Himalayas, to heights at which every breath becomes a conscious act of self-preservation. Porters were commonly used to transport tea bricks, not only to Tibet but to ports and other trade centers along the coast, up to the beginning of the twentieth century.

Brick tea, as opposed to loose-leaf tea, is commonly used throughout central Asia to prepare the beverage. Tibetans still make tea as in Lu Yü's time: they boil powdered brick tea in water, then add yak butter, salt, and *tsampa*, a ground barley or buckwheat cereal, which turns tea into more of a soup. Tea bricks can also be purchased in specialty tea shops in Europe and North America, but they are rarely used to brew tea. On the other hand, compressed teas of different kinds and shapes, mostly from China, are gaining favor in the West among an increasing number of sophisticated tea lovers. A few rare ancient tea bricks have become a numismatic collector's item. They are coins, after all. But, because they are "drinkable" coins, not many are left in circulation. Some Tartar prince must have used up all the good brick tea, enjoying a hot cup of it on a chilly evening, tucked under his bear covers, gazing at the millions of stars overlooking his desert kingdom.

The Guessing Game

In idle moments
When bored with poetry
Thoughts confused
Beating time to songs
When the music stops
Living in seclusion
Enjoying scholarly pastimes
Conversing late at night
Studying on a sunny day
In the bridal chamber
Detaining favored guests
Playing host to scholars or pretty girls
Visiting friends returned from far away
In perfect weather
When skies are overcast
Watching boats glide past on the canal
Midst trees and bamboos
When flowers bud and birds chatter
On hot days by a lotus pond
Burning incense in the courtyard
After tipsy guests have left
When the youngsters have gone out
On visits to secluded temples
When viewing springs and scenic rocks.

—A list of appropriate occasions for drinking
 tea in China, according to the Ming tea
 manual *Ch'a-shu* by Hsü Tz'u-shu

The head servant surveyed the setup one last time. The bowls and the salt dish were lined up on the stand, the whisk brushes and the water ladle lay beside them. The teas, carefully roasted and

Doucha, or Tea Contest, album leaf, color on silk, China, Ch'ing dynasty. Freer Gallery of Art, Smithsonian Institution, Washington, D.C. Gift of Charles Lang Freer.

ground by his master, were ready to be used, the water was warming up in the cauldron. Distant voices from under the banyan tree and the gentle splashing in the nearby stream fused into a placid, indistinct sound. The head servant didn't dare close his eyes lest he should be lulled to sleep by it. Soon his master walked over to the fire, ladled out some of the water from the cauldron, and set it into a jar. He placed one type of tea into each bowl, poured hot water over it, and offered it to his guests. Each guest vigorously whisked his own tea, added some of the cooler water that had been set aside in the jar, and then compared. Which froth was the foamiest? Which lasted the longest? They all tasted the teas, discussed them at length, and finally

declared the best. Then they returned to the banyan tree and impro-
vised poems until dark when it was time to go home. By then, the servants had cleaned all the tea utensils, put all the tea dregs in the
appropriate container, and packed everything in the portable basket.

Such gatherings took place hundreds of thousands of times
among T'ang and Sung tea lovers. While Tartar princes and herdsmen
alike enjoyed coarse brick tea, all of China, it seems, practiced tea appreciation in those days. Poets, scholars, and literati would congre-
gate, either in natural settings or in their new garden teahouses,
especially built for the purpose of tasting and enjoying different varieties of tea and discussing art and literature. These were delightful
small garden houses, the latest fashion in T'ang tea culture, which
would later provide the inspiration for the Japanese tearooms. Because this type of tea gathering developed a form of intellectual enjoyment, it came to be known as "scholar tea," which was later also
imported to Japan as the more secular form of tea ceremony called
sencha.

With the increasing popularity of tea and the expansion of tea
culture to the general population, scholar teas grew into veritable "tea
contests." These were regular tea competitions—with a judge and an
audience—in which teas would be tasted, winners chosen, and
awards assigned. Instead of watching Olympic athletes, the audience
would enjoy the spectacle of several gentlemen sipping tea, observing how much froth the bamboo whisk would produce and how long
the froth would maintain its consistency—teas whose froth did not
last were considered worthless—all the while politely exchanging
opinions with one another, and finally declaring the winning "froth
of the liquid jade." As a popular form of group entertainment tea contests began to decline only in the Ming era (1368–1644 C.E.), when
both the compressed and the powdered, whipped tea were abandoned in favor of the loose-leaf infusion, commonly in use today.

Over time, this practice spawned the figure of the tea master, a
prototype of the modern tea taster, with the difference that T'ang
and Sung tea tasters sometimes became the stuff of legends, while today's tea taster is a common mortal like the rest of us. One such leg-

end was Ts'ai Hsiang (1012–67 C.E.). Not only was he a scholar and a poet, like most government officials, but he was also one of the greatest calligraphers of his time. Later he became tea commissioner, responsible for the production and delivery of the tea destined for the imperial table. In this role, Ts'ai Hsiang wrote a report for the emperor, which then became an important tea record, the *Ch'a-lu*. He participated in many tea contests, and his tea-tasting skills were so exquisite that he could determine the region of provenance of a particular tea just by one sip. On one famous occasion he was even able to discern the presence of a small quantity of lower-grade tea in a bowl made with a very rare and expensive tea. His host's servant had apparently added the cheap tea when a second, unexpected guest had put the servant in a quandary about how to make enough tea for three.

As with most everything else that originated in China, the tea contests were later imported and imitated by the Japanese. Begun as tea gatherings (*cha-yoriai*) among the aristocratic and the warrior classes, they evolved into tasting contests known as *tōcha* during the Kamakura period (1192–1333 C.E.). *Tōcha* were different from the Chinese tea contests: here the objective was to distinguish what was considered the only "true" tea (*honcha*)—grown in Togano-o and later in the Uji district near Kyoto—from all other teas (*hicha*, "non-tea"). Usually contestants would be served four bowls containing four different teas, but competitions varied, and sometimes the number of bowls would rise to ten (called *juppuku-cha*) or even fifty (*gojuppuku-cha*). Along with *tōcha*, the leisure classes often practiced *soradaki*, the profound and delicate art of incense appreciation, which challenged the participant to identify different mixtures of incense by inhaling their aroma. The competitive spirit was sometimes also expressed in a more literary type of contest, the *renga*, a linked-verse competition that consisted of improvising verse linked to the last person's verse.

One of the most consistent character traits of the human species is that we don't know when to leave well enough alone. So it was that *tōcha* came to lose their original meaning of appreciation of unique teas in an aesthetic context. Then, they often became either a forum to display extravagant wealth and power in the face of widespread poverty, or they turned into wild affairs, also known as *basara*. These lasted for days and included vast amounts of sake drinking, gambling, and generalized debauchery, which would leave the participants in predictable disarray, both in body and pocketbook. So frequent did such gatherings become throughout Japan that the authorities grew seriously concerned. During the Muromachi period (1338–1573 C.E.), the shoguns established laws to try to limit the social and economic damage caused by *basara* excesses. But they were only partially successful. It was Zen Buddhism and the evolution of the tea ceremony that in the end helped tea out of the dregs of society and into a new era of spirituality.

The Eyelids of
Bodhidharma

Emperor Wu, hopeful: "What merits have I achieved by building all these temples?"
Bodhidharma: "None whatsoever."
The emperor, bewildered: "Then what is the teaching of Buddhism?"
Bodhidharma: "Vast emptiness."
The emperor, infuriated: "Whom do I have standing before me then?"
Bodhidharma: "I don't know."

—A famous exchange on the merits of secular versus spiritual achievements passed
  on in Buddhist tradition

Zen Buddhists have their own story about the beginnings of tea. Bodhidharma was a Brahman prince from the south of India and a follower of the Buddhist doctrine of sudden enlightenment. This is the so-called wordless dharma, the path of the void, which seeks an intuitive attainment of "Buddha-mind" through meditation rather than through devotional rituals and the study of scriptures. Bodhidharma traveled to China, where he spent many years teaching his own approach to Buddhism, and around 520 C.E. he was invited to an audience with Emperor Wu of the Southern Liang dynasty (502–57 C.E.). The emperor had made great efforts in spreading Buddhism in China by building temples and having sutras translated from Sanskrit. But he did not understand Bodhidharma's doctrine of the void. After the exchange reported above, Bodhidharma left and traveled north to the famed Shaolin Temple near Loyang in Honan

Province. There he sat in meditation
for nine years facing the wall of a cave
and "listening to the ants scream." Because of this, he is also known as "the
wall-gazing holy man."

Bodhidharma was a master but he
was human. One day, during a seven-
year meditation, he was overtaken by
sleep. When he woke up he was furious. In order to never shut his eyes
again, he cut his eyelids off and threw
them on the ground in a rage. Where
the eyelids touched the soil, a tea bush
grew. Since then, meditating monks
have been blessed with the gift of the
sacred beverage as an aid during their
long hours of meditation practice. And
since then, Bodhidharma is always
portrayed with intense, lidless eyes in
artistic renderings.

This story tells as much about the
birth of Zen as about the birth of tea.
Bodhidharma may have been instrumental in spreading the practice of sitting meditation (*zazen*) in China, and
he was certainly a radical proponent of
the spiritual practice of the fearless

*Bodhidharma (Daruma) Seated in Medita-
tion*, by Hashimoto Gaho, hanging
scroll, ink and color on paper, Japan,
c. 1885. Freer Gallery of Art, Smithsonian Institution, Washington, D.C.
Gift of Charles Lang Freer.

warrior. But Taoist monks had been meditating and drinking tea for
centuries before Bodhidharma arrived. It was the fusion of the two
disciplines—meditation and the love of nature, wordless teaching
and spontaneity, the unity of all things and the incommensurate
void—that gave birth to the new form of "Ch'an" Buddhism. The
word itself is testimony to the way the philosophies traveled. *Ch'an* is
the Chinese version of the Sanskrit *dhyana*, which means "eliminating
distracting thoughts" or "meditation." *Ch'an* in turn became *Zen* when

Bodhidharma (Daruma) is always depicted without eyelids.

Tea Bowl with Design of Daruma and Inscription, Kyoto stoneware, Japan, Edo period or Meiji era. Freer Gallery of Art, Smithsonian Institution, Washington, D.C. Gift of Charles Lang Freer.

it was imported to Japan. Bohidharma is known in China as Pu-ti ta-mo, or simply Ta-mo, and in Japan as Bodai Daruma or, in short, Daruma. Because he was a catalyst of this convergence of disciplines, Bodhidharma is considered the father of Zen Buddhism.

Aside from tea and meditation, Zen Buddhism and Taoism also share the emphasis on physical health as an integral element of the path to enlightenment. Some stories credit Bodhidharma with the introduction of physical activity as part of daily practice. According to their version, Bodhidharma realized that the monks were in poor shape because of the immobility during meditation and instituted a regimen of vigorous exercise based on the yoga principles he had brought with him from India. This, along with the mind discipline acquired during meditation, developed into the practice of kung fu, for which Shaolin Temple is famous in the West. Yet it is unlikely that Bodhidharma invented kung fu. Some scholars doubt that Bodhidharma even existed. Taoists had been studying how to use energy for health and longevity since Confucian times. The result of their effort was the discipline of tai chi. Bodhidharma's strength, instead, was meditation. With his "barebones Zen" he was a warrior of the spirit rather than of the body. The traditional explanation of why he is often depicted in a seated posture without arms and legs is that his long periods of meditation caused his limbs to fall off—which doesn't quite testify to his alleged practice of physical exercise.

Like many Zen parables, the story of Bodhidharma has symbolic meaning: nothing is more important in life than attaining enlightenment through meditation, not even our eyelids or our limbs. And the sprouting of the tea bush is an indication of how important tea was in a monk's life. From a healing herb and practical aid in meditation, tea became part of the daily routine. Over time, the gestures around tea as well as the utensils and room arrangements evolved into elements of religious rituals. Monks would offer tea to the image of Bodhidharma, then drink from a single bowl and pass it around to the next monk before settling in for *zazen*. Other Buddhist practices also included tea, such as making tea offerings to the whole congregation or drinking tea after chanting in special ceremonies. These gestures and rituals are what the first Japanese monks traveling to China observed and took home with them. They also took home the seeds of the precious plant as well as the Zen and Taoist philosophies. This is the knowledge that amalgamated and evolved into what is known in the West as the Japanese tea ceremony.

Thirteen centuries have passed since then. The piercing, unblinking gaze of the lidless Bodhidharma surveys the scurry of worldly activity, seeing and not seeing, looking beyond into the Unknowable Void. Tea and Zen remain inextricably linked.

Zen and the Tea Masters of Japan

Meanwhile, let us have a sip of tea. The afternoon glow
is brightening the bamboos, the fountains are bubbling
with delight, the soughing of the pines is heard in our
kettle. Let us dream of evanescence, and linger in the
beautiful foolishness of things.

—Kakuzo Okakura, *The Book of Tea*, 1906

On February 28, 1591, a seventy-year-old man, an immensely influential and respected member of Japanese society, committed
seppuku, ritual suicide. At the request of Toyotomi Hideyoshi, the
ruler of Japan, he drove a sword through his bowels after serving tea
to his friends and writing his death poem: "This life of seventy years /
Shout out! A towering roar: / By this hallowed blade of mine, / All
Buddhas and masters are slain." The man was Sen no Rikyū
(1522–91), an icon of Japanese culture. Considered the greatest tea
master of Japan, he is the man who forever embedded tea and Zen in
Japanese consciousness.

The First Monks

Centuries before Rikyū, Japanese monks and scholars had traveled to mainland China and had brought back architectural designs, artistic techniques, governmental models, and many other Chinese ideas and concepts, which Japan admired deeply. They also brought back Buddhism and tea, along with the tea rituals then commonly practiced in Chinese monasteries. These first teas, which reached Japan during the eighth century, were tea cakes or bricks, or other kinds of compressed teas. Because the introduction of tea to Japan occurred mainly through religious channels, tea was limited to monastery life at first, but over time it gradually spread to the aristocracy. Emperor Shomu (701–56), himself a Buddhist, is said to have served tea to a hundred priests in Todaiji Temple in Nara. Emperor Saga (786–842), who had great respect for Chinese culture, contributed to the popularization of tea by having a tea plantation built in the imperial palace and including tea in his official banquets. These teas, often com-

The translation of the verse is: "The pine breeze fills the tea bowl with moon and stars. One sip awakens you from the long dream sleep." Kuga Kankei was the sixty-first head abbot of the great Zen temple Eihei-ji and the spiritual leader of the Soto School of Buddhism during the turbulent period at the end of the Tokugawa (Edo) period. Under his guidance Zen Buddhism entered the modern world.

Tea Bowl and Verse on the Theme of Tea, by Kuga Kankei (1817–1884), detail of scroll, ink on paper, Japan, nineteenth century. Private collection, Los Angeles.

pressed into spherical shapes, were known in Japan as *dancha*. The tea ball shavings were boiled in hot water, and a souplike brew was served with salt for seasoning, as was common in T'ang China.

After a period of general waning interest for Chinese culture, the Buddhist priest Eisai (1141–1215) traveled to the mainland in search of inspiration to renew Japanese Tendai Buddhism and brought back the powdered tea known as *matcha*, which had by then become the preferred tea of Sung China. This is the brilliant green, whipped tea still in use in the tea ceremony today. Eisai also brought back the teachings of Zen and became the founder of the Rinzai Zen sect of Buddhism in Japan. The *Kissa Yojo Ki*, a treatise extolling the medicinal benefits of tea according to ancient Taoist principles, is Eisai's work. Tea, health, and Zen meditation were further endorsed by Eisai's friend Myoe—also a Buddhist priest and a poet who cultivated tea—and by priest Eison (1201–90), who was the first to take tea out of the monasteries and introduce it to the common folk. Eison traveled across Japan spreading the word of Zen and curing the poor and sick with tea, thereby following the tradition of the first Taoist monks as healers and protectors of the poor.

The Samurai

While Eisai moved in high circles and established Zen and tea rituals among the nobility, Eison brought both to the population at large. Over time, two forms of tea drinking developed: the lavish tea party of the upper classes, which retained the ritual forms but was mostly a social affair centered around the proud displaying of expensive Chinese tea utensils, and the simple tea of the monks and the lower classes, associated with the search for spiritual harmony in everyday life. These two extremes gradually came together in a new style of "shogun tea." As figures of the emerging social class, the samurai sought social status and used the social function of tea gatherings to achieve it. As warriors, they favored the austere Zen style and discipline over the court-approved and more conservative Tendai Buddhism. Zen priests often became important advisers to the shoguns and acted as ambassadors and "cultural attachés."

As the shogunates became more powerful over the increasingly insignificant imperial court, so did Zen Buddhism—and with it, tea. Generals were often accompanied by clergy on the battlefield. The portable tea hut, where tea would be served by Zen priests according to the prescribed rituals, provided a much needed opportunity for retreat away from the combat zone. When not at war, the samurai, often of humble origin, also used the tea gatherings as a means to establish a social identity in the unstable and turbulent atmosphere of the Muromachi era (1338–1573). The *shoin*, originally a study room in a Zen monastery, evolved into a large, formal reception room, which became the traditional setting for samurai tea gatherings. Monks were employed to evaluate and catalog art objects and tea utensils and to advise the lords in questions of taste and culture. They defined and compiled rules for room decoration, display of utensils, and flower arrangements during tea gatherings, often basing their decisions on the temple practices they had brought with them. Thus, temple culture merged with the salon culture of the samurai, and Zen masters often became tea masters.

Shuko and Jōō

One such master was Murata Shuko (1423–1502), a gambler turned Zen practitioner. He saw the tea gathering—the act of preparing and drinking tea, arranging the utensils, and choosing the decorations— not as a social event but as a Buddhist path, an opportunity to seek enlightenment in the gestures of everyday life. With his contribution, the tea ceremony became a Way, *chado* (*cha* means "tea," *do* means "way"). He also favored simple surroundings, a thatched hut, over the lavish *shoin*-style tearooms, and rustic Japanese tea ware over luxurious Chinese items. With his influence, the tea ceremony evolved from a Chinese import to a truly Japanese practice, *chanoyu*, which literally means "hot water for tea."

Master Takeno Jōō (1502–55) further developed the style of the tea ceremony along Shuko's ideas by introducing the concept of *wabi*, the appreciation of primitive simplicity, sincerity of heart, and the beauty of imperfection—an element as central to Zen as to Japanese aesthetics to this day. He thought the tearoom should be small and simple and introduced the idea of the four-and-a-half-mat tea hut. Sizes were measured in terms of the standard tatami straw mat, which was three by six feet (about $1.80m^2$). But after Shuko and Jōō, Japan would have to wait for the third and grandest of tea men, an individual who would bring these concepts and innovations together into the highest expression of spiritual and aesthetic sophistication, turning *chanoyu* into a national art form. This was Sen no Rikyū, the first *sadō*, grand master of tea.

Sen no Rikyū

Born into a wealthy merchant family of Sakai, near Osaka, Rikyū studied Zen at the main Rinzai temple, Daitokuji, near Kyoto. He also learned tea and the principle of *wabi* from Master Takeno Jōō himself. Rikyū was a gifted and self-confident pupil and soon rose to a position of prominence in the world of tea, both among the prosperous merchant class and the warrior elite. He was chosen as tea master by Oda Nobunaga, one of the most powerful shoguns after the fall of the Ashikaga. After Nobunaga's assassination, Toyotomi Hideyoshi, the man who unified Japan, took on Rikyū as tea master. The association of Hideyoshi and Rikyū would prove ideal for the flourishing of the art of *chanoyu*.

Hideyoshi was a patron of the tea arts. He supported and encouraged any activity relating to tea and studied the art of serving tea himself, a humble act for the most powerful man in Japan. Like other shoguns, he was close to Zen and appreciated and respected the *wabi* style, although during his meetings with official delegations he had tea served in the ostentatious *shoin* rooms. Undoubtedly, he used these tea gatherings politically, to forge alliances and to impress visi-

This type of hand-formed bowl originated through the collaboration of Tanaka Chojiro, a maker of roof tiles, and Sen no Rikyū. Simple, thick-walled black raku tea bowls by Chojiro are considered by many to be the ideal vessels for drinking tea.

Black Raku Tea Bowl, pottery with black raku glaze, Kyoto, Japan, Momoyama period, c. 1585–89. Freer Gallery of Art, Smithsonian Institution, Washington, D.C. Gift of Charles Lang Freer.

tors with his power and wealth. When Hideyoshi invited the emperor to tea, he had an entire tearoom built of gold, including walls and tea utensils. As Hideyoshi's tea master, Rikyū was involved in *shoin*-style tea and played an important role as a diplomatic adviser and go-between. How much or how little he enjoyed the role is unclear. Those were times of despotic rule, and servants—even a highly regarded tea master was a servant, after all—did what their lords told them to do. But Rikyū's real contribution to the world of tea, both in style and in spiritual substance, lies in creating and bringing to national prominence *wabicha*, the tea of simplicity and sincerity.

Rikyū was a creative spirit and not afraid to stand up for what he believed. For him, the ceremony of preparing and drinking tea was not entertainment. It was a unique opportunity to find harmony within oneself and thus experience the essence of life, an occasion for togetherness with purity of heart, a moment to transcend everyday reality and be at one with the One. To achieve this, the tearoom required simplification in the *wabi* spirit of restraint and frugality. Following Jōō's teachings and his own Zen training, Rikyū further reduced the size of the tearoom from the already small four-and-a-half-mat size to a two-mat size (about thirty-six square feet, or 3.60m^2), a small hut indeed. The interior was to be free from showy decoration, often asymmetrical to emphasize naturalness, and built only with natural and unfinished materials. No display of expensive Chinese painting, only a simple calligraphy scroll on the wall. No rare and costly imported utensils, but rustic Japanese ware; he introduced raku ware, the coarse, handmade ceramic ware so uniquely Japanese. No extravagant flower arrangements, only one flower perhaps, magnificent in its solitude. As the ideal retreat from the world, the two-mat tea hut represented the connection to nature in the Taoist sense and offered the opportunity for host and guest to share a spiritual intimacy. The famous Taian Hut, built by Rikyū for Hideyoshi in 1582 and now a national treasure in Japan, follows these principles. Rikyū did not hesitate to serve tea to high-ranking officials in a *wabi* hut instead of the *shoin* room. Hideyoshi himself became a passionate *wabi* tea man under Rikyū's guidance.

The way of entering the tearoom was another courageous innovation. Before Rikyū, tearooms had a main entrance, the *kiniguchi*, for guests of rank. Through this door people could enter walking upright. But common people had to enter through a much smaller door, the *nijiriguchi*, barely two and a half square feet, which obligated them to crouch to get into the room. Rikyū eliminated this inequity and decreed that all guests—nobles and merchants, warriors and commoners—enter through the *nijiriguchi*. This meant that social hierarchies were not recognized; in the tearoom all were equal. In addition, the extremely small entrance obligated everyone entering the tearoom to deposit swords and other weapons outside. This was as Rikyū had intended, for he believed that the tearoom was a place of peace and brotherhood, no matter how many wars were being fought outside. That Rikyū was able to challenge the establishment and bring such concepts as social equality, fraternity, and peacefulness into the consciousness of feudal Japan at such turbulent times is nothing less than a miracle. His values reverberate through the practice of *chanoyu* to this day and throughout the world.

The peak of Rikyū's public success came in 1587, when Hideyoshi declared that a great tea party would be organized, to which all tea men, high and low, from all over Japan would be invited. This was the *Kitano dai chakai* (The Great Kitano Tea Meeting), which took place in the Kitano pine grove in Kyoto at the beginning of October. Eight hundred tea men came, nobles and commoners from near and far, and built eight hundred tea huts, each in a different style and according to each tea master's aesthetic inclinations and budget. Utensils and paintings of all sorts were displayed, and different types of tea were served in various fashions. Hideyoshi himself served tea in his *wabi* hut. A grand affair, organized masterfully by Rikyū, the Kitano Tea Meeting was indicative of how important tea had become in Japanese culture, and also of how it was used for political purposes. Undoubtedly, Hideyoshi intended Kitano not only as a tea meeting but also as a massive display of power.

In the context of power, Rikyū lived a life in delicate balance. While his lord displayed his golden tearoom, Rikyū advocated the *wabi* hut. While his lord used tea gatherings for his political machinations, Rikyū made high officials crawl through the *nijiriguchi* to enter the tearoom. Yet, though Hideyoshi was indeed an adept of the art of *wabi*, he was also the ruler of Japan and an unpredictable and cruel man. Why he gave Rikyū a death sentence remains somewhat of a mystery. Scholars suggest several possibilities. Some say that Rikyū openly defied Hideyoshi's authority by opposing his lord's plans to invade China and Korea, and he may thereby have written his own death sentence. Others say that a statue of Rikyū, built in his honor by one of his admirers, irritated Hideyoshi to no end because he was forced to walk under it. Still others suggest that Hideyoshi was distraught by the loss of his first son and reacted impulsively by punishing one of his closest men. And last, the general perception was that politics and *wabi* had become mutually exclusive, and Rikyū's position untenable.

All along, Rikyū had been aware of the narrow path he was walking. A few years before his death he was pessimistic about the future of *wabi*, and perhaps he sensed that his own end was near: "In less than ten years, the true way of tea will decline and when that time comes people will think on the contrary that it is prospering. Tea will be reduced to a pitiful state, serving merely as a worldly amusement. Now this is so obvious that it makes me sad." Perhaps this is why he refused to save his life by requesting a pardon from his lord. Hideyoshi later regretted his action. He, too, walked a narrow path, torn between his spiritual awareness and his political ambitions, his life a magnificent study of human contradictions. A true *wabi* man occupied the same body as the capricious despot. Hideyoshi's most profound *wabi* spirit comes through in his own definition of *chanoyu*:

> When tea is made with water drawn from the depths of Mind
> Whose bottom is beyond measure,
> We really have what is called cha-no-yu.

Chanoyu

I heard from the monks of Daitoku-ji and Nanshu-ji
that they . . . open the realm of the Pure Land by proceeding through the roji-path, and by making wabi tea
in a two-mat grass hut, and by undergoing the discipline of gathering firewood and boiling water, they
come to realize that the Truth lies in a bowl of tea . . .

—Nambō Sōkei, *Nampōroku,* a seventeenth-century classic of
Japanese tea literature

After tea master Sen no Rikyū's death, the spiritual and aesthetic
pursuit of *chado,* the Way of Tea, spawned several schools and
practices in Japan. Three of them—the Urasenke, the Omotesenke,
and the Mushanokojisenke—were founded by three of Rikyū's great-
grandchildren. Best known in the West is the Urasenke school of tea,
which adopted the tea practices passed on by Rikyū to his son. Since
then, the *iemoto,* the grand master of the Urasenke school, has always
been a member of the Sen family, a descendant of Sen no Rikyū. The
present *iemoto,* Zabosai Soshitsu, is the sixteenth-generation successor
in the Urasenke line.

Chanoyu, the tea ceremony, is practiced in a variety of ways, depending on the season, on the tea master's individual choices, and on
the level of skill of the practitioners and of the guests. The fairly
short, but by no means simple, tea gathering is called *chakai* and is
practiced regularly. The full ceremony is *chaji,* complex and rarely

Matsukaze (pine wind) waits as water boils in the iron kettle. Her tea utensils are arranged nearby. Even her kimono alludes to tea, with its pattern of tea-storage jars.

Matsukaze of Yamashiroya, Courtesan Preparing Tea, by Harunobu Suzuki, woodblock print, Japan, Edo period, c. 1770. Freer Gallery of Art, Smithsonian Institution, Washington, D.C. Gift of the family of Eugene and Agnes E. Meyer.

performed, yet profound and the most complete expression of the spirit of *chado*. Beginning practitioners, and even some teachers, do not perform *chaji*. As with life's challenges, so with *chaji*: it takes many years to master both.

When guests are invited to *chaji*, they first arrive to the waiting room (*machiai*) where they are served simple hot water and where one of the guests is designated as the main guest who will lead the way from then on. The guests then proceed through the garden surrounding the tearoom along the *roji* path, the water-sprinkled, mossy stepping stones that lead to the teahouse. On the *roji* path one walks away from the noise of the outer world toward the stillness of the inner world: "Proceeding along the *roji*-path to the teahut, one cleanses oneself of the dust of the world, and host and guests relate to each other with pure hearts." So says the *Nampōroku*, the sacred book of tea in Japan. Throughout the development of *chanoyu*, tea masters took great care in arranging the *roji* path to guide the guest through this "passage," and each master did it according to his beliefs and aesthetic sense. In *The Book of Tea*, Okakura says that Kobori Enshu, for example, "wished to create the attitude of a newly awakened soul still lingering amid shadowy dreams of the past, yet bathing in the sweet unconsciousness of a mellow spiritual light, and yearning for the freedom that lay in the expanse beyond."

At the *koshikake machiai*, the resting arbor, the guests sit on a bench and wait for their host to invite them into the teahouse. Here they have the opportunity to admire old trees, often present near teahouses, and to enjoy the beauty of nature. Not many words are spoken. The host then appears at the middle gate (*chumon*) and invites the guests in. The main guest, or guest of honor, is the first to go through the gate, as prescribed. He or she follows the host to the *tsukubai*, the stone water basin, where host and guests wash their hands and rinse their mouths. Sen no Rikyū said that the *tsukubai* should be low, closer to the earth and closer to nature. Everything around a Japanese tearoom is either close to nature or nature itself, the gnarly tree, the water splashing in the basin, the clay of the walls, the thatched grass roof, the bamboo holding the teahouse together. No artificial materials are used inside the tearoom, only the five elements of the Taoist universe: earth, wood, fire, water, metal.

For *chaji*, guests generally crawl through the *nijiriguchi*, the small "humbling" door of the teahouse, the great social equalizer. Entering the teahouse is like entering a womb. The door is so small one forgets it exists as soon as one is inside. The windows are covered with white paper. This creates a separation from the rest of the world. And yet, there is a sense of simple comfort and of being safe, a feeling that one has "arrived." The room is small, around eighty square feet (8.10m²) or the standard four and a half tatami mats, and essentially empty. A water kettle—the yin—a small hearth with a charcoal fire—the yang. Everything in a tearoom is yin or yang. A calligraphy scroll hangs in the small alcove called the *tokonoma*. An emptiness that feels complete and pure. In this sense, *chanoyu* best reflects the Zen notion that emptiness, the Void, is the same as the All. Indeed, the spirit of Zen is present everywhere in *chanoyu*. As Sen Sotan, grandson of Sen no Rikyū and first Urasenke tea master, said: "The taste of tea and the taste of Zen are the same." The aim of both is to expand awareness through a practice governed by four main principles: harmony (*wa*), reverence (*kei*), purity (*sei*), and tranquility (*jaku*). The belief is that a ritual executed with mindfulness of these principles has the power to transform human consciousness.

Entering the tearoom marks the beginning of the first of three sequences of the ceremony: *shoza*. The host arranges the charcoal fire (*shozumi*), an act that takes place at the beginning of *shoza* during winter and at the end during summer. The guests make some brief admiring comments about the scroll, the alcove, the hearth, as is expected of them. Then they kneel down, each at their designated places on the tatami mats, and they are offered the *kaiseki*, a light and elegant meal of soup, rice, broiled fish, vegetables, and sake in a specified sequence of servings. The meal menu varies according to the seasons, but in essence it is meant to be the simple, nutritious meal of a Zen monastery kitchen, not a gourmet feast. It is a perfect *wabi* meal, in that material insufficiency is an opportunity to experience spiritual freedom. Some polite comments are made, but for the most part silence reigns. No tea is served. The tea master is very quiet during preparation and arrangements. The guests are quiet and observe the master. The silence unites all. This, too, the Zen masters—practitioners of the wordless dharma—know well.

After cleaning the bowls, the chopsticks, and the dishes and returning them to the host, the guests are offered rice sweets and then are invited to proceed to the second, and shortest, sequence: the *nakadachi*, a short break during which the guests go back outside to the waiting arbor, and the host has a chance to make preparations for serving thick tea (*koicha*). During *nakadachi*, the host also takes away the calligraphy scroll from the alcove and sets up a flower arrangement in its place. When everything is ready, the guests are called back to the tearoom with a gong. The sound of the gong varies depending on how many guests are present.

What follows is *goza*, the third and last sequence of *chaji*, in which tea is finally served. The tea setting, with the water jar, the tea caddy, and the tea utensils, is ready. The host now prepares thick tea, which will be served only one time and with only one bowl, shared among guests. The host does not eat or drink during the ceremony and ded-

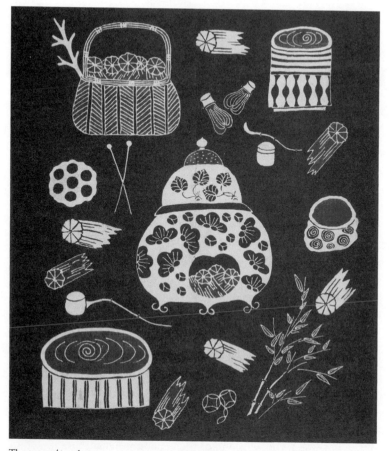

The *tsutsugaki* technique is a process by which designs are drawn freehand in a rice paste that resists the indigo dye and colored pigments. These textiles, which traditionally formed part of a bride's trousseau, were often decorated with bold designs that carry auspicious meaning.

Futon Cover Showing Tea Ceremony Utensils, plain weave cotton with rice-paste resist design (*tsutsugaki*), Japan, nineteenth century. Philadelphia Museum of Art.

icates all the attention to the guests. Again, no words are spoken, with the exception of a few appreciative comments on the part of the main guest. Each action, each moment is a meditation in itself. *Koicha*, thick tea, is made with *matcha*, the brilliant green powdered tea, and amalgamated with water into a creamy, frothy mixture, almost like a soup. The host hands the bowl of tea to the main guest who sips the prescribed three and a half sips, wipes the bowl, and hands it over to the next guest. This gesture of passing the bowl is an ancient one, perhaps two thousand years old. The healer-monks in Taoist China shared their tea bowls during rituals in their drafty mountain monastery halls. Sharing the bowl was then, as it is now, a symbol of togetherness in peace and harmony, a gesture that has overcome wars, class distinction, international boundaries. A gesture that says: we are all One.

After thick tea, the host prepares the *gozumi*, the refreshing of the charcoal fire, for *usucha*, or thin tea. During thin tea, the atmosphere is more casual than during the rigorous thick-tea procedure. *Usucha* is still made with *matcha* but is prepared with only a third of the powder used for thick tea, and it is therefore much less dense. For thin tea, each guest receives a separate bowl. First, lighter sweets are served, and then the host whisks the tea in each bowl and offers it to each guest. If a guest particularly appreciates the tea, the host will make as many bowls as the guest desires. Because in each of the activities the host's movements are swift and confident, one tends to assume that the procedures are simple. Yet, how many years of regular practice, how many mistakes, how much patience and rigorous discipline lie behind every little move: the scooping of the tea powder, the pouring of the hot water, the whisking of the tea and water into the "froth of the liquid jade," then the rinsing of the bowl, the folding of the silk cloth. Executed mechanically, these are movements devoid of all meaning. But for a true *chanoyu* practitioner, each gesture is an opportunity to be fully in the present moment, a dance of concrete practicality to gracefully connect everyday life with the most abstract and ephemeral of human notions, the No-thingness of the Void. The flow of gestures is one long and complex moving meditation, the result of superior levels of focus and concentration. The precision of the moves and the ease with which the master accomplishes them bring to mind an old Zen story:

A long time ago, an old tea master accidentally hurt a samurai. He had not intended to cause any harm and apologized, but the samurai insisted that he had been offended and that the matter be settled in a sword duel. The tea master had never used a sword before and decided to invite a fellow Zen practitioner, who was also a swordsman, to tea and ask him for advice. During the tea ceremony the Zen swordsman noticed the profound concentration and lightness of spirit with which the tea master executed his movements. He knew then what advice to give the tea master: "When you will stand in front of the samurai, hold your sword high above your head, as if you were ready to strike, and gaze at him silently, but with the same concentration and tranquility you have when you serve tea." This the tea master did. For a long time the samurai was unable to act, staring into the focused yet calm eyes of the tea master. Then he lowered his eyes and apologized for his arrogance. Not a blow was struck.

The thin tea signals that the end of the ceremony is approaching. The host takes all the utensils away to the *mizuya*, a small separate area where supplies are kept, and closes the door. The guests are left alone for a short while. When the host comes back, the guests express their appreciation for the tea and admire the host's art and skill. Then they leave. The host kneels in front of the *nijiriguchi* and watches them walk away. No words of farewell are exchanged.

Viewed from a lay perspective, *chanoyu* appears to be a fairly simple, if exacting, sequence of household-oriented actions—preparing a meal, serving tea, cleaning up. In reality, it is a complex art in which each single act is the result of a long and difficult path toward reaching what in Zen is considered the highest achievement: an expansion of consciousness. In *chanoyu*, the conscious act may not be easy, though it does manifest as simple. Yet, even the most experienced practitioner cannot fully express the essence of *chanoyu*, and of Zen, if all he or she knows is technical execution; there is always the danger of slipping into meaningless and rigid formality. To explain what

the essential element of the ceremony is, Sen Soshitsu XV, the predecessor of the present Urasenke tea master, tells the following story:

> Once a tea grower invited Rikyū to have tea. Overwhelmed with
> joy at Rikyū's acceptance, the tea grower led him to the tearoom
> and served tea to Rikyū himself. However, in his excitement his
> hand trembled and he performed badly, dropping the tea scoop
> and knocking the tea whisk over. The other guests, disciples of
> Rikyū, snickered at the tea grower's manner of making tea, but
> Rikyū was moved to say, "It was the finest."
>
> On the way home, one of the disciples asked Rikyū, "Why
> were you so impressed by such a shameful performance?" Rikyū
> answered, "This man did not invite me with the idea of showing
> off his skill. He simply wanted to serve me tea with his whole
> heart. He devoted himself completely to making a bowl of tea for
> me, not worrying about errors. I was struck by that sincerity."

A sincere heart is at the center of tea. A sincere heart is what may
have moved the first Chinese healers to cure with tea, Taoist monks
to adopt the sacred beverage into their practices, and Zen warriors to
learn discipline with it. Daisetz Suzuki, the great Zen master and
scholar, says that *chanoyu* brings together the tradition of togetherness and respect for ritual of Confucianism, the purity and harmonious relationship with nature of Taoism, and the quest for truth and
self-knowledge of Buddhism. In this view, tea becomes the distillation
of two thousand years of Eastern wisdom, and *chanoyu* the most complete and profound celebration of such wisdom. Three centuries before Suzuki, tea master Sen Sotan (1576–1658), and Rikyū's
grandson, gave his own definition of *chanoyu* in more poetic terms:

> If asked
> The nature of chanoyu,
> say it's the sound
> of windblown pines
> in a painting.

Part 2

❖

. . . to West

Foreign Devils

Whatsoever person or persons come to any man's house of quality, hee hath a custome to offer him . . . a kind of drinke called ch'a, which is somewhat bitter, red, and medicinall, which they are wont to make with a certayne concoction of herbes.

—Portuguese missionary Gaspar da Cruz—one of the first Europeans to taste tea—on discovering the use of tea in Oriental households, 1560

And then the "barbarians" arrived from the sea. And they had not the faintest idea of what tea was. The fragrance of cinnamon and nutmeg and cloves and the rustling of silk brocades and taffeta had lured them to the Asian shores. But a peaceful arrival it was not to be. The sound of the barbarian guns and the smell of their gunpowder interrupted tea tastings and tea ceremonies, meditations and poetry.

Asia's traumatic encounter with the first Western maritime powers—Spain, Portugal, Holland, and England—marked the beginning of a profound shift in the economic world order. With the promise of fortunes to be made, scruples crumbled, and the age-old excuse for plunder—"they are not like us"—unleashed the basest of humanity, creating chaos from Batavia to Canton, from Nagasaki to Manila. Powerful Asian kingdoms and potentates found themselves in the grips of tiny, insignificant European nations, which would rise

The term *namban* (southern barbarians) came to be used in Japan to designate Europeans—*namban* art refers to Japanese art influenced by European culture. Six-panel *namban* screen depicting the arrival of a Portuguese ship (detail), ink, colors, and gold leaf on paper, Japan, c. 1630s. Private collection, New York.

to be the uncontested masters of the world. The balance between East and West would never be the same.

In 1494, Pope Alexander VI had established a north-south demarcation line, the Tordesillas Line, in the middle of the Atlantic Ocean.

Along this line and in the name of God, he divided up the non-Christian world between Spain and Portugal, the two superpowers of the time: the lands to the west of the line, except Brazil, were to go to Spain, while the Portuguese would have possession of Brazil and the lands to the east. May they explore the world, he said, spread the Christian faith, and bring home the precious pepper and spices on their blessed caravels, now that the land routes to Asia had been blocked by the infidels of the Ottoman empire. The division effectively settled a dispute between the two nations as to who should plunder where. Spanish ships sailed westward and began God's work in the New World, pillaging and massacring and bringing home untold riches. The Portuguese traveled east, circumnavigating the Cape of Good Hope and setting up trading posts along the way on the African coasts, in Goa and Ceylon, along the Malay Peninsula, and in Macao.

The Eastern kingdoms were not especially aware of being an object of partition at the time. China had had its ups and downs but still considered itself the greatest power on Earth. From that vantage point, it had confidently come in contact with many foreigners from the West, the most famous one being Marco Polo. Over the centuries, there had been other, lesser known visitors, such as the Nestorian Christians—who had been allowed to settle in the Middle Kingdom long before Polo—and later the Franciscan missionaries. And even before that, there were the countless Persian and Arab traders who, century after century, had braved the central Asian desert and mountain routes to bring exotic Chinese items to the West. The Romans had particularly valued Chinese silks and had come to rely on the camel caravan traders.

In the first half of the 1400s, Ming China not only received foreigners but also went out to "meet" them. The celebrated Admiral Cheng Ho, a court eunuch and a Muslim, was the mastermind of China's maritime adventures and a fascinating character in Chinese history, but little known in the West. He set up a naval program of unprecedented scope, with at least thirty thousand men, seventy ships, and advanced shipbuilding technology. The size of the ships

was imposing: nine masts and an average length of 440 feet (134m).
A Chinese illustration shows nothing less than a giraffe being transported on one of the ships to be delivered as a gift to the emperor!
For comparison, Columbus's *Santa Maria* had three masts and was 87
feet (26m) long. Cheng Ho's objective was to explore the "Western
Oceans" and bring distant kingdoms under the Chinese tributary system. In a massive display of Chinese superiority, the fleet sailed to India, along the African coast, and into the Red Sea. But for political
reasons the program was canceled after Cheng Ho's death. This put
an end to China as a naval power. When the first European ships arrived in the Chinese harbors in the 1500s, all they found were a few
fishermen's junks. History might have been written very differently if
they had been met by Cheng Ho's fleet instead. On the other hand,
had that been the case, the intruders might have been chased away
unceremoniously, and we might not have tea in the West.

Thus, Ming China was not the xenophobic, isolationist kingdom
it is often portrayed to be. And when it came to trading, most of the
dealings the Chinese had with the Arab traders from the West had
been peaceful. Together they danced the same bargaining dance that
has been danced all over the world from time immemorial. The Arab
merchants haggled over prices, which the Chinese had set too high
because they knew the Arab merchants would haggle over prices.
Upon completion of the first dance movement, the Chinese initiated
the second movement and lowered the prices to where everyone
knew they should have been in the first place. The third movement
entailed complaining on the part of the Arab buyers that the mer-
chandise was still too expensive, while at the same time proceeding
to the opening of the money purses. This indicated the satisfactory
completion of the dance. The Arabs then loaded their purchases on
their camels, ready to start the long trek back, and the Chinese had a
bowl of tea and waited for the next customers.

But when the first Portuguese ships entered Canton harbor, something was ominously different. Instead of money purses and camels,
these "traders" came with ships, guns, and missionaries. China scholar
C. P. Fitzgerald described Portuguese behavior thus: "Trade was only

the weaker alternative to a plundering foray. When the enemy was weak or unprepared the Portuguese plundered his ships and cities, massacred the 'heathen' and seized the harbours as bases. When he was strong or ready for battle they traded—always ready to assume the more congenial role of marauders if opportunity presented itself."

Seeing how rich the Portuguese had become with this particular trading technique, other nations followed. The Dutch, who at first limited their business to transporting goods from Lisbon to northern Europe, set up their East India Company, the Verenigde Oostindische Compagnie (VOC), and began sailing eastward themselves. England, whose East India Company had been chartered by Queen Elizabeth on New Year's Eve 1600—two years before the Dutch—also wanted a share of the goods. Both companies were set up as joint-stock ventures and, as such, they were different from their Spanish and Portuguese competitors. The latter answered only to their monarchs, whereas the former had an additional boss to satisfy: the investor.

Where there is money, there is greed. Where there is greed, there is violence. Ferocious trade wars ensued, with the Dutch attacking the Portuguese, the English attacking the Dutch, the Portuguese retaliating on both, and all of them attacking whatever Asian tribe or country they had planned to conquer, from Java to Formosa, from Canton to the Spice Islands. They killed and pillaged, enslaved the local populations, used deception and intrigue to gain favor with the local chiefs and authorities in order to eliminate the competition. And when all else failed, they plundered one another's ships on the high seas with the blessing of their kings and queens. In addition to avarice, religious opposition between Catholic and Protestant nations further fueled the already intense rivalries. In 1618, Jan Pieterszoon Coen, the merciless VOC governor-general, described the situation with frightening clarity: "There's no trade without war; no war without trade." Five years after this dictum, the escalating tension between the Dutch and the English would culminate in what history books call the Amboyna Massacre, in which twenty-one Englishmen were tortured and later executed by the Dutch.

When the dust settled, the Dutch concentrated their efforts in Indonesia, which remained under Dutch control until the middle of the twentieth century. In 1667 Holland struck what was considered a very advantageous deal with England at the time: it kept the rich nutmeg island of Pulo Run, east of the Philippines, and gave England in exchange that inconsequential small island of Manhattan it had bought from the natives a few years before. The Portuguese held their trading post in Macao—it was not given back to the People's Republic of China until 1999—and did whatever they could to keep their head above water. This included acting as interpreters for other traders, which spawned a strange hybrid pidgin English, and which explains why we have words like *mandarin* (from the Portuguese *mandar*, to impart orders) in our vocabulary today. The English, after trying to establish themselves as main traders in Amoy, consolidated their activities in Canton, from where they soon dominated the trade.

The Chinese no doubt thought back with longing to the innocent haggling of the Arab traders. These were no traders. "Ocean devils"

European Traders in China: Port Scene in Which Tea Is Being Weighed and Loaded into a Sampan, last of a series of twelve images depicting the Chinese tea industry from planting to shipping, attributed to Tinqua, watercolor and gouache, China, c. 1850. © Mystic Seaport Museum, G. W. Blunt Library Collection, Mystic, Conn.

they were, with their ships and their cannons. "Red devils" others called them, on account of their reddish hair, which made them look like the devil, often depicted with red hair in Buddhist iconography. And at the very least, they were referred to as "foreign devils." Yet devils they were, wherever they came from and whatever they looked like. And worse, much worse, was yet to come. But for the time being, the Chinese decided that, however dangerous, trade was too profitable, and the new Manchu rulers were not willing to shut it down altogether. Instead, they would maintain strict control over it and limit all contact with the foreigners to one port, Canton. There, they set up what came to be known as the Factories, trading establishments built on a thin strip of land between the river and the city walls, to which the foreigners were confined during their stay for the trading season (October to March).

Life and trade for the foreigners were governed by austere regulations. No foreign warships nor firearms were to enter Canton harbor. No foreign women were allowed into the Factories. There was to be no contact whatsoever between the foreigners and any Chinese subject unless it was through the intermediary of an appointed Chinese official, and that only for reasons of trade. On the Chinese side, the hong merchants—the only ones allowed to conduct trade with the foreigners—were under no circumstances allowed to accrue debt with any foreign party. When it came to leisure, the foreigners could stroll up to one hundred yards from their Factory but no farther. On the eighth, eighteenth, and twenty-eighth of each month they were graciously permitted to visit the nearby flower gardens, but they were not allowed to row on the river nor ride sedan chairs. The foreigners were also not permitted to learn the Chinese language or buy Chinese books. Traders resented the cramped lifestyle but were forced to accept it; it came with the job. Later, when tea became the main item of the China trade, disgruntled employees would walk up and down the one-hundred-yard circuit and rail against the herb that fetched millions but made them miserable, referring to it as "that blasted vegetable."

Japan solved the "foreign devils" problem in an even more extreme way. After allowing the Portuguese to settle on Japanese shores in 1543 and watching the growing influence of the Jesuit missionaries, the Japanese shoguns decided that Christianity brought with it the danger of colonization and therefore expelled the Portuguese from the country. A minuscule artificial island was built in the port of Nagasaki: Deshima—about six hundred feet long and two hundred feet wide (about 180 × 60m)—to which the Portuguese were relegated at first, but from which they were ultimately chased away altogether. From 1641 on, only the Dutch were allowed to stay on in Deshima and maintain minimal trade relations with Japan. As Protestants and practical businessmen, the Dutch were not interested in proselytizing and were therefore not perceived as threatening. Aside from Deshima, the Japanese shutdown from the rest of the Western world was complete and stayed in place until 1853 when American Commodore Matthew Perry arrived in Edo (as Tokyo was then called), demanding that Japan open its doors to trade.

During this era of trauma and turmoil, tea maintained its place in Chinese households, where it was counted as one of the seven daily necessities, along with fuel, rice, oil, salt, soy sauce, and vinegar. But the foreign devils didn't understand tea. In Europe, tea was mentioned briefly in the *Navigazioni et viaggi*, a 1559 account of world explorations by the Venetian Giambattista Ramusio. Some of the first Jesuit priests who had traveled to the East—among them the Portuguese Gaspar da Cruz as well as the Italians Matteo Ricci and Giovanni Botero—wrote about the strange medicinal herb and how the Chinese and the Japanese made use of it. And the Dutch Hugo van Linschooten, who sailed to the East with the Portuguese and who may have motivated the Dutch to enter the competition for the Eastern markets, also mentioned tea in his 1598 travel accounts on Japan. But overall, Europe was ignorant in matters of tea, a fact that greatly amused the Chinese. A story still circulates in Chinese tea circles. A Portuguese sailor once brought home some tea from China and gave it to his mother. Not knowing how to prepare it, the mother boiled it and served it to her guests, who found it bitter and not in the least attractive. When her son later inquired about what she had done with the water, the mother answered impatiently, "The water? Why in the world would I save the water if the stuff itself was so dreadful? I threw it away!"

Therefore, it was as a curiosity of secondary importance, the ugly duckling next to the star commodities of the time—nutmeg, pepper, cinnamon, cloves, and silks—that the traders threw the first satchels of tea in their ships, betting on its exotic novelty value. Little did they know that the dried-up, shriveled leaves would one day sustain or destroy economies and cause wars. The generally accepted date of the first tea import to Europe is 1610. The Dutch are credited with bringing some from Japan, although most likely the first shipments were Portuguese but went unacknowledged—except for the story of the sailor's mother. Within a short time, tea would burst onto the scene, becoming a central topic of medical disputes, and raising tempers all across Europe in indictment or defense of the new concoction.

The Impertinent Novelty of the Century

I must desire you to procure the chaw [*tea*], if possible. I care not what it cost. 'Tis for a good uncle of mine, Dr. Sheldon, whome some body hath perswaded to study the divinity of that herbe, leafe, or what else it is; and I am soe obliged to satisfy his curiosity that I could willingly undertake a viage to Japan or China to doe it. . . . *And when it didn't arrive:* For God's sake, good or badd, buy the chaw if it is to be sold. Pray favor me likewise with advise what 'tis good for, and how to be used.

—From a letter written by Daniel Sheldon urgently requesting a sample of the latest novelty, tea, for his uncle, the Archbishop of Canterbury, 1659

Can anyone imagine a world without tea? Or coffee? Or cocoa? A world without a hot, comforting, stimulating beverage to start the day or to move past the early afternoon slump? A world without the pleasure of a tea break, a quick espresso, or the delicious treat of a cup of hot cocoa on a cold day? Such a world was the Europe of the 1600s. A dreary Old World, from this perspective. But precious gifts were on their way, from distant lands and truly older worlds: tea from the Chinese, cocoa from the Aztecs, coffee from Yemen. They all landed on European tables within a few years of one another, brought by traders and explorers unleashed to the four corners of the globe.

Tea, so casually added to the precious spices, was to make quite a name for itself before long.

At first, tea was an expensive item afforded only by a restricted elite. Availability was contingent upon shipments arriving safely, and then only in apothecaries as a remedy. But as tea became more popular, the opinions about it multiplied. All across Europe, doctors, clergymen, and naturalists had something to say about the strange brew. One of the most famous advocates of tea was the Dutch Cornelius Decker, better known as Dr. Bontekoe, who in 1683 stated: "It must be a considerable and obstinate fever that cannot be cured by drinking every day forty to fifty cups of tea, about twenty of which are strong and bitter. This is an effect that we have proven recently on several patients and this is why we now reject all the remedies we used to use to cure such sicknesses. . . . We recommend in particular the use of tea for all sorts of people of both sexes, young and old, for all this nation, and all other peoples, and we advise them to drink it every day, at all times, all hours, as much as they can drink, beginning with eight to ten cups and eventually augmenting the dose to whatever amounts the stomach can hold. . . ." Dr. Bontekoe was rumored to be on the payroll of the Dutch merchants and may simply have been carried away in his endorsement fervor. Or perhaps he was carried away by his own caffeine high, as he claimed to drink that much tea himself.

The German physician Dr. Simon Paulli had expressed quite the opposite view a few years earlier, in 1665: "As to the virtues they attribute to it [tea], it may be admitted that it does possess them in the Orient, but it loses them in our climate, where it becomes, on the contrary, very dangerous to use. It hastens the death of those who drink it, especially if they have passed the age of forty years." It is doubtful whether they applied double-blind studies to ascertain the validity of medical assertions in those days. Another critic, the Austrian Jesuit Martino Martini, who lived in China from 1643 to 1650 is said to have shouted: "Down with tea! Send it back to the Garaments and Sauromates!" Clearly, he didn't develop a tea habit during those seven years, whoever the Garaments and the Sauromates may have

The Tea-Table, England, illustration for a broadside, England, 1709.
Courtesy of the Bramah Museum of Tea and Coffee, London.

been. And in 1648 France, the famed doctor Guy Patin, intrigued but
distrustful of anything new, made the following dismissive commentary on a thesis entitled "Does Tea Increase Mentality?" presented to
the medical community: "One of our doctors who is more celebrated
than able, named Morissot, wanting to bestow favor upon that impertinent novelty of the century, and trying in the process to take
credit for himself, has had presented here a thesis on tea. Everyone
disapproved, some of our doctors burned it, and the deans were re-
proached for having approved it." Following the controversy, the
Collège de France dismissed any medical value connected with the
Chinese herb.

Yet Cardinal Mazarin took tea for his gout, ignoring the opinions of the illustrious Collège de France, as did the poet Racine who was also fond of taking tea in the morning. The controversy was still alive two hundred years later, and no matter how many French celebrities loved tea, there would always be the hard-core Anglophobic, tea-hating Gaul who would not miss an opportunity to take a potshot at the archenemy across the Channel. Said A. Saint-Arroman in 1846: "The best tea of the Celestial Empire cannot bear a comparison with Bordeaux, Burgundy and Champagne . . . ," and he explained why the English simply had to drink tea: "The Englishman is naturally lymphatic; stuffed with beefsteaks and plum-pudding, he remains for two hours almost annihilated by the painful elaboration of the stomach; one might call him a boa quasi-asphyxiated by a gazelle that he has just swallowed. Tea alone can draw him from his lethargic sleep. . . ."

But back in the 1600s, when the English were not eating gazelles yet, tea was still finding its way into the heart of the island. Hypotheses abound as to how the first tea arrived in England. Did the Dutch traders bring it? Or the officers on board the cargo vessels bringing silks and spices, doing a little business on the side? Did the Jewish merchants from Amsterdam take it along when they were allowed back into England after Cromwell? And what about the Portuguese Catherine of Braganza who was wedded to Charles II, the Restoration king, in 1662? She did indeed bring Bombay as part of her dowry—royalty brought territories, not linen—but, more important, she brought a stash of tea along with it. Though often quoted, Queen Catherine was not the initiator; tea was known in England when she arrived. But she played her part in spreading the tea-drinking habit at court, not just as a remedy but as a leisure drink. The English ladies were only too eager to catch up on the latest fashions from the Continent. And the lonely queen found solace in the ever-comforting cup of tea, while her Charles made merry with that "other woman" at court, Barbara Villiers (additional cups would be necessary for all the subsequent other women).

Adulterers aside, England was slow to catch up to tea, compared to the rest of Europe. But once it did, the tea habit took over the

Garway's Slightly Skewed View on Tea and the Resulting Broadside

Tea! Thou soft, thou sober, sage, and venerable liquid, thou innocent pretence for bringing the wicked of both sexes together in a morning; thou female tongue-running, smile-smoothing, heart-opening, wink-tipping cordial, to whose glorious insipidity I owe the happiest moment of my life, let me fall prostrate thus, and . . . adore thee.

—Colley Cibber, *The Lady's Last Stake,*
an eighteenth-century play

In the down-to-earth circles of 1660s Stuart England, away from royalty and the medical establishment, shop owner Thomas Garway (also known as Garraway) was the tea man of the day. He is credited with being the first to spread the use of tea in England using modern methods: advertising. Garway had something to sell and went about it with great gusto. He distributed a broadside listing an impressive number of "vertues" possessed by the novelty beverage, the achievement of lust and of gentle vomit being among the desirable results of tea drinking. His marketing logic seems to have fol-

Silver Teapot, cast panels with chased and applied decoration, China, c. 1679. Peabody Essex Museum, Salem, Mass.

lowed the principle that if an ad covers absolutely everything, then absolutely everyone will buy the product.

Considering the prominent status tea gained in England within a very short period, Garway may just have been right. Around 1670, after doing business in several parts of London and surviving the Great Fire of 1666, Garway opened a shop on Exchange Alley in the financial district of London. The shop survived the owner by many decades and was immortalized as "Garraway's" in Victorian engravings. Tea was served there until the establishment closed down in 1866. Here are the essential parts of this extravagant and delightful piece of "shameless promotion."

An Exact Description of the Growth, Quality and Vertues of the Leaf TEA

*by Thomas Garway in Exchange Alley near the
Royal Exchange in London, Tobacconist, and Seller and
Retailer of TEA and COFFEE.*

. . . The said Leaf is of such known vertues, that those very Nations so famous for Antiquity, Knowledge and Wisdom, do frequently sell it among themselves for twice its weight in silver, and the high estimation of the Drink made therewith hath occasioned an inquiry into the nature thereof among the most intelligent persons of all Nations that have travelled in those parts, who after ex-

act Tryal and Experience by all wayes imaginable, have com-
mended it to the use of their several Countries, for its Vertues and
Operations, particularly as followeth, viz:

The Quality is moderately hot, proper for Winter or Summer.
The Drink is declared to be most wholesome, preserving in perfect health untill
extreme Old Age.
The particular Vertues are these.

* It maketh the body active and lusty.
* It helpeth the Head-ach, giddiness and heavyness thereof.
* It removeth the Obstructions of the Spleen.
* It is very good against the Stone and Gravel, cleansing the
  Kidneys and Uriters, being drank with Virgins Honey instead
  of Sugar.
* It taketh away the difficulty of breathing, opening Obstruc-
  tions.
* It is good against Lipitude Distillations and cleareth the Sight.
* It removeth Lassitude, and cleanseth and purifieth adult Hu-
  mors and a hot Liver.
* It is good against Crudities, strengthening the weakness of the
  Ventricle of Stomack, causing good Appetite and Digestion,
  and particularly for Men of a corpulent Body, and such as are
  great eaters of Flesh.
* It vanquisheth heavy dreams, easeth the Brain, and strengtheneth the Memory.
* It overcometh superfluous Sleep, and prevents Sleepiness in
  general, a draught of the Infusion being taken, so that without
  trouble whole nights may be spent in study without hurt to
  the Body, in that it moderately heateth and bindeth the mouth
  of the Stomack.
* It prevents and cures Agues, Surfets and Feavers, by infusing a
  fit quantity of the Leaf, thereby provoking a most gentle
  Vomit and breathing of the Pores, and hath been given with
  wonderful success.

❀ It (being prepared and drank with Milk and Water) strengtheneth the inward parts, and prevents Consumptions, and powerfully asswageth the pains of the Bowels, or griping of the Guts and Looseness.

❀ It is good for Colds, Dropsies and Scurveys, if properly infused, purging the Blood by sweat and urine, and expelleth infection.

❀ It drives away all pains in the Collick proceeding from Wind, and purgeth safely the Gall.

And that the Vertues and Excellencies of this Leaf and Drink are many and great is evident and manifest by the high esteem and use of it (especially of late years) among the Physitians and knowing men in *France, Italy, Holland* and other parts of Christendom. . . .

The Penny Universities

So great a Universitie
I think there ne'er was any
In which you may a scholar be
For spending of a Penny.

—"News from the Coffee-House,"
a 1667 broadside

"**A**nd afterwards I did send for a cup of tea (a China drink) of which I never had drank before, and went away." It was the Lord's Day, September 25, 1660, when diarist Samuel Pepys committed to written memory his first cup of tea. But if there was a Pepys to send for a cup, there must have been a place he sent *to* for same. Alas, the place was not a teahouse. It was a coffeehouse—or better yet, a "cophee house," as it was called in those days—named after the drink first served in those establishments. Before long, tea would take over and overshadow the Yemenite drink that gave the shops their name.

The first coffeehouse opened in Oxford in 1650, only ten years before Pepys's take-home order. Two years later, the Pasqua Rosée's Head—the first London coffeehouse—opened in St. Michael's Alley in Cornhill, serving coffee, tea, and chocolate, the novelty drinks of the day. After that, the deluge. Within a dozen years, there were more than eighty coffeehouses in London, and by the turn of the century that number had risen to five hundred. Not even the 1665 plague, which killed sixty-eight thousand people, nor the Great London Fire the year after, which nearly wiped out the city, could stop their proliferation. One reason for the success was good timing. In those years, London was a city bustling with activity. A city in which one could get stuck in a traffic jam (Pepys did, and complained about it in his diary)—a city on the way to becoming the center of world commerce. A city that was in sore need of public places for the emerging middle class, where the merchant, the office boy, the lawyer, the tailor, or the clerk could all stop and catch their breath on their way to their next meeting or errand.

It was in these coffeehouses—and not at Queen Catherine of Braganza's table—that tea was chosen over coffee and chocolate to become the national drink of England. Here is where store owners propagated, advertised, and sold tea. Here is where the average English citizen first tasted tea. One might say that the English cuppa and the English middle class were born in the same place at the same time.

The coffeehouse created a revolution not only in drinking habits but also in England's social life. The new stimulating beverage activated the brain chemistry in more ways than one. Along with tea, customers had access to newspapers, broadsides, gossip, the latest news too fresh to be printed, and vivacious conversation on all possible topics. For a mere penny, one could receive the comfort of a hot drink as well as an education of sorts, which is why the coffeehouses came to be known as the "penny universities." In a very short time they became lively social centers and an essential element of daily life in London. "Man is a sociable creature, and delights in company. Now, whither shall a person, wearied with hard study, or the laborious turmoils of a tedious day, repair to refresh himself? Or where can young gentlemen, or shop-keepers, more innocently and advantageously spend an hour or two in the evening, than at a coffee-house? . . . To read men is acknowledged more useful than books; but where is there a better library for that study, generally, than here; amongst such a variety of humours, all expressing themselves on divers subjects according to their respective abilities?" With these words the 1675 broadside "Coffee Houses Vindicated" confirmed the trend.

As humans are tribal in nature, people soon gravitated to one coffeehouse or another according to their interests, political inclinations, literary pursuits, or the type of business they were in. The poet John Dryden, for example, could be found at Will's, his home away from home for thirty years. Jonathan Swift and Alexander Pope frequented Button's, the new literary spot after Dryden's death. The Grecian was for scientists such as Isaac Newton and Edmund Halley; Jonathan's hosted money people; St. James's attracted politicians. Some of the coffeehouses became the starting point of businesses that are still in operation today. Lloyd's of London got its start by posting the latest shipping news and cargo information on the walls of a coffeehouse. The London Stock Exchange was conceived at Jonathan's. And *Tatler's*, the first modern magazine, started as a weekly compilation of the best gossip from all the coffeehouses.

Some people used the coffeehouse as their office, conducted their business from it, and even gave it as their permanent address. In his *History of England*, Thomas B. Macaulay noted "that the coffee-house was the Londoner's home, and that those who wished to find a gentleman commonly asked, not whether he lived in Fleet Street or Chancery Lane, but whether he frequented the Grecian or the Rainbow." As an example, people who were at home in more than one coffeehouse and wanted to be found wherever they were would give out their address as follows: "Dr. Tom Saffold at the Black Ball and Old Lilly's Head, next door to the Feather Shops that are within Black-Fryers Gateway, which is over against Ludgate Church, just by Ludgate in London." What a fascinating address, full of promises of mystery and adventure and feather-tickling, far more interesting than our bland street names and numbers.

Coffeehouses were open to everyone; the penny entrance fee ensured access even to low-income customers. Mixing social classes was a new thing in England, a sort of petri dish for democracy. This is how the author of a 1673 broadside, The Character of the Coffee-House, saw it: "As you have a hodge-podge of drinks, such too is your company, for each man seems a leveller, and ranks and files himself as he lists, without regard to degrees or order; so that often you may see a silly fop and a worshipful justice, a griping rook and a grave citizen, a worthy lawyer and an errant pickpocket, a reverend nonconformist and a canting mountebank, all blended together to compose an oglio [medley] of impertinence." However impertinent this particular author thought the medley to be, it was also vibrant humanity enjoying company and freedom. Visiting French author Abbé Prévost noted that London coffeehouses were the "seats of English liberty . . . where you have the right to read all the papers for and against the government."

And this is precisely what worried Charles II. However merry the Merry Monarch was, he was not so merry as to condone possible seditious behavior. Besides tea, there were rumors of anti-Stuart talk, secret plots, and general trouble brewing in the coffeehouses. Something needed to be done. On December 29, 1675, a "Proclamation for the Suppression of Coffee Houses" was issued:

> Whereas it is most apparent that the multitude of Coffee Houses of late years set up and kept within this Kingdom . . . and the great resort of Jdle and disaffected persons to them, have produced very evil and dangerous effects . . . in such houses and by occasion of the meetings of such persons therein, diverse, False, Malitious and Scandalous reports are devised and spread abroad, to the Defamation of His Majesty's Government, and to the disturbance of the Peace and Quiet of the Realm; his Majesty hath thought it fit and necessary, That the said Coffee-houses be (for the future) put down and suppressed . . . and doth . . . Strictly Charge and Command all manner of persons, That they or any of them do not presume from and after the Tenth Day of *January* next ensuing, to keep any Publick Coffee-house, or to Utter or sell by retail, in his, her or their house or houses (to be spent or consumed within the same) any Coffee, Chocolet, Sherbett or Tea, as they will answer the contrary at their utmost perils. . . .

Selling tea and "Liquors of the sort" remained an act punishable by law for exactly eleven days. The popular outcry against the closure of the coffeehouses was such that on January 8, 1676, a new

proclamation was hurriedly issued that recalled the previous
one "out of princely consideration and royal compassion." Most
likely, the recall had more to do
with lost revenues than with royal
compassion. Either way, the People of the Coffeehouses had won.
Compassionees could go back to
their cups of tea and conversations, however seditious they may
have been.

The coffeehouses lasted for
two hundred years, after which
many of them fell in disrepute,
shut down, or turned into private
clubs, betraying their democratic,
all-inclusive beginnings. Nothing
in the world is more restrictive
than the institution of the British
club, to which the privileged few
can repair, with their cigar, their
sherry, and their copy of *The Times*.
But, as far as the tea story goes,
the coffeehouses had fulfilled their
function. They had transformed tea
from an exotic curiosity for the
aristocratic leisure class to a restorative beverage for the rest of the
population.

Pots à preparer le Thé, engraving, France, 1687.
Reprinted from *Le bon usage du thé, du café et
du chocolat pour la préservation & pour la guérison
des Maladies* (The Good Use of Tea, Coffee,
and Chocolate for Preserving Health and
for Treatment of Maladies), by Nicolas de
Blegny, engraving, France, 1687. Bitting
Collection, Rare Books, Library of Congress, Washington, D.C.

The Revenge of the Fair Sex

Her two red lips affected Zephyrs blow,
To cool the Bohea [tea], and inflame the Beau;
While one white Finger and a Thumb
Conspire
To lift the Cup and make the World
Admire.

—Edward Young, "Love of Fame," 1725

At the height of their popularity, the seventeenth-century coffee-houses in England were off limits to women. The social order dictated that wives yield to their husbands and daughters to their brothers, fulfilling their expected roles at home. But times were changing, and the power structure was beginning to be questioned. The more men went to the coffeehouses, the more women resented staying at home. In time, the aggregate discontent grew to the point of giving birth to a pamphlet entitled "The Women's Petition Against Coffee." The object of indictment was indeed coffee, but the real complaint was quite another.

The main issue was clearly stated in the subtitle: "Humble Petition and Address of several Thousands of Buxome Good Women, Languishing in Extremity of Want." The subsequent text didn't mince words, either. In it the female collective reminisced about the good old times when England was a "Paradise for Women" and its men were the "Ablest Performers in Christendome." They recalled that there was a "Golden Age when Lusty Ladds of seven or eight hundred years old got Sons and Daughters," and that in countries other than England they had the opposite problem. They cited Spain where men had to be restrained and a law was issued "that Men should not Repeat the Grand Kindness to their Wives above NINE times in a night."

But now that the English male was spending so much time in the coffeehouses, the women noticed a "sensible Decay of that true Old English Vigour; our Gallants being every way so Frenchified that they are become meer Cock-sparrows . . . and in the very first Charge fall down flat before us." They come home, the women complain, "with nothing moist but their snotty Noses, nothing stiffe but their Joints." None of the "arts" the women used could "revive them from this Lethargy, so unfit they are for Action, that like young Trainband-men when called upon Duty, their Amunition is wanting; peradventure they Present, but cannot give Fire, or at least do but flash in the Pan, instead of doing Execution." Such a petition was indeed published and circulated in London in 1674.

Specifically, the chosen scapegoat was that "little base, black, thick, nasty, bitter, stinking nauseous Puddle water"—in other words, coffee. The women were convinced that it was "the Excessive Use of that Newfangled, Abominable, Heathenish Liquor called Coffee, which . . . Eunucht our Husbands." Nor was the lacking in "nocturnal benevolencies" the only complaint. The women were also concerned that by spending so much time talking to one another, the men would "usurp on our Prerogative of Tatling, and soon learn to excel us in Talkativeness: a Quality wherein our Sex has ever Claimed preheminence: For here like so many Frogs in a puddle, they sup muddy water, and murmur insignificant notes till half a dozen of them out babble an equal number of us at a Gossipping."

The men were not going to take it lying down—literally—and published their own "Mens Answer to the Womens Petition Against Coffee" in response to that "scandalous pamphlet" so many "ungrateful women" had dared to circulate. "Talk not to us of those doating

Fumblers of seven or eight hundred years Old. . . . That our Land is a Paradise for Women is verified by the brisk Activity of our Men," they stated flatly and went on to expound on their obliging efforts to satisfy their women: "Have we not with excess of Patience born your affronts, been Sweated, Purged, Fluxed between two Feather-beds, flog'd, Jib'd, and endured all the rest of the Devils Martyrdoms, and will you still offer to Repine? Certainly, experience'd Solomon was in the right when he told us that the Grave and the womb were equally insatiable." And so what if the men didn't spend much time at home? If anything, they offered the women a gracious opportunity for a little extramarital exploration: "You will not think it Impertinent, when you consider the fair opportunities you have thereby of entertaining an obliging friend in our Absence."

Coffee, that "harmless and healing liquor," was certainly not the problem, the men's reply continued. On the contrary, and to speak in plain English: "Coffee collects and settles the Spirits, makes the erection more Vigorous, the Ejaculation more full, adds a spiritualescency to the Sperme, and renders it more firm and suitable to the Gusto of the womb, and proportionate to the ardours and expectations too, of the female Paramour." If things still didn't work out, "the occasion of the defect" must be due to the "Husband's natural infirmity," the men considered, or, most likely to "your own perpetual Pumping him, not drinking Coffee." And as far as the gossiping was concerned: "You may well permit us to talk abroad, for at home we have scarce time to utter a word for the insufferable Din of your ever active Tongues." After a last attempt to appeal to the women's reason by reminding them that "the Coffee House is the Citizens Accademy," the men closed their argument with a not-so-subtle threat: "And let all our wives that hereafter shall presume to Petition against it, be confined to lie alone all Night, and in the Day time drink nothing but Bonny Clabber [sour buttermilk]."

And that was that. What was probably the largest en masse episode of public marital bickering the world had ever witnessed was over. It wasn't the coffee per se, and certainly not tea, which was not even a defendant in the trial, even though it was widely consumed in the coffeehouses. Most likely, women were simply resentful of being excluded from the company and reacted by attacking men in their most vulnerable area. Today we consider sitting around a table sipping tea and having a conversation with friends as an activity any human being should be entitled to, regardless of gender. Yet, three hundred years ago women fought for it and lost. For the time being, at least, it appeared that the men had won the battle; they continued to go to the coffeehouses, and the women stayed home. By extension, since coffee, tea, and chocolate were served only in the establishments, women had no access to the beverages, either. Only sour buttermilk for them.

Then something happened. Colonial imports were rapidly gaining significance, and tea became too big to be contained within the four walls of a coffeehouse. Thomas Twining, the first of a three-hundred-year-old uninterrupted succession of Twinings in the tea trade, had started Tom's Coffee House in 1706. He was doing so well that in 1717 he opened a second shop next door, the Golden Lyon. Twining must have sensed an untapped market in tea and set up the Golden Lyon not as a coffeehouse but as the first true English tea shop, where patrons could buy dry-leaf tea to brew at home. The revolutionary element of the Golden Lyon was that ladies were welcome to come in and taste the blends. Soon "great ladies flocked to Twining's house in Devereaux Court in order to sip the enlivening beverage in small cups for which they paid their shillings," quotes William Ukers in *All About Tea*. Protofeminism or good business? We'll never know. Thomas Twining may have been one of the first agents of change, but tea was ready to make the transition from the male public establishment to the English home, from where it would soon reign over the vast lands of the British empire—with women the masters of ceremony.

In a short time, dry-leaf tea was everywhere. Along with the newly emerging figure of the tea grocer, women's shops selling textiles, hats, or sewing supplies also started selling dry-leaf tea on the side. One Yorkshire Quaker woman, Mary Tuke, made tea history in 1725. A single woman with no family connections, Mary was harassed in various ways, including being fined for selling tea without a license; but she went on with determination to become the first female tea dealer in a business dominated by men. Women were selling, and women were buying. The lady of the house had her preferred grocer and her preferred blends. The lady of the house kept her precious tea locked away in the newly acquired tea caddy, the key to which hung safely around her neck. And before long, the lady of the house decided who got invited to tea and what the topic of conversation would be.

Now it was the men's turn to complain. The ladies sat and conversed while the men had to stand behind them, preferably listening in polite silence. The ladies spent too much money on that wretched leaf, the men said, and even more on the newly imported chinaware. In a 1722 pamphlet condemning the excessive spending on tea, a "Whipping-Tom" writing "in order to touch the Fair Sex to the Quick" stated that a husband "had better trust his Hand in the Mouth of a Lion, his Substance to the Management of a Whore, his Conscience to a Horse-Courser, or his Religion to a Synagogue of Jews [anti-Semitism was a fact of life then], than his Purse in the Hands of his Wife, that's a Tea-Drinker." In addition to wreaking havoc on finances, tea was encouraging idleness, as the ladies spent endless hours at the tripod table and neglected house duties—and their spouses.

As if that were not enough, the conversation was desperately boring, and the gossip simply intolerable. "Then to hear insignificant Chit-chat, and dull impertinent Discourse, which these Tatterdemalions . . . have over their Tea, would make the lunatick Inhabitants of Bedlam laugh at 'em; their gossiping over their Sippings, would make a fool loath their Conversation," added Whipping-Tom a little later in his pamphlet. Real men—and the author of said pamphlet must surely have seen himself as one—also had scathing words for the other kind of men, the ones who still, after all this, attended tea parties. These were the same kinds of "real men" who, a century earlier, had fought against the use of the fork in England—a common practice in Italy at the time—labeling it an unmanly affectation and an "excessive delicacy." Every century has its particular brand of "real men." The eighteenth-century ones considered that any man choosing to participate in such debauched habits as tea drinking with the ladies, and submitting to the strictures and etiquette dictated by them, was a man who had lost his manly virtues and was nothing more than an effeminate fop gobbling down cucumber sandwiches, or else a dandy intent on seduction and abandonment.

But it was too late. Anyone who was anyone had to be seen at the latest, fanciest tea party, not at the coffeehouse. It was tea parties that conferred social status—to the guest, who knew that by being invited he or she "belonged." And to the hostess who confirmed her position by showing off the latest tea sets or the grand new canvas depicting the family. It was at tea parties that activities such as social climbing or matchmaking occurred, and the latest society news was apprehended. The coffeehouses had descended to the level of tavern. And when women were done conquering the parlor, they went on to extend their dominions to other territories: the pleasure gardens, such as Vauxhall, Ranelagh, or Marylebone, and the many others opening around London. These were the newly fashionable centers of social activity, where polite society would go and listen to the latest compositions by Haydn or Handel, take tea in the tearooms or at a table outside, admire the elaborate fountains, enjoy the fireworks at night, or simply walk along the paths and take in the fresh air. Just like the coffeehouses, the eighteenth-century pleasure gardens—or tea gardens, as they were also called, for every entertainment was accompanied by tea—were open to people of all walks of life. Their success was clear evidence of the ascent of the English middle class and its increasing wealth and access to leisure. By including the women as patrons, the pleasure gardens became the first public spaces that welcomed the presence of mixed company, not only in terms of social status but also where gender was concerned.

With that, women had come full circle, and victory for the fair sex was complete. Exclusionary coffeehouses discredited, full control over the tea party at home, unlimited access to flirting at tea garden outings, away from the surveillance of stern tutors and great-aunts.

The verse accompanying the illustration reads:
All innocent within the Shade you see,
This little Party sip salubrious Tea,
Soft Tittle-Tattle rises from the Stream,
Sweetn'd each word with Sugar & with Cream.
The Tea Gardens, illustration published by Robert Sayer,
England, 1788. Courtesy of the Bramah Museum of Tea and
Coffee, London.

And tea flowing for everyone. Did the commercial success of tea unwittingly foment women's emancipation? Or did women simply use tea as one of the vehicles for their agenda, thereby furthering tea's commercial success? The question is open to debate. Either way, the womanly touch had pervaded the world of tea, and there was no going back.

Smuggling and Smouch

A little Tea; one leaf I did not steal.
For guiltless bloodshed I to God appeal.
Put Tea in one scale, human Blood in t'other,
And think what 'tis to slay thy harmless Brother.

—On the gravestone of Robert Trotman, allegedly a
member of a smuggling gang, who was
"barbarously murdered on the shore near Poole,
the 24th of March, 1765"—St Andrew's Church,
Kinson, Bournemouth, England

A shadow steals through the night. A rapping, the usual signal. A woman opens the window, careful not to make a sound. She hands down money, takes in a satchel of tea. No words are exchanged, just a smile in the dark. The shadow disappears, the window is closed; for the time being, tea provisions for the family are secured. Back in the warmth of her bed, the woman looks forward to the morning cup she has been missing since her tea stash ran out. The sweet anticipation far outweighs the fear of punishment for once again having committed the crime of purchasing "run" (smuggled) tea.

Such a scene took place thousands of times every night in eighteenth-century England. Back then, tea was an item of contraband, along with tobacco, alcohol, silks, salt, and all sorts of spices. Sell or buy any of these items other than at the official outlets and you would end up behind bars. Why would such a harmless substance as tea trigger condemnation? All contraband develops either because governments impose high taxes on import items or because the trade is controlled by monopolies, which set high prices for the items to maximize profits. Tea smuggling was a consequence of both.

The Tax

The success of the coffeehouses, the true birthplace of the English tea habit, brought with it an unintended consequence. The more people enjoyed the fashionable beverage and flocked to the stimulating atmosphere of the coffeehouses, the more they became noticeable as an excellent source of tax revenue. The English monarchy needed money to fund its after-Cromwell administration. When Charles II became king in 1660 he wasted no time in instituting an excise tax of eight pence per gallon of tea sold. The owners of the establishments were also required to obtain and pay for a business license and found themselves double-taxed from one day to the next.

The natural result of the new measure was that the tea containers (brewed tea was kept in kegs and heated as needed, alas) were refilled at night so as to appear full to the government inspector. And of course, it was impossible to go around and measure how many cups of tea each customer gulped down in the overheated and overcrowded rooms. The tax was soon converted to an import tax on dry tea. This is the very tax that triggered most unfortunate consequences for the British empire, the most famous one being the American Revolution and the loss of a major colony. In the course of time, the percentage of the tea duty fluctuated, depending on the political atmosphere and the needs of the government. But from the initial, fairly innocuous eight pence per gallon it reached an exasperating 119 percent of the sale price, a figure that would turn even the most law-abiding citizen into a "tea criminal."

The Monopoly

While the English were paying good money for reheated keg tea, the Dutch East India Company, the main tea importers into England, were raking in the profits. The English East India Company was busy trading spices and silks and was slow to catch on to the business potential of tea. At the time of the first English official purchase of tea in 1664, the Dutch had been importing tea and selling it all around Europe for more than fifty years. But once the English East India Company machine was set in motion, the tables turned.

Anglo-Dutch trade tensions were ongoing, and the English government did not hesitate to take measures against the Dutch. The first move was to increase the duty on Dutch imports. But this was not enough. Soon a more extreme measure was taken: in 1667 all Dutch imports were simply declared illegal by the English government. Meanwhile, the English East India Company had secured, against fierce commercial competition with both the Dutch and the Portuguese, a Chinese trading post at Amoy. From there, the first Company tea shipment made its way to England in 1669. With its government charter and the trade measures protecting it at home, the Company found itself the holder of a monopoly on Far Eastern trade. The initial myopia soon turned into trading frenzy. In a few decades, tea became the Company's main commodity. But monopolies have a habit of sending prices up, and soon only the very rich could afford to buy legal tea. For the majority of the population, officially imported and taxed tea remained an unattainable item, and regular folks were forced to look elsewhere for alternatives.

The Contraband

High taxes, high prices: Perfect conditions were now in place for a flourishing smuggling business. Legal imports of tea went from about twenty thousand pounds annually at the beginning of the eighteenth century to twenty million pounds a year by the end of the century. Half—or even two-thirds, by some estimates—of all the tea consumed in England was smuggled. Hence, a staggering ten to fifteen million pounds of bootlegged tea were consumed in English households. The trade was by no means restricted to bandits and hoodlums. Fishermen unloaded the tea cargo from ships waiting off the southern coasts of Cornwall or Kent. Farmers and laborers transported it on land. Clergymen stored it in their church vaults. Bribed customs officers looked the other way. East India Company ship captains and various and sundry petty officers dropped off their own smuggled stash, before sailing into the Thames to deliver the official company cargo. And members of the very board of trade that was trying to control the smuggling business bought and consumed smuggled tea at a fraction of the price of the legally imported one.

"A quite peculiar elasticity of conscience universally prevailed throughout the kingdom" wrote Henry Shore in 1892 in *Smuggling Days and Smuggling Ways*. By some accounts, the smuggling business

Loading Tea Junks at Tseen-tang, by Thomas Allom, engraving, England, c. 1840s. Reprinted from Wright, *The Chinese Empire: Historical and Descriptive*, 1843.

was so lucrative that at one point the fishing and farming trade experienced a shortage of labor. This was hardly surprising, considering the conditions of extreme poverty, and sometimes starvation, in which the great majority of the English rural population lived. Honesty, as they say, was not a luxury many of them could afford. And there were also those who supported the practice on principle: "I like a smuggler. He is the only honest thief. He robs nothing but the revenue—an abstraction I never greatly cared about. I could go out with him in his mackerel boat, or about his less ostensible business, with some satisfaction," wrote Charles Lamb, who saw no contradiction between his statement and the fact that he was on the payroll of the East India Company.

Outside of England, whole countries were involved in the business. The Dutch continued to import tea into England just as before, if not more so, simply by "adjusting" their deliveries from official daytime company dockings to nighttime offshore drops into the holds of fishing boats turned smuggling vessels for the night. They also furnished almost all of the tea to the American colonies, where tea drinking was as popular as in the mother country, and where smuggled tea was preferred to taxed tea, as if in anticipation of things to come. The Swedish East India Company, hurriedly formed with Dutch, English, and even Austrian employees, did not even bother with any other trade but the smuggling of tea into England via Scottish shores.

All this activity was by no means a peaceful one. Smugglers formed powerful and well-armed gangs, some of which accrued legendary status: the Hawkhurst Gang, the Mayfield Gang, the Groombridge Gang. Armed conflicts between smugglers and customs officers were frequent and bloody. The smugglers, who were supported and protected by the general population, generally outnumbered the customs officers and did not hesitate to kill any one of them to carry on their trade. If a smuggler killed an officer and was caught, he was executed, and his body hung on a gibbet along the coast as a warning. But this did not happen often.

Smugglers were particularly brutal with informers, or "King's evidence," as they were called then. One of the most famous cases involves the Hawkhurst Gang, which successfully attacked the Custom House at Poole to recover thirty-seven hundred pounds of tea seized by customs officers. Sometime after the attack, the gang grew suspicious about two men, Galley and Chater, possibly being informers. The two were caught and questioned but, instead of being tied to a tree, whipped, and then put on a boat to France—a common practice, in those days, to remove anyone interfering with smuggling procedures—they endured days of hellish torture. They were held captive and beaten, and then tied to their horses and whipped by the whole gang, particularly by their ringleader Jackson. When they fell over in agony they were forced to continue to ride with their heads under the horse's belly for a while. Then they were set upright, and the whole thing started again. At one point, a wretched Galley is reported to have murmured: "For God's sake, shoot me through the head." But this was not to be. Galley's body was buried in a sandpit, and it is unclear whether the smugglers were aware that he was still alive when he was buried. When the corpse was exhumed, his hands were found held over his face, as if to protect it. Chater was hanged, headfirst, into the bottom of a well and stoned to death.

Ultimately, this ferocious behavior is what lost the smugglers the much-needed support of the local population. An anonymous letter denounced members of the Hawkhurst Gang who were caught, put on trial, and executed. Jackson is said to have died of fear in his cell before his execution.

The Smouch

The demand for tea was so great that along with the smuggling a second and also very profitable trade developed: tea adulteration. Started by the Chinese, who were unable to meet the growing demands of the European market but unwilling to lose any business, adulteration of tea proceeded into England and became a serious industry. Several shops were set up in London, and a young tea importer of the time, Richard Twining—grandson of Thomas, the founder of the Twining house—complained that there was a whole village near London where the adulteration of tea was the main occupation, producing as much as twenty tons of it yearly. According to Twining, the recipe and ingredients of the adulterating compound, commonly called "smouch," were quite shocking: "When the [ash tree] leaves are gathered they are boiled in a copper with copperas [ferrous sulfate to obtain a green dye] and sheep's dung; when the liquor is strained off, they are baked and trod upon, until the leaves are small, after which they are fit for use."

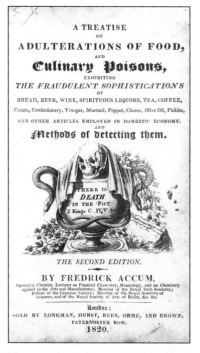

A TREATISE
ON
ADULTERATIONS OF FOOD,
AND
Culinary Poisons,
EXHIBITING
THE FRAUDULENT SOPHISTICATIONS
OF
BREAD, BEER, WINE, SPIRITUOUS LIQUORS, TEA, COFFEE,
Cream, Confectionery, Vinegar, Mustard, Pepper, Cheese, Olive Oil, Pickles,
AND OTHER ARTICLES EMPLOYED IN DOMESTIC ECONOMY.
AND
Methods of detecting them.

THERE IS
DEATH
IN THE POT
2 Kings C. IV. V.

THE SECOND EDITION.

BY FREDRICK ACCUM,
Operative Chemist, Lecturer on Practical Chemistry, Mineralogy, and on Chemistry
applied to the Arts and Manufactures; Member of the Royal Irish Academy;
Fellow of the Linnean Society; Member of the Royal Academy of
sciences, and of the Royal Society of Arts of Berlin, &c. &c.

London:
SOLD BY LONGMAN, HURST, REES, ORME, AND BROWN,
PATERNOSTER ROW,
1820.

There Is Death in the Pot, frontispiece illustration, England, 1820. Reprinted from *A Treatise on Adulterations of Food and Culinary Poisons Exhibiting the Fraudulent Sophistications of Bread, Beer, Wine, Spirituous Liquors, Tea, Coffee . . .* by Fredrick Accum, 1820. Bitting Collection, Rare Books, Library of Congress, Washington, D.C.

Other accounts listed additional smouch ingredients such as spent and dried tea leaves, or leaves from entirely different plants; gypsum, clay, iron filings, or sand to increase the weight; and Prussian blue, turmeric, soapstone, or plumbago to improve the appearance. Sawdust was another preferred adulterant and became such a problem that the government expressed concern about "the injury and destruction of great quantities of timber, wood, and underwoods," not to mention the "prejudice of His Majesty's subjects, the diminution of the revenue, the ruin of the fair trader, and the encouragement of idleness."

One can only imagine how tea must have tasted then. And yet, people drank enormous amounts of it every day. Conceivably, the well-known prejudice about Englishmen having trouble distinguishing good food from bad might date back to these days of mass acceptance of such a staple into the daily diet. According to William Ukers in *All About Tea*, one unintended and unfortunate consequence of the adulteration business has survived to our days. Green tea was much easier to adulterate than Bohea tea, as black tea was called in those days. Consequently, Europeans lost confidence in green tea and switched to black tea, which might explain in part why 80 percent of all tea consumed in the world today is black.

How It All Ended

A 1725 law against adulteration with a one-hundred-pound fine did not make much difference. Nor did the 1766 penalty of imprisonment added to it, or the subsequent Act of 1777. On the smuggling front, neither the 1736 Smuggling Bill nor the numerous acts of Parliament against smuggling in general were of much help, often because of the dim wit exhibited by the legislators who devised them. The reasoning behind one of these measures, passed in 1781 in an attempt to control smuggling by controlling transport, is worth mentioning as a particularly good example of "brilliant" legislating. Denys Forrest describes it thus in *Tea for the British*: "Next to Charles II's attempt to tax tea by liquid measure, this last was about the most fatuous piece of legislation in the history of our subject. It laid down that no package of tea weighing more than 6 lb. could be brought into London from outside, or more than 40 lb. (later 20 lb.) could be moved from A to B in the country. Removals *from* London were unrestricted. The cheerful response of the smuggling interest was to set up 'shops' in the suburbs, whence a steady flow of 6 lb. packets streamed day and night into the Metropolis."

What really put an end to most of the illicit activities relating to tea was William Pitt's 1784 Commutation Act, which reduced the tea duty from 119 percent to 12.5 percent. The smugglers and the domestic adulteration shops were virtually put out of business overnight. But, as Forrest added, the tea trade owed the smugglers a thank-you after all, because "it was largely due to their clandestine enterprise and cut rates that the habit of tea-drinking spread to the remotest corners of the Kingdom and into the least opulent homes." As far as the government was concerned, no revenues were lost with the Commutation Act. The tea duty was not repealed altogether; it was simply "commutated" into a new tax—this one on . . . windows. Innovative legislators must have considered that it was easier to count the number of windows on people's homes, and then charge them a duty according to how many were built into the walls, than track down smuggled tea. As an aside, the Commutation Act initiated the new fashion, for the wealthy, of designing buildings with unusually large windows, while the poor walled up as many windows as possible, no matter how small they were.

A subsequent Food and Drug Act in 1875 also eliminated what remained of the Far Eastern adulterated teas, the *maloo*, which was made up of spent leaves, and the spurious tea called *li*. They were simply sent back to manufacturers and middlemen, who did not survive long trying to sell surpluses of bad teas. On the nonlegislative end of things, the tea merchant John Horniman, an English Quaker, came up with an ingenious idea to counter the danger of adulteration. In a world where tea was sold loose from bulk, he reasoned, why not sell tea weighed, sealed, and packaged with a recognizable and trusted grocer's name—for example, Horniman's Tea—on it? It was a good idea, but it took time to gain acceptance. Horniman peddled his tea packages around the countryside traveling on his bicycle for years before he established himself as a major player in the tea trade. But in the end he did start a worldwide trend, which produced the sumptuous tea boxes of the turn of the century. Nowadays we are left with the rather forgettable mass-marketed tins and cardboard packages anonymously lined up on the store shelves. At least they don't contain sheep's dung.

Sugar, Anyone?

Slaves were a "false commodity" because a human being is not an object, even when treated as one. In this instance, millions of human beings were treated as commodities. To obtain them, products were shipped to Africa; by their labor power, wealth was created in the Americas. The wealth they created mostly returned to Britain; the products they made were consumed in Britain; and the products made by Britons—cloth, tools, torture instruments—were consumed by slaves who were themselves consumed in the creation of wealth.

—Sidney Mintz, *Sweetness and Power: The Place of Sugar in Modern History*, 1985

The great Queen Elizabeth I had rotten teeth. Foreign ambassadors visiting the royal court whispered their amazement to one another with regards to the unseemly appearance of Her Majesty's mouth. It was said that the Queen had a powerful sugar habit, a luxury only few could afford at the time.

Before the arrival of cane sugar into Europe, honey had been used as a sweetener, but the dissolution of the English monasteries—the main honey producers—during the Reformation had seriously diminished supplies. The first cane sugar was imported from Venetian and Arab traders and later from the Spanish and Portuguese South American plantations. It was used in minimal quantities, mostly by apothecaries to reduce the bitterness of herbs and concoctions, or as an exotic delicacy in such privileged households as the queen's. Sugar might have been limited to this marginal role had it not been for the arrival on the scene of a commodity that was to exert, directly or indirectly, a major influence over the lives of millions of people. That commodity was tea.

It is unclear when and why the English first started putting sugar in their tea. Perhaps because they sometimes added sugar to their wine, or perhaps because tea itself was first used for medicinal purposes and therefore sweetened. The practice surely did not arrive from China along with the tea chests. A Chinese, so keenly aware of the delicate balance between taste sensations, would have fainted watching an Englishman pour several teaspoons of sugar into the heavenly beverage; to this day, the Chinese do not use sugar in their tea. But pour it in the Englishmen did, in great amounts and with great consistency—hence the word *teaspoon*. As to when the practice started, history is equally fuzzy. It was possibly around the last quarter of the seventeenth century. Though by the 1750s, when tea, and to a lesser extent the other two colonial beverages, coffee and chocolate, had spread from aristocratic circles to the urban population and to the countryside, stirring sugar into a hot beverage had become a customary and, for many, an essential element of the day's functioning.

The English climate may have contributed to the sugared-tea habit. Can anyone imagine a more perfect antidote to a perennial gloomy drizzle and an insistent, bone-penetrating humidity than the reassuring comfort of a steaming cup of tea? And when sugar and a few biscuits were added to the equation, the sun came out from behind the clouds! It was as if the Chinese had custom-designed tea as a remedy against England's winters (and even some summers). Yet aside from the weather, important social developments contributed to the growing popularity of sweetened tea. According to anthropologist Sidney Mintz in *Sweetness and Power: The Place of Sugar in Modern History*, the nobility may have introduced tea to England, but it was the working class that turned the consumption of tea with sugar into a national mass habit. Although expensive within the general household budget, tea was relatively cheap when compared to coffee and chocolate, and more easily adulterated. Only a few leaves, often treated with questionable ingredients, were enough to make a hot drink. As such, tea solved an important budgetary problem. A pinch of it went a long way, and, with a little sugar, it provided much needed, though not nutritious, calories.

Cheap and energetic, sweetened tea became not only the preferred but the essential beverage of the working poor in late-eighteenth-century England. Within a diet that consisted mainly of bread and potatoes with the very occasional piece of bacon or cheese, sweet tea became the cheap alternative to real food and offered the temporary illusion of a hot, nutritious meal. When there was butter for the bread, it was a treat, but the bread slice was always thin. As a visitor to London commented: "The Butter and Tea which the Londoners live upon from morning until three or four in the afternoon, occasions the chief consumption of bread, which is cut in slices, and so thin, that it does as much honour to the address of the person that cut it, as to the sharpness of the knife." In addition, Mintz argues that in a rapidly industrializing society, tea and sugar became necessities for another practical reason. When women became factory workers, putting on some water for tea consumed very little fuel and was also a quick thing to do in the evening coming home from work. Sweet tea with bread often became the main meal of the day for simple lack of time. As a whole, nutritional standards declined sharply, especially for women and children, who renounced what little protein was available for the benefit of the working males in the family.

Tea was clearly the pied piper of English sugar addiction, which expanded from sweet tea to the copious amounts of sweet breads, tarts, puddings, jams, and biscuits that came to be its ideal accompaniment. In time, sugar became more affordable, and annual per capita sugar consumption in England rose by 350 percent, from four pounds in 1700 to eighteen pounds in 1800. The phenomenal success of the beverage had triggered a demand for the condiment, the two by then considered inseparable companions. China was able to provide tea to

England throughout the eighteenth century. Yet how could tiny Barbados and the other Caribbean sugar islands under British management keep up with the massive amounts of sugar the English sweet tooth required? The answer is in all the history books. The commercial success of a commodity was achieved at the cost of the irreparable human failure and horror of the slave trade. It is said that up to 70 percent of slave traffic supported the sugar industry. And tea, that most innocent of beverages, was the main, albeit accidental, trigger of the disaster.

While British citizens sipped their tea, British merchant ships were busy crossing the Atlantic with human cargo. During the eighteenth century alone, they transported 3 million Africans from their home countries to the Caribbean. For comparison, in 1800 the entire population of England and Wales was 9 million. Imagine kidnapping a third of the strongest, most able-bodied English and Welsh men in their prime. During the three hundred years of the international slave trade, 15 to 20 million Africans were forced onto the nightmare of the Middle Passage, the traumatic sea voyage from Africa to the New World. As the antislavery movement gained momentum, and sugar was identified as the main cause of the slave trade, the Antisaccharites, as the activists came to be known, encouraged the public to abstain from consuming sugar: "Think but for one minute at what a trifling sacrifice the redemption of 800,000 of our fellow creatures from the lowest condition of degradation and misery can be accomplished. Abstinence from one single article of luxury would annihilate this West Indian Slavery," suggested a British 1826 appeal.

Opponents of slavery circulated pamphlets, signed mass petitions, and organized boycotts of West India sugar. This prompted such competitors as the East India Company, which imported sugar from India, to adjust their marketing angle and advertise their own ware as "Sugar not made by Slaves . . . A Family that uses 5lb. of Sugar a Week will, by using East India instead of West India, for 21 Months, prevent the Slavery, or Murder, of one Fellow Creature! Eight such Families in 19½ years will prevent the Slavery, or Murder of 100!!" Of course, the East India Company well knew that slavery and bonded labor were common practice in India as well, which made East Indian sugar not very different from West Indian sugar in that respect. But the general public was not aware of this, and the Company wasn't going to tell.

Slavery in the British dominions was abolished during 1834–38, in part due to the pressure of the antislavery reform movement, but to a great extent because the economics of slavery had become less profitable. This did not slow down tea consumption. On the contrary, the industry continued to grow unperturbed, especially after the 1850s, when tea became an empire product from British India. Where tea went, sugar followed. In 1800, 30 million pounds of tea and 300 million pounds of sugar were imported to England. Fifty years later the yearly figures grew to 56 million pounds of tea and 1 billion pounds of sugar. Before the century was over, England imported 300 million pounds of tea, and annual sugar consumption had reached nearly ninety pounds per person.

Sugar was never in short supply. After emancipation, "free" laborers, who were possibly even worse off than when they had been slaves, continued to produce West Indian cane sugar. But the truly slave-free source of sugar came from Berlin, where the German scientist Andreas Marggraf had succeeded in extracting sugar from the root of the sugar beet. His discovery lay dormant for half a century until, in 1811, France put it to use. Napoleon encouraged domestic beet sugar production to get around the British blockade of French ports during the Napoleonic Wars. Sugar beet plantations and refineries sprang up across France and Europe, and by the end of the nineteenth century beet sugar was firmly in place as the main sweetener.

Tea, the unwitting vector of boundless human misery on an intercontinental scale, had survived yet another historical permutation and could now be enjoyed with a clean conscience. At least, as far as sugar was concerned.

Gin Lane, Tea Lane

Wine, Beere, and Ale, together by the Eares

Wine:	I, iouiall Wine, exhilirate the heart.
Beere:	Marche-Beere is drinke for a king.
Ale:	But Ale, bonny Ale, with spice and a tost,
	In the morning's a daintie thing.
Chorus:	Then let us be merry, wash sorrow away,
	Wine, Beere, and Ale shall be drunke to-day.
Wine:	I, generous Wine, am for the Court.
Beere:	The Citie calls for Beere.
Ale:	But Ale, bonny Ale, like a lord of the soyle,
	In the Countrey shall domineere.
Chorus:	Then let us be merry, wash sorrow away,
	Wine, Beere, and Ale shall be drunke to-day.

—Drinking song by John Grove, 1629

In addition to sugar, tea's rise to stardom in British life was linked to another substance, also sugar related and also addictive but with a different societal impact: alcohol. In different forms and concentrations, alcoholic beverages were part of the British diet to an extent that is hard to imagine in our day. For example: What did the English have for breakfast before tea existed in their world? On the table of a wealthy man you might find a good pottage of mutton or beef, bread, and biscuits, accompanied by ale, beer, or wine. Some added seafood to the menu: in his diary, Samuel Pepys recorded serving his New Year's guests a breakfast of a "barrel of oysters, a dish of neats' [beef] tongues, and a dish of anchovies, wine of all sorts and Northdowne ale." A merchant might have herring, rye bread, and ale. A cobbler perhaps just rye bread and beer; for a boy sent away to school it would be porridge, bread and butter, and beer. The one constant was alcohol.

The explanation of alcohol's ubiquitous role on the breakfast table was not the old stereotype of all Englishmen, Scots, Welsh, and Irish being natural drinkers, which perhaps was more of a consequence than a cause. As strange as it may seem, part of the choice was dictated by health concerns: one of the most dangerous things to drink in those days was not beer but water. As early as 1542, a doctor Andrew Boorde wrote in his *Dyetary of Helth* that "water is not wholesome, sole by itself, for an Englishman. . . . Water is cold, slow, and slack of digestion." This was putting it mildly. Before the development of filtration and purification systems, water was scarce and carried all sorts of bacteria, some of them deadly. This was a problem in rural areas, but even more so in London, which had grown into one of the largest cities in Europe but continued to have wildly inadequate sanitation and water supply systems (wooden pipes!) up until the end of the nineteenth century. Milk, another breakfast alternative, was expensive and, without refrigeration, also unsafe to drink, often carrying diseases such as tuberculosis.

Beer, on the contrary, was a mild antiseptic thanks to the hops in it, and, as an added but significant benefit, both beer and ale contained valuable nutrients. "Small" beer, so called because of its slightly lower (2 or 3 percent) alcoholic content, was brewed in every home and given to men, women, and children. Distilled spirits, in general, were considered necessary to provide energy for hard physical work and were therefore an important element of the daily diet of the working class. They were also commonly used as painkillers and to dress wounds. Hospitals served alcoholic drinks to their patients. Colleges brewed their own beer; Eton College did so until 1875. Royal Navy sailors were issued one gallon of beer a day as part of their diet. Fathers celebrated their sons' coming of age with the so-called rearing, in which the sons would get solidly drunk for the first time at the tavern in front of their fathers' friends and peers; it was considered a sign of virility to be able to do so. Tradespeople and the working class generally observed Saint Monday, a day devoted to recovering from Sunday drinking. And things were not much different in the upper echelons of society where, according to a chronicler of court life, both the ladies and the gentlemen "stupefied their brains morning, noon, and night."

The daily, grinding exposure to the side effects of intoxicating beverages didn't seem to be an issue. Perhaps it was considered just that: a side effect, nothing more, and a rather pleasant one at that. Building ships, drafting laws, drawing carriages, sewing dresses, signing contracts, writing plays, running countries—activities at all levels of society were performed under the influence. Queen Elizabeth I had large amounts of strong ale for breakfast and, when traveling, sent tasters ahead to make sure the quality of the local ale measured up to her expectations. From this perspective, one would have to be nothing less than astounded at how well English society still functioned, and perhaps understand better why sometimes it didn't.

At the beginning of the 1700s, a new, aggressive drink arrived from Holland and carried alcohol consumption to a whole new level. Genever, it was called—better known as gin—and it flooded England. Cheap, easily accessible, and deadly—it was, as Jessica Warner says in her excellent book, *Craze: Gin and Debauchery in an Age of Reason*, the original urban drug and the drug of choice of London's poor. "You may here get drunk for one penny, dead drunk for two pence, and clean straw for nothing," said the banners advertising gin shops. The clean straw was added, most likely, so people could sleep off their high on a somewhat softer surface. With cheap and fast-acting gin, the poor were able to forget for a moment hunger, cold, and the general feeling of desperation that pervaded all aspects of their lives. Gin was not only drunk by men and women but also given to children, either directly to help a baby fall asleep, or indirectly by gin-drinking wet nurses. By the time the "gin epidemic" was in full swing in the 1750s, a yearly per capita gin consumption of 2.2 gallons was added to a stable per capita beer consumption of around 30 gallons a year. Put simply, this meant that every man, woman, and child living on the British Isles consumed a shot of gin one day and almost a pint and a half of beer the next. Throughout the year, no vacations taken.

Enter tea, the savior beverage. The growing concern over what was now seen as a national emergency—and a threat to the country's productivity and capital investments in an increasingly industrialized society—led to the formation of the temperance movement, devoted to the eradication of alcoholism. The Chinese, devout rice wine drinkers, had known about the salutary effect of tea to counter alcohol intoxication for a long time: "The Chinese have an herb from which they press a delicate juice which serves them instead of wine. It also preserves the health and frees them from all those evils that the immoderate use of wine doth breed in us," wrote the Venetian author Giovanni Botero in 1589. Now the Victorians discovered this, too. By the end of the eighteenth century, tea was a popular and easily accessible article. What better tool could the temperance movement have chosen for its crusade than a cheap, hot, sobering cup of tea? And so it was that tea became "the temperance reformer's N. 1 weapon" in the crusade against alcohol abuse.

Temperance associations were formed in every town in Britain. Temperance halls, temperance clubs, and even temperance hotels—"dry" locations—sprang up all over the country. Large meetings were held in which, upon purchase of an entrance ticket, people gathered around long tables, and copious amounts of tea were served while a speaker, often a reformed drinker, gave a motivational talk on the advantages of giving up liquor. Sometimes the tea meetings were so large that the tables were hundreds of feet long, seating up to twelve hundred people, and "the N. 1 weapon" came in the form of a two-hundred-gallon tea boiler or a series of three-foot-square brewing containers connected to a pipe delivering boiling water. But, of course, all the bustling was focused on curing the symptom and ignoring the cause. Charles Dickens, that supreme chronicler of Victorian society, made fun of the tea meetings in *The Pickwick Papers*, in which an astonished Mr. Weller stares at excessive tea drinkers "swellin' wisibly before my wery eyes" and "this here old lady next me . . . a drowndin' herself in tea."

Although a devoted tea drinker himself, Dickens knew where the real problem was, and drinking "nine breakfast cups and a half" of tea in one sitting, as the "wisibly swellin'" lady did, was not going to make it go away. To the moralists of the time who pointed the finger at the lower classes and their lack of willpower, he later gave a terse illustration of his view on the subject: "Gin-drinking is a great vice in England, but wretchedness and dirt are a greater; and until you improve the homes of the poor, or persuade a half-famished wretch not to seek relief in the temporary oblivion of his own misery, with the pittance which, divided among his family, would furnish a morsel of bread for each, gin-shops will increase in number and splendour. If Temperance Societies would suggest an antidote against hunger, filth, and foul air . . . gin-palaces would be numbered among the things that were."

Gin and other distilled liquors—some home brewed, awful tasting, and often laced with highly toxic ingredients—were the target of the temperance movement at first. Beer consumption, on the other hand, was tolerated and even encouraged because of its nutritive value. The enemies of tea—there were such beings—who considered tea an unnecessary and expensive item as well as pernicious to nerves and digestion, touted the benefits of beer for this very reason. Some of them, like social reformer William Cobbett, went so far as to assert that tea made people lazy, "render[ing] the frame feeble and unfit to encounter hard labour. . . . Hence succeeds a softness, an effeminacy, a seeking of the fireside, a lurking for the bed . . . ," and that "the gossip of the tea table is no bad preparatory school for the brothel." Hard to believe, but Cobbett's honest and charitable intent was to improve the conditions of poor farm laborers by counseling on nutrition—drink good beer—and economy—eliminate expensive tea.

Cobbett aside, soon the failure of this moderate approach was recognized, and the teetotalers—the more extreme advocates of total abstinence from any alcohol including beer—went into action. But they never had much success in Britain, either. The reality was that the temperance movement was in large part a middle-class effort to reform the working classes and turn them into "productive" members of society, instead of having them loaf around drinking beer. Apparently, the working man could never get it right: if he drank tea he was lazy, if he drank beer he was lazy. But for factory workers, cleaning women, and chimney sweeps, spending time at the pub with friends and a cheap drink was essentially the only affordable form of entertainment after a hard day's work. They were not about to give it up.

So it was that tea and the well-intentioned reformers who served it, although successful in bringing the issue of alcoholism to consciousness, were not as successful in eradicating it. What the temperance movement, with its festivals and gigantic teapots, did succeed in doing was to increase tea consumption to levels never reached before. In the end, British subjects were hooked on both—tea *and* alcohol. This produced handsome profits, both for private entrepreneurs and government excise tax collectors, the latter never the ones to be left behind. By the time Queen Victoria died in 1901, marking the end of the era to which she had given a name, yearly per capita tea consumption had risen to 5.7 pounds, and hard liquor consumption to just below three gallons—greater than at the height of the gin epidemic.

Yet, some reasoned, every problem had a solution—of sorts. If tea didn't help drinkers kick the habit, the popular Victorian journal "The Family Oracle of Health" had precious suggestions on how to deal with the "morning after" effect:

Feaster's morning Draught

Take two drachms of Rochelle salts,
one ounce of infusion of senna,
one teaspoonful of compound tincture of cardamoms,
and (*if you can get it*), a small wine glass of Ratafia of Eau de Cologne.

Mix, for a draught; and during the morning . . . take an occasional glass of *strong* ginger beer. It will also be of great advantage to sit in a snug fauteuil before a good fire, with your feet in carpet shoes, planted comfortably on the hobs. This position tends to keep the head *erect*, which is of the utmost importance, while the warmth of the feet draws the superabundance of blood downwards from the brain, and consequently renders the nerves strong, the spirits light, and the whole man cheerful and buoyant.

The Porcelain Secret

. . . Oh, had I now my Wishes,
Sure you should learn to make their China Dishes.

—Coryat's Crudities, 1611

The enormous popularity of tea spawned the import of yet another commodity: porcelain. Brought to Europe from China on
the first sea routes as a companion import to tea, spices, and silks,
porcelain was identified as very valuable cargo in more ways than
one. First, it was the perfect ballast material. Heavy and impervious
to water, it was stowed at ship's bottom and helped stabilize the sailing. Second, the packing cases were used as insulating platforms on
which the moisture-sensitive tea cargo could be placed, farther up
and away from the dank holds. And third, unlike deadweight ballast,
porcelain could be sold at a profit when it was done fulfilling its other
two purposes. As the trade intensified, more and more East Indiamen,
the large supercargo ships used by the English and the Dutch for the
Orient trade, sailed home from China, heavily loaded with what
came to be known as "chinaware."

Along with the growing demand for tea, the public was enthusiastic about porcelain and about Chinese imports in general, a passion
that spread all over Europe and gave rise to the chinoiserie craze. Establishing collections of valuable pieces became a fashionable pastime among the European aristocracy. Demanding customers sent in

Painting in Underglaze Blue, gouache on paper, one of a series of twenty-four images illustrating porcelain manufacture, China, c. 1820. Peabody Essex Museum, Salem, Mass.

orders with specific requirements regarding color, shape, design, or the inclusion of the family's coat of arms, all of which Chinese potters on the other side of the world skillfully carried out and delivered. Everyone wanted Chinese porcelains; a ship's cargo log typically listed teapots, cups, and saucers in the order of tens of thousands of each. The trade grew to such an extent that the market was flooded with Chinese porcelain. Prices fell, and eventually even modest households could afford porcelain sets.

Before maritime trading, Europeans had come in touch with earlier Chinese porcelain, brought by Arab traders on the land routes, and had long been fascinated by the exquisite shapes and the mysterious opalescence. Thin and delicate yet stronger and more heat-resistant than earthenware; light and translucent and yet not made with glass. What was porcelain? How was it made? A story circulated, possibly spread by shrewd Chinese traders intent on protecting their secrets. Oh, it's a very long and complicated process, they would say to the Portuguese travelers who first landed on Chinese shores. And at the beginning of the 1500s, one of these travelers, Duarte Barbosa, reported the story thus: "They make in this country [China] a great quantity of porcelains of different sorts . . . in this way. They take the shells of sea-snails, and eggshells, and pound them into a powder, and with other ingredients make a paste, which they put underground to refine for the space of 80 or 100 years, and this mass of paste they leave as a fortune to their children, and they always have some that was left to them by their predecessors, with memory of each of the places where it is deposited." History doesn't record if someone actually sat and crushed large amounts of eggshells and mixed them with seashells, but the story made the rounds of Europe, and many believed it.

The reality of porcelain making had nothing to do with eggs and snails. The Chinese had been producing high-quality porcelain long before the Europeans became curious about it. Around the middle of the seventeenth century Dutch potters imitated the blue-and-white Chinese designs and produced "delftware"—named after Delft, the town where the manufactories were located. But it was earthenware, not porcelain. It was pretty, but not translucent, not thin and hard, not pure white, and if struck lightly, it made a dull sound, not the pure ringing tone characteristic of porcelain. The same was the case with the faience and majolica developed in France and Italy. Beautiful, but not the real thing. The effort to reproduce porcelain's translucence led some to believe that glass was an ingredient and to add vitreous substances to the clay. This resulted in a type of soft-paste porcelain that was more similar to Chinese porcelain but still not the same. What was the secret?

There were several. One was kaolin, named after the deposits found near Kaoling Mountain in southeastern China. Kaolin is a very pure, easily moldable white clay, also called china clay, that stays white when fired. The other was *petuntse*, or china stone, a kind of feldspathic mineral rock that melts and vitrifies when fired. The third was high baking temperatures (up to 2,600°F, or 1,450°C), much higher than the ones used to bake earthenware (1,800°F, or 1,000°C). And, of course, the secret of all secrets in any quality endeavor is practice. Chinese potters had a thousand years of it, honing their skills on porcelains for customers around the world and for the most demanding customer of all, the emperor himself, for whom nothing less than perfection was acceptable.

It was Ehrenfried Walther von Tschirnhaus (with such a name he was destined for great things) who finally solved the arcanum of porcelain in Europe in 1708. He was a German mathematician, physicist, and philosopher, a friend of Spinoza, Newton, and Leibniz, and the first German to be accepted into the Académie Royale des Sciences in Paris. Tschirnhaus's long-standing interest in porcelain manufacture led him to travel around Europe, where he studied methods and learned from other people's failures. Back home in Dresden, Tschirnhaus convinced King Augustus the Strong of Saxony to finance his porcelain laboratory where he experimented with different materials and firing temperatures. Augustus the Strong, who was an avid collector of Chinese porcelain, no doubt also saw the economic potential of being the first one to produce European porcelain.

Tschirnhaus's long years of research were finally brought to a successful conclusion by a stroke of luck: a deposit of the one elusive element, kaolin, the white clay, was found in Colditz near Dresden, and the first true porcelain made on European soil saw the light of day. But no sooner had Tschirnhaus unlocked the secret than he contracted dysentery and died. As a result, his assistant, Johann Friedrich Böttger, and not Tschirnhaus, is generally credited with the findings. A self-proclaimed alchemist, boasting about being able to transform lead into gold—a claim that landed him in jail for a time—Böttger was a man of dubious morals who suspiciously proclaimed to have invented porcelain a short time after his mentor's death. Nonetheless, he was named director of the Meissen porcelain manufactory, the first and most famous true porcelain factory in Europe, which is why his name is forever associated with the beginnings of European porcelain.

The utmost secrecy was maintained at Meissen for a time, but it could not be kept forever. In 1719 the details of the porcelain recipe were leaked to Vienna. Additional information was provided by the

Jesuit priest Père François Xavier d'Entrecolles, who spent many years in China doing missionary work as well as some industrial detective work on the side. Along with saving souls, d'Entrecolles collected details on the porcelain materials and production processes while in Ching-te-chen, the porcelain capital of the world, and sent two long reports back to Paris. These were greatly appreciated by the nascent porcelain-manufacturing community in Europe. Kaolin deposits were then found in other parts of Europe, and factories opened in Sèvres and Limoges, in Vienna and Berlin, in Capodimonte near Naples, in St. Petersburg, and in other parts of Germany. The English developed a special type of porcelain called bone china—thus named not because it is as strong as bone but because it contains up to 50 percent actual animal bone ash, which, according to manufacturers, offers a variety of technical advantages.

Before the century was over, porcelain making had become a European trade like any other. Unique styles were developed that veered from the Chinese prototypes. Teapots, originally designed to imitate the small, individual-size Yixing teapots that were brought to Europe with the first imported China teas, changed shape and became larger and puffier. Imported Chinese wine jugs with lids were also used as inspiration for teapot design. Novelties, such as strainer-holes at the base of the teapot spout, were added. The tea bowl developed into a teacup on account of the added handle, which became necessary to hold the cup while drinking hot black tea. The Chinese to this day drink tea in bowls because their tea of choice is green tea, which is served at lower temperatures. The saucer, which existed in China but was not of common usage, became an indispensable element of the European tea set. Before it became unfashionable and inelegant, it was fairly common to pour the tea into the saucer to let it cool and then drink from it—hence the expression "a dish of tea." The Chinese must have wondered about the logic of inventing a handle to hold hot tea and then using saucers to cool it. Logic or not, it is indisputable that the Europeans, and the English in particular, had come of age in matters of tea and porcelain use, developing their own tastes, preferences, and aesthetic sensibilities.

There was a downside to all this. As the European porcelain industry grew in size and sophistication, the English East India Company saw its warehouses fill with unsold imported chinaware, once so in demand. The Company secretly discontinued bulk imports altogether in 1791, selling warehouse overstocks for several years pretending they were new arrivals. For China, this meant that two centuries of porcelain trade with Europe came to a grinding halt. Manufactories had to look elsewhere for sales of their enormous surplus. Thousands of pottery workers, clay miners, carriers, and shippers were left to find alternative means of support. But the porcelain arcanum was solved. Young Europe had wrested another secret from the old Celestial Empire.

The Willow and
the Lovers

Two doves flying high,
Chinese vessel sailing by,
Weeping willow hanging o'er
Bridge with three men, and not with four,
Chinese teahouse there it stands
Seems to take up all the land,
Orange tree with fruit thereon,
A pretty fence to end my song.

—An English children's rhyme describing
the willow pattern, nineteenth century

In the world of porcelain decorations, the willow pattern is unlike
any other and deserves a special mention. This queen of blue-and-
white porcelains holds the memory of a love story, tragic and beautiful, as the best love stories always are.

Kung-hsi, the young daughter of a wealthy mandarin, lived with
her father in a two-story pagoda along a river. In the garden surrounding the house, a little teahouse had been built for Kung-hsi's
leisure. A fragrant orange tree nearby offered cooling shade, while a
graceful willow framed the footbridge leading to the main entrance.
A powerful businessman, the mandarin had a large staff. One of his
employees was Chang, his secretary and accountant. Chang was very
efficient in taking care of all the mandarin's affairs, but he was of a ro-

mantic nature, a poet at heart. One early morning, Kung-hsi and Chang caught a brief glimpse of each other, and from that moment on they could not forget the depth they spied in each other's eyes. After that, they would see each other from far away, Kung-hsi escorted by her lady-in-waiting and Chang attending to his master. Yet distance was a feeble obstacle, and in time their longing gazes grew into a deep, powerful love.

Willow pattern, from a hand-engraved copper plate, England, nineteenth century. Courtesy of the Spode Museum Trust, Stoke on Trent, UK.

Kung-hsi lived in a world of privileged segregation, Chang in that of subordinate duty. In their separate solitudes, they both learned to love birds and talk to them. Two doves became their favorite messengers, carrying letters and love poems from one lover to the other. One day, Kung-hsi's father intercepted one of the messages. Angered by what he considered a foolish liaison between a great mandarin's daughter and a lowly secretary, he sent Chang away and forbade Kung-hsi to go beyond the little teahouse in the garden. He built a fence around the property to keep Chang out and betrothed his daughter to Ta-jin, a wealthy and dissolute old duke. Ta-jin was so happy to be the chosen groom that he immediately sent a box of jewels as a gift for his bride-to-be.

As is often the case with forbidden loves, the feelings the young lovers had for each other grew even stronger. Chang stayed up all night writing beautiful letters and poems, and in the morning he let them float downstream in a coconut shell into the hands of his beloved. Kung-hsi waited for them in her garden at the river's shore.

She read the precious words under the orange tree. Sometimes she cried, longing for her lover, and the doves kept her company. Alas, the day came for Kung-hsi to wed the old duke. Lovers' blindness to impending doom knows no limit, but now the doom was upon them. What to do? Kung-hsi sent a message to her beloved: "Gather thy blossom, 'ere it be stolen."

Chang sent a message back with the dove asking Kung-hsi to meet him under the willow tree that same night. Under the moonlight they concocted a plan. They kissed and stroked each other's cheeks, they whispered and cried and laughed in silence. Kung-hsi felt safe in her lover's arms.

The next day at the wedding banquet everyone feasted and drank copious amounts of wine. But not Kung-hsi. She was alert and ready, her box of jewels hidden in her shawl. Chang walked into the banquet hall disguised as a servant and quietly led Kung-hsi out of the building and toward the bridge. When they had almost reached the other side of the bridge, the mandarin realized what was happening and gave chase. But Chang had a boat ready, and the lovers pushed off before the guards could reach them.

The stream carried them to an island far away, where they built a house and started a new life. They sold the jewels and worked the land. Chang continued to write and, in time, his poems made him famous. But this was the lovers' undoing. Chang's fame traveled far, and although the mandarin had died, it reached Ta-jin. The old duke had not forgotten. He found the lovers' hiding place and dispatched his guards to the island. Chang was killed. Kung-hsi, in desperation, set fire to the house and burned herself to death.

The gods saw all this. They cursed the duke and, touched by the lovers' devotion to each other, they transformed their spirits into immortal doves, the lovers' favorite birds. If you are sitting by your window someday, you may see them kissing and flying together in a dance of joy. They want to remind us that love is stronger than hate and stronger than death itself.

*

Though the story is apocryphal, the familiar blue-and-white willow pattern is one of the most popular landscape decorations ever to be used on porcelain and chinaware. The pattern as we know it today generally includes the main elements of the story: a willow, an orange tree, a two-story pagoda and a smaller building (the teahouse), a footbridge with three figures running across it (the lovers and the mandarin), a boat, an island, and two birds. It is commonly believed that Thomas Minton, founder of the famous Thomas Minton & Sons pottery, created it around 1780 while he was a young apprentice potter in Shropshire, England. Some say he was inspired by an already existing Chinese design, while others insist it was the Chinese who later copied Minton. Robert Copeland of Spode Ltd., the other well-known English porcelain manufacturer based in Stoke-on-Trent, believes that it was Josiah Spode who first started producing English porcelain with the willow pattern to satisfy a growing demand for replacement pieces of broken Chinese originals.

Whoever may have been first, willowware porcelain has been extremely popular around the world over the last two hundred years. Potters and porcelain manufacturers in many countries have reproduced variations of the pattern. Several books have been written about it. And enthusiastic collectors worldwide have formed organizations, attend yearly conventions, subscribe to newsletters, trade pieces, and discuss the minutest details of each variation. The more practically oriented believe that the legend of the lovers was nothing but a marketing tool to boost sales. The detail-driven determine the value of a piece by the shade of blue or by counting the number of oranges hanging from the tree in the pattern. Others are on an unending quest for the first piece of willowware that ever existed.

Kung-hsi and Chang smile and say nothing.

A Large Cup of Tea for the Fishes

They's been a row about this yer tea, I expect you
heerd tell of it. A tax or something. And bung me if I
don't think the province is right, what I understand of
it. Anyhow, I like to see 'em stand up against England.
It looks good. I'm for shutting down on tea. But what I
says is, shut down on it in a general way, but a little tea
never done no harm to no one. 'Specially on a chilly
morning like this yer.

—James Boyd, *Drums*, 1925

On the other side of the Atlantic, the success story of a tea would
take a rather different turn, even though it had started under
the most propitious auspices. At a time when Londoners still drew a
blank at the mention of the word *tea*, New Yorkers had already been
sipping the beverage at elegant tea tables while conversing affably
about the weather and the latest society news. How could that be? To
be precise, they were not called New Yorkers at the time, but citizens
of Nieuw Amsterdam. As Dutch colonists, they were well acquainted
with the pleasures of tea long before the English caught on, and it
was they who first introduced tea to the New World. They brought
their delftware and their windmill decorations and faithfully re-
created the atmosphere of the rich tea parties of The Hague. Perhaps

Susanna Truax, by the Gansevoort Limner, possibly Pieter Vanderlyn, oil on bed ticking, Colonial America, 1730. Image © 2006 Board of Trustees, National Gallery of Art, Washington, D.C. Gift of Edgar William and Bernice Chrysler Garbisch.

this was due to the colonist's inherent homesickness—to do everything just as it is at home, and even more so, may help the immigrant recapture the feeling of home for a fleeting moment. Or perhaps it was just for sheer palatal enjoyment. Washington Irving seems to lean toward the latter explanation in his memorable—and mouthwatering—description of a Dutch tea table in "The Legend of Sleepy Hollow":

Fain would I pause to dwell upon the world of charms that burst upon the enraptured gaze of my hero, as he entered the state parlor of Van Tassel's mansion. Not those of the bevy of buxom lasses, with their luxurious display of red and white; but the ample charms of a genuine Dutch country tea-table, in the sumptuous time of autumn. Such heaped-up platters of cakes of various and almost indescribable kinds, known only to experienced Dutch housewives! There was the doughty doughnut, the tender oly koek, and the crisp and crumbling cruller; sweet cakes and short cakes, ginger-cakes and honey-cakes, and the whole family of cakes. And then there were apple-pies and peach-pies and pumpkin-pies; besides slices of ham and smoked beef; and moreover delectable dishes of preserved plums, and peaches, and pear, and quinces; not to mention broiled shad and roasted chickens; together with bowls of milk and cream, all mingled higgledy-piggledy, pretty much as I have enumerated them, with the motherly teapot sending up its cloud of vapor from the midst— Heaven bless the mark! I want breath and time to discuss this banquet as it deserves, and am too eager to get on with my story. Happily, Ichabod Crane was not in so great a hurry as his historian, but did ample justice to every dainty.

When the English arrived in 1674, and Nieuw Amsterdam became New York, they found these sorts of tea tables waiting for them and were only too happy to add their own teapots and kettles to the picture. Whether it was the beverage itself, the cakes that went with it, or being far away from home that functioned as a motivating force, it didn't take long for tea to become *the* social beverage in America. Not only was tea served at every occasion as a sign of hospitality, but teatime was a prime opportunity for courtship, gossip, or playing cards, not to mention showing off the latest tea equipage. Just as in England, one could not be in society without incessantly being invited to tea parties. "My health continues excellent," wrote Louis Philippe, the comte de Ségur, to his French wife while traveling in

America, "despite the quantity of tea one must drink with the ladies out of gallantry."

In public life, pleasure gardens like the ones in London, where one could drink tea and socialize at any hour of the day, opened in what were then the outskirts of New York City. Sometimes the gardens even had the same names as their London counterparts. Not one but three Vauxhall Gardens were opened in New York. The most fashionable one was near what is now Lafayette and Astor Place. Ranelagh Gardens was on Broadway between Duane and Worth Streets. Niblo's Garden was at the corner of Broadway and Prince Street. And there were others. The colonists in New York were so serious about their tea that they even had a special pump built over a spring to get good water to brew. It was aptly named the Tea-Water Pump and was located near Park Row and East Broadway on Chatham Square. Naturally, there was a tea garden next to it. The pump yielded 14,300 gallons of water a day, and home delivery was offered for a penny per gallon. According to Ukers in *All About Tea*, the business of water peddlers filling New York streets with their carts and their cries of "Tea water! Tea water!" grew so much that the city had to put in place a regulating act for the "Water Men."

The passion for tea was by no means limited to New York. Grocers from Boston to Philadelphia to Charleston did brisk business selling tea; the tea ritual was practiced as fervently in those cities and anywhere else in the colonies as in the middle of Manhattan. In short, Americans were frenetic tea drinkers and, by some accounts, even more so than their relatives across the ocean.

Onto this lively tea scene descended the famous Tea Act of 1773, triggering the beginning of that enormous power shift in the world from which Great Britain never recovered. The colonists had been already variously inflamed by other acts the mother country had imposed on them: the Sugar Act, the Stamp Act, the Townshend Acts. All these acts levied duties on sugar, paper, paint, oil, glass, lead, and, of course, tea at three pennies per pound. Additional acts, not involving taxes but limitations and obligations, fueled the rebellious spirit even further: the Currency Act, prohibiting the colonies from issuing their own currency, and the Quartering Act, which required settlers to provide food and shelter for British troops.

The widespread colonial reaction was to call a general boycott of British goods. Consumer items became politicized, and tea acquired privileged status as *the* symbol of rebellion. Anything but British tea was the motto. Tea substitutes began to appear on the market: Labrador tea was one, made with the leaves of a native shrub. Hyperion tea, made with leaves of the raspberry plant, was also a popular alternative. And other, aptly named Liberty teas were invented by resourceful colonial housewives, using strawberry leaves, sage, sassafras bark, berries, and other herbs. But when it came to the real thing, buying Dutch smuggled tea—at half the price of British tea—was the only principled thing to do. Dutch traders, and their American business partners, benefited a great deal from that principle: more than half of all the tea consumed in the colonies was smuggled. And consume the Americans did: 2.5 million colonists drank as much tea in a year as the entire population of England and Wales, which was three times larger. Tea was big business in the New World.

On the other side of the pond, kings, ministers, and East India Company officials watched in consternation as smuggler's ship upon smuggler's ship loaded with the precious cargo made the happy voyage from Rotterdam to New York. This represented enormous tax revenue losses for the British coffers, and equally enormous income losses for the Company. Seventeen million pounds of Company tea lay in London storages unsold. This was not only due to the fierce competition from the smugglers. Company mismanagement had something to do with it. In addition, the government requirement that the Company import a prescribed amount of tea every year, regardless of market conditions, had thrown things off balance even more. The British government relied heavily on domestic tax revenues on tea and wanted to ensure sufficient stock in case of delivery problems from China. Besides, no British subject should ever run out of tea: there was no telling what could happen in a Britain on tea withdrawal!

The situation called for action. Britain had emerged victorious from the Seven Years' War in 1763, acquiring Canada and the territories east of the Mississippi from France. But the war effort had left the government cash-poor and heavily indebted. On the trade side, the East India Company risked bankruptcy. British policy makers thought they might solve two problems at once if they allowed the Company to export its excess tea to the American colonies and sell it at prices lower than the smugglers' while at the same time collecting taxes on it.

Instead of solving problems, the Tea Act created two new ones. It incensed the already irate colonists even further on the well-known issue of "no taxation without representation." And, it turned the tea business upside down. Not only did the act deprive people of the pleasure of drinking smuggled tea to spite the British Crown—that was bad enough. Worse yet, it took away the profits American businessmen had grown accustomed to deriving from smuggled Dutch tea. For the colonists the whole thing was simply preposterous. They were asked to buy official tea *and* pay a tax on it, from none other than East India Company agents, brought in for the express purpose of enforcing a trade monopoly. In the process, merchants and middlemen on both sides of the Atlantic—British trade had long resented the East India Company monopoly and was on the side of the colonists on this one—would be put out of business overnight. And all this only to help the despised East India Company extract herself from the financial quagmire she had gotten herself into.

The Tea Act was the last straw. Every American child knows what followed that December 16, 1773, on board the *Dartmouth*, the *Eleanor*, and the *Beaver* docked in Boston Harbor. Three hundred and forty-two tea chests thrown overboard, about 120,000 pounds of tea leaves floating in the ocean. In the words of George Hewes, a participant in the action: "They divided us into three parties, for the purpose of boarding the three ships, which contained the tea, at the same time. . . . We then were ordered by our commander to open the hatches and take out all the chests of tea and throw them overboard, and we immediately proceeded to execute his orders, first cutting and

A satirical depiction of the Edenton Tea Party of 1774, in which fifty-one ladies of Edenton signed a pledge not to use East India Company tea and, moreover, engaged "not to conform to the Pernicious Custom of Drinking Tea."

A Society of Patriotic Ladies, at Edenton in North Carolina, by Philip Dawe, mezzotint, England, 1775. British Cartoon Collection, Library of Congress, Washington, D.C.

splitting the chests with our tomahawks, so as thoroughly to expose them to the effects of the water. In about three hours from the time we went on board, we had thus broken and thrown overboard every tea chest to be found in the ship, while those in the other ships were disposing of the tea in the same way, at the same time. We were surrounded by British armed ships, but no attempt was made to resist us." When Hewes went home and told his wife what happened, she asked: "Well, George, did you bring home any of it?" But George, patriot that he was, did not bring home any tea and recounted how the citizens caught trying to slip some tea into their pockets were seized and punished with "a kick or a stroke." Only an elderly gentleman, in consideration of his age, "was permitted to escape, with now and then a slight kick." After having emptied his pockets, of course.

In the subsequent months, the Boston Tea Party was followed by other, lesser-known tea parties. In Greenwich, New Jersey, protesters burned the tea in the middle of the town square. In Philadelphia, the citizens threatened tar and feathers to any pilot who should help the ship into the harbor, and convinced the captain to take the tea cargo back to London. In Charleston, South Carolina, the ship owners were so concerned about the public outrage that they destroyed the tea cargo and threw it overboard by themselves in order to save the ship from being damaged. Citizens of Chestertown, Maryland, followed the Boston example and threw the tea in the water. So did New Yorkers after discovering they had been deceived by the captain who insisted there was no tea in the cargo. And in Annapolis a threatening crowd accomplished the destruction of both ship and tea by forcing the owner of the brigantine *Peggy Stewart* to set her on fire, pending his life.

In a matter of a few years, Americans had gone from being fanatical tea drinkers to throwing tea away and being "merry, in an undertone, at the idea of making so large a cup of tea for the fishes . . . ," as Joshua Wyeth said when recalling his participation in the events of the Boston Tea Party as a sixteen-year-old journeyman blacksmith. Clearly, East India Company officials would have to look elsewhere for business opportunities. And this they did. They concentrated their efforts on the East, on China and India, countries with their own sets of instabilities and ill prepared to withstand the power and machinations of such a powerful entity. In the name of tea, they turned one country into a drug producer and the other into a drug consumer, and they drew untold profits from both.

The Opium Factor

The blissful cloud of summer-indolence
Benumb'd my eye; my pulse grew less and less;
Pain had no string, and pleasure's wreath no flower:
O, why did ye not melt, and leave my sense
Unhaunted quite of all but-nothingness?

—John Keats, "Ode on Indolence," 1819

Toward the end of the eighteenth century, Great Britain had become the leading colonial and maritime power in the world. This was in part due to the enormous success of the East India Company's commercial ventures in the East, in particular the tea trade. And yet, tea seemed to have an odd way of undermining the very power it had helped create, the prime example of this being the loss of a major colony such as America. Now tea seemed to be at the root of another problem developing in the China trade.

The good news was that, thanks to the mercantile efficiency of the East India Company, tea consumption in England had risen to unprecedented levels. Between 1730 and 1790 imports had gone from 1 million to nearly 20 million pounds a year. The increased business was good for the Company and for the government, which relied on the tea trade as a major source of tax revenue. The bad news was that China held the reins of the market and was not interested in the Company's repeated offers of trading other goods in exchange for tea. Chinese merchants wanted to be paid in nothing but cash, preferably silver bullion. European silver was in great supply since

Spain had found silver in the New World, particularly in Peru and Mexico.

In 1793 Lord Macartney had journeyed to Peking's imperial court as King George III's ambassador in hopes of convincing the emperor to expand trade with Britain. But the mission was a failure, as was the later Lord Amherst mission in 1816. "Strange and costly objects do not interest me," Emperor Ch'ien-lung clarified in a letter to the British monarch after Lord Macartney's visit. "As your Ambassador can see for himself, we possess all things. I set no value on objects strange or ingenious, and have no use for your country's manufactures." China's ancient, self-sufficient culture and advanced technology did not need much from the West. In China, people carted things around on a wheelbarrow a thousand years before the Europeans first used it in the building of the Chartres cathedral. The Chinese invented the stirrup, without which the English would have had trouble playing a decent game of polo many centuries later. Not to mention paper, cast iron, and the suspension bridge—all Chinese inventions. As was the match, the umbrella, the fishing reel, the zoetrope, the clock, and many other advanced medical, scientific, and agricultural practices firmly in place in Chinese society at a time when Europeans were just emerging from the Dark Ages.

Clearly, trading goods was not an option. This state of things had created a chronic trade imbalance for the British, who exported some cotton to China, but certainly not enough to make a difference. In addition, with the loss of the American colonies, Britain had lost access to the precious South American silver supply. And all this was happening in the context of a mounting debt the East India Company had accumulated since its successful but costly expansion of control in India in 1757. What could help turn the tides?

The answer was opium. Lightweight, not perishable, and extremely profitable, opium was the ideal trade item. The Portuguese and the Dutch had preceded the British by several decades in the opium trade and were amassing fortunes. The Chinese had been using opium mainly for medicinal purposes ever since the Arabs had introduced it in the eighth century. But when the Dutch brought tobacco and the pipe to China, the practice of smoking opium mixed with tobacco took hold. This increased the demand, which in turn increased imports. In 1729, concerned about the spreading habit, China had issued an edict prohibiting the practice of smoking opium. But if the smoking of opium became illegal, the importation of it was not. The edict had no effect whatsoever, and traders rationalized that if customers really didn't want the product they would not buy it. This type of circular thinking appeased many consciences at the time.

Thus started Britain's tea-for-opium balancing act, one of the most sinister chapters of Western imperialist history. As historian and Asian studies professor Frederic Wakeman Jr. explains in *The Fall of Imperial China*: "For it was opium which bought the tea that serviced the E.I.C.'s [East India Company's] debts and paid the duties of the

Stacking Room, by Captain Walter S. Sherwill, fifth in a series of seven engravings on opium production, England, 1851. Reprinted from *Illustrations of the Mode of Preparing the Indian Opium Intended for the Chinese Market,* Walter S. Sherwill, 1851. Courtesy of the Wason Collection on East Asia at Cornell University Library, Ithaca, N.Y.

British crown, providing one-sixth of England's national revenue." It was simple: sell opium for cash, use cash to pay for tea. The Company had been selling small amounts of opium to China since the 1720s. Now the goal was to expand the opium trade enough to balance the tea trade—create one addiction to support another. This the Company did with great efficiency and soon became the leader in the field, raising international drug trafficking to unprecedented levels, both in terms of sheer quantities sold and in the development of sophisticated production and distribution systems.

Warren Hastings, India's governor-general, had been setting up operations for some time in Bengal, where small opium plantations were already in place. In 1773, Hastings abolished the Indian opium syndicate and established a Company monopoly for the cultivation, production, and sale of opium. As a result, other crops with smaller profit margins were destroyed. Indian farmers were forced to work for poverty wages, often wasting away as opium addicts themselves. Growers were not allowed to sell their crop to anyone other than the East India Company, which processed the raw opium in the Company factories in Patna and Benares. The finished product in the form of opium balls was packed in chests and shipped down the Ganges and the Hooghly to Calcutta and on to China. Before long, Bengal became an important opium producer, and its high-quality Patna opium an important international commodity.

In a renewed effort to limit opium consumption, China issued a new edict in 1796 declaring not just the smoking but also the import of opium illegal. Thus the East India Company, and any other country or organization importing opium to China, was now officially considered to be performing an illegal operation. But the Company continued its imports undisturbed by using an efficient system of independent smugglers, the so-called country traders or agency houses, to deliver the drug to Canton. Some of these—Jardine, Matheson & Co., for example—later grew into international holdings and are still in operation today, albeit with "diversified" purposes. A vast network of corrupt and heavily bribed Chinese officials then made sure to look the other way when the smugglers dropped off the drug in the Chinese port. As Harvard professor and eminent China expert John King Fairbank says in *China Watch*: "The basic rule of foreign activity in China was that nothing really could be done without Chinese assistance. . . . The Chinese component of the Western invasion was of course composed of desperadoes, opportunists, and dissidents of the worst sort." Ironically, bribe money was called "tea money," an expression still used today to describe the practice of gaining favors through bribery. At the distribution end, dealers used the familiar technique of giving away free samples to increase their clientele. Delegating this whole operation to middlemen, runners, and dealers had a double benefit for the Company: it ensured the continuation of extraordinary profits from the opium trade while being able to officially maintain that it was not responsible for the opium scourge in China, for it was not they who brought it into the country. This in turn allowed it to continue operating the tea trade as the legitimate British enterprise that it was.

At the beginning of the 1800s and for about two decades, the Company maintained a balance between opium exports to China and tea imports from China, limiting—if such a term may be used in this context—yearly opium production to 280 tons (one ton is two thousand pounds). But this was not to last. The trade was so fantastically lucrative that competitors were pressuring to get a piece of the pie. When the Company relaxed its regulations and allowed the distribution of Malwa opium, China's yearly imports increased to seven hundred tons per year. After the Company lost the China trade monopoly in 1834 and trading was open to all, the imports shot up to twenty-five hundred tons per year. The hungry American traders—Charles Cabot, John Cushing, John Jacob Astor, Russell & Co., and others—were the newcomers to the trade, but no less aggressive. Cut out from the Indian opium supply, they were making new fortunes bringing in Turkish opium, which rose from seven tons in 1805 to one hundred tons in 1830. Throughout these developments, the Dutch East India Company never stopped selling opium at an average of five to seven tons per year through Java, its preferred trade port.

Competition notwithstanding, the Company had succeeded in

Opium-Fleet, by Captain Walter S. Sherwill, sixth in a series of seven engravings on opium production, England, 1851. Reprinted from *Illustrations of the Mode of Preparing the Indian Opium Intended for the Chinese Market,* Walter S. Sherwill, 1851. Courtesy of the Wason Collection on East Asia at Cornell University Library, Ithaca, N.Y.

addressing the grave trade imbalance caused by the heavy tea imports. "During the first decade of the nineteenth century . . . ," writes Wakeman, "China's balance of trade was so favorable that 26,000,000 silver dollars were imported into the empire. As opium consumption rose in the decade of the 1830s, 34,000,000 silver dollars were shipped out of the country to pay for the drug." All this happened with the approval of the British government. An 1832 parliamentary report on Indian revenue stated that it was not advisable to abandon such an important source of revenue as the Bengalese opium industry, since it represented a sixth of the gross national product of British India. Lord Palmerston, then foreign secretary, refused to recognize the validity of Chinese anti-opium edicts on the argument that if the Chinese were unable to enforce them, why then should the English respect them? In a similar style of colonial double standards, Warren Hastings condemned the use of opium by English citizens while encouraging its export: "Opium is not a necessity of life but a pernicious

article of luxury, which ought not to be permitted except for purposes of foreign commerce only, and which the wisdom of the Government should carefully restrain from internal consumption."

Britain was just making too much money in too many ways. The
East India Company covered 80 percent of the opium trade, had a monopoly on the China trade—at least until 1834—and controlled revenues in India. On all this the British government collected fantastic
amounts in taxes. Accounting books silenced morals. And people
whose business it was to promote morals, like the Reverend George
Newenham Wright who traveled to China, often had a somewhat
skewed view on how to solve the opium problem: "It may be asked,
can no remedies be discovered for a vice so deplorable, a disease so
corroding to the heart of the nation? Yes, let the Chinese abolish des-
potism, enlarge the liberty of the people—remove prohibitory duties,
cultivate foreign commerce—establish philanthropic institutions—
and receive the Gospel; then will the distinction between virtue and
vice, truth and falsehood, honour and shame, be understood, and the
duties of the public censor become less onerous and more valuable."

By the 1830s, it was estimated that 1 percent of the Chinese
population—about 3 million people, mostly young and middle-aged
men—was addicted to opium, particularly in the coastal regions
where the drug was more easily available. The workforce was beginning to be weakened by addiction. The nation's silver reserves were
being drained by cash payments for opium, which was affecting the
currency. Opium use transcended class structure. Farmers, merchants, mandarins, poets, and high-court officials were equally affected. Opium dens were filled with hollow-eyed, emaciated men
oblivious to anything but their daily dose. Broken families with no
means of sustenance were a common sight, land went untilled, state
affairs untended. The social fabric of Chinese society was slowly dis-
integrating.

At the most advanced stages of addiction, nothing could compete
for the attention of the user but the next pipe. A Chinese official, sent
to observe conditions on the island of Formosa, stated: "The limbs

grow thin and appear to be wasting away; the internal organs col-
lapse. The smoker, unless he be killed, will not cease smoking." Besides being one of the most addictive substances in the world, some
sources also attribute the widespread use of opium to its qualities of
powerful appetite suppressant. In an overpopulated and famine-
ravaged China it may at some point have been more cost-effective to
buy opium than food. In any case, it was perhaps more pleasant to die
of opium addiction than of hunger.

Several times Chinese court advisers suggested to the Emperor

A Visit to an Opium Den, stereograph, Canton, China, 1901. Keystone-Mast Collection
UCR/California Museum of Photography, University of California at Riverside.

Tao-kuang that legalizing the opium trade might resolve some of the problems. Eliminating the profit factor might finally rid the Celestial Kingdom of the Western barbarians and reduce the level of corruption among Chinese officials, which had reached epidemic proportions. Controlling the supply might help limit the abuse; and taxing the now lawful import might replenish the state coffers. But the emperor could not bring himself to do that: "It is true, I cannot prevent the introduction of the flowing poison; gain-seeking and corrupt men will for profit and sensuality, defeat my wishes; but nothing will induce me to derive a revenue from the vice and misery of my people." The emperor had lost his own son to opium.

In 1839 the situation had reached dramatic proportions. The atmosphere was tense. Something had to be done. In a last desperate effort, Emperor Tao-kuang decided to send Commissioner Lin Tse-hsü, an official with the fame of being incorruptible, to Canton to solve the problem. The foreign traders at Canton were not particularly worried. They had been able to bribe all the previous officials, so why would Lin be different? But Commissioner Lin *was* different: courageous, efficient, loyal, and highly ethical. The emperor had chosen the right person. And yet, what the emperor did not foresee was the force with which Britain was ready to respond. Engaging Lin to combat a well-armed drug empire firmly motivated to maintain its power was like setting up a matchstick barrier against a tsunami.

China Pried Open

No Dogs or Chinamen.

—Sign allegedly hanging above the entrance of a park in
Shanghai after Western traders settled in the city

Liquid Opium

The smell was unbearable. On June 3, 1839, 2.5 million pounds of opium balls—about half the yearly imports for the Chinese market—were being crushed and mixed with lime and salt. The nauseating concoction was diluted with water and poured into stone-lined trenches especially constructed for the purpose of destroying the entire opium stock possessed by the foreign traders. The inactivated sludge was then released into the Canton estuary. Hundreds of coolies stirred the mixture with long poles for the twenty-three days it took to complete the process. Workers were systematically inspected and executed on the spot if found in possession of any amount of opium. The message was clear: China was going to be rid of the opium scourge once and forever. The barbarian merchants would finally learn their lesson. From now on, they would have to turn to an honest trade and pay their tea, silk, and porcelain imports with legitimately acquired silver, not with dirty opium money.

Commissioner Lin Tse-hsü, the man chosen by the emperor to solve the opium problem, was pleased. The fifty-three-year-old scholar and high government official had successfully implemented strict opium laws and rehabilitation programs in other Chinese provinces. He was known for being competent and just, and he was so thoroughly incorruptible that he wouldn't even allow his porters to accept tips. Within two months of his arrival in Canton, Lin's actions left no doubt in the minds of anyone involved in the opium trade that this imperial official was unlike any of his predecessors: he was not to be bribed and he meant business.

Lin had arrested several well-known hong merchants involved in the opium trade; announced that the death penalty for opium offenses was now applicable to Chinese and foreigners alike; blockaded the Factories and locked up fifteen of the most infamous foreign opium dealers in their own offices, including the recently arrived British superintendent of trade, Captain Charles Elliot; and obtained the handing over of the entire opium stock from all traders in Canton. He succeeded in his endeavor without resorting to violence and was now in the process of destroying the staggering pile of opium chests, 20,283 in total. The task assigned to him by the emperor seemed well under way to being accomplished. He could allow himself to smile. Or so he thought.

Address to the Spirit of the Sea

Once the opium destruction was under way, Lin turned his attention to what he considered a serious concern of a different sort. Eliminating the opium by liquefying it had been the only efficient and politically acceptable solution, but dumping it into the ocean was not an act in harmony with nature. Lin addressed the problem in the only way a Confucian scholar, well versed in poetry and steeped in the principles of Taoism, knew how to do. He composed an "Address to the Spirit of the Sea," begging forgiveness for his act, and performed a sacrificial ceremony two days before starting the process. "Early this morning I sacrificed to the Sea Spirit," he wrote in his diary, "announcing that I should shortly be dissolving opium and draining it off into the great ocean and advising the Spirit to tell the creatures of the water to move away for a time, to avoid being contaminated." He apologized for polluting the sea and asked the spirit to help rid China of the barbarians. Little did he know that his action was going to mark the end of China as he knew it. Instead of ridding the country of drugs and foreigners, the opium destruction would precipitate a massive invasion of both.

The turning over of the opium to the Chinese authorities had succeeded in great part because of Captain Elliot's efforts. Elliot was personally opposed to the opium trade, but he knew what happened to Crown subjects who spoke out against it. His predecessor, Sir George Robinson, had clearly stated that not only was he ready to "prevent British vessels from engaging in the traffic, whenever H. M. Government direct us to," but he also dared to suggest that "a more certain method would be to prohibit the growth of the poppy, and manufacture of opium in British India." He was fired for this. Whether or not his decision was motivated by personal belief, Elliot managed to convince the foreign merchants, among whom were representatives of Jardine, Matheson, and Dent, to hand in the opium with the promise that the British government would compensate them for their loss. Due to Lin's efficient crackdown the merchants had overstock in their warehouses and were only too happy to sell their entire supply in one swoop to none less than the government itself, a customer with a guaranteed pocketbook.

Collision Course

The conflict was about more than just the spread of opium and the payment of tea bills. For several decades Britain had tried to convince China to accept the Western notion of free trade, but it felt repeatedly rebuffed and humiliated, most spectacularly with the failures of Lord Macartney's mission in 1793 and Lord Napier's in 1834. The Chinese emperor considered foreigners in general mere tributaries to the Celestial Kingdom, and merchants in particular a lower class of human beings. From his point of view there was no reason why they should receive any preferential treatment. China would stay closed, and the barbarians relegated to their Factories.

This view was in dramatic opposition with the way Britain saw China: 300 million new customers. Writes Wakeman in *The Fall of Imperial China*: "China was being viewed by restless country traders and Manchester industrialists as a potential market. To Midlands manufacturers struggling against German competitors for the European market, China seemed to offer boundless economic opportunities." Alas, the Chinese administration would simply not collaborate. For a nation at the height of its military and economic power as Britain was, the Chinese stubbornness was too much to bear. Two different worlds, based on radically opposed economic concepts, were in direct confrontation: Chinese Confucianism versus Victorian pragmatism; one, an ancient, static, centripetal tributary system, the other, an aggressive, profit-driven, colonial expansionary machine. The urgency of the opium problem combined with the accumulated tension of the larger issues was like a dynamite stick ready for a match. And the match soon materialized.

When a brawl broke out in Kowloon between drunken British sailors and Chinese peasants, and one villager died, Commissioner Lin demanded the culprit be handed over to be tried under the Manchu penal code. Captain Elliot refused on extraterritoriality grounds. Although the destruction of the opium stock had brought a momentary sense of satisfaction, Lin realized that the problem was far from resolved. The merchants had refused to sign a bond prohibiting the trade of opium under penalty of death by strangulation, and instead were continuing their smuggling operations from Hong Kong. The lack of supply and the desperation of addicts had succeeded in driving the price of opium to unprecedented highs. With this last incident the tension had become unbearable. Lin blockaded the Factories again, halted all trade, and deployed some war junks around Macao, to which the British had retreated.

A Letter to the Queen

In a last effort to resolve the impasse without violence, Lin wrote a lucid and somewhat desperate letter to Queen Victoria. The queen was twenty years old at the time and had been in power for only two years.

> Even though the barbarians may not necessarily intend to do us harm, yet in coveting profit to an extreme, they have no regard for injuring others. Let us ask, where is your conscience? I have heard that the smoking of opium is very strictly forbidden by your country; that is because the harm caused by opium is clearly understood. Since it is not permitted to do harm to your own country; then even less should you let it be passed on to the harm of other countries. . . . Suppose there were people from another country who carried opium for sale to England and seduced your people into buying and smoking it; certainly your honorable ruler would deeply hate it and be bitterly aroused. We have heard heretofore that your honorable ruler is kind and benevolent. Naturally you would not wish to give unto others what you yourself do not want . . .

The letter was carried to London by a British trader, but it is unclear whether the queen ever read it. By some accounts, Lord Palmerston, then foreign secretary and nicknamed the "gunboat diplomat," made sure it never reached her. He saw the situation as the perfect opportunity to finally pry China open and began lobbying Parliament for military action. From his point of view, China stubbornly refused a civilized offer of fair and free trade and was now making things really difficult for British businessmen by halting commerce altogether. The fact that opium was one of the items of commerce was not specifically stated. And yet, as John King Fairbank says in *China Watch:* "The plans for the campaign . . . came to Palmerston directly from leading British free-traders like Dr. William Jardine, who was also the chief opium merchant." And describing the arrangements to come: "Vessels of the opium fleet were hired to help carry the expeditionary forces from India. Opium ship captains were employed as pilots, opium firm translators as interpreters. The expedition's military and diplomatic leaders benefited from the opium traders' hospitality and advice. . . . From the beginning it was intended that a Chinese indemnity should pay the full costs of the expedition. The war was really a speculation expected to pay for itself and also to make indirect profits."

War

The young Tory M.P. William Gladstone was one of the few who spoke against military action in China, saying that such a war was "morally indefensible" and that he did not know "a war more unjust in its origin, a war more calculated to cover this country with permanent disgrace." Perhaps he was motivated by his own sister's opium addiction, or by the increasingly widespread opium use in all social strata of Victorian England, of which authors and poets like Thomas de Quincey, Samuel Taylor Coleridge, John Keats, and Elizabeth Barrett Browning were only the most visible. In any event, he was not able to stop Palmerston. In addition, Queen Victoria asserted that the Chinese behavior was harming the dignity of her empire. Parliament voted in favor of the war by a margin of nine votes, and in June 1840 a British fleet of sixteen warships, four armed steamers, and four thousand troops sailed into Canton Bay.

Had this happened four hundred years earlier, the British might have hastily retreated when faced with the massive ships of the eunuch Admiral Cheng Ho. But the present rulers were Manchus, foreigners themselves, who had controlled China by keeping it isolated and ignorant of world developments for the last two centuries. Their navy was no match for the British. Although Lin had tried to prepare by buying and arming an American ship, the British firepower and war technology were so far superior that the war was fought and won in a few skirmishes. The British fleet sailed north up the Chinese coast, sacking cities on the way, taking Shanghai, and finally subduing the Chinese into signing the first of the "Unequal Treaties," the Treaty of Nanking, in August 1842. The treaty required the Chinese to open four more ports, besides Canton, to foreign trade: Shanghai, Ningpo, Amoy, and Foochow. Trade concessions in these ports were to be immune from Chinese jurisdiction. Furthermore, China was to pay the sum of 21 million silver dollars—astounding at the time—in war restitutions and compensation for the destroyed opium, and cede the island of Hong Kong to the British government. The only demand China refused to honor was the legalization of opium.

Epilogue

Before the war was over, Commissioner Lin was demoted by an irate emperor, who blamed Lin for his incapacity to avoid the conflict and exiled him to Sinkiang, near the Russian border. Ten years later Lin's true contribution was recognized, and he was reinstated in his role as imperial commissioner in a different province. June 3, the day on which Lin started the destruction of the opium, became opium prohibition day in China. Captain Elliot was removed from office for not having demanded enough in his negotiations with the Chinese and was sent to Texas as a British representative. Jardine collected his opium reimbursement money from the government, became a member of Parliament, and created a business empire in Southeast Asia. Donald Matheson, one of Jardine's younger partners, was among a growing number of Englishmen with moral qualms about the opium trade; he resigned from the firm in 1849.

Lord Palmerston went on to fight a second Opium War (the Arrow War) to open China even more. As was the British wish, the opium trade was finally legalized in 1858. From the 2,500 tons of yearly opium imports at the beginning of the First Opium War, the now legal imports rose to 4,800 tons and peaked at seven thousand tons in 1880. Wakeman writes that in the latter part of the nineteenth century, as much as ten percent of China's total population may have used the drug. From a desolate rock in the middle of the South China Sea, Hong Kong developed into one of the greatest trade centers in the world, thanks to virtually every business on every square inch of land being directly or indirectly connected with the opium trade. As a legal transaction, the trade was not brought to an end until 1917, and then mostly because Indian opium was not competitive with the growing Chinese production anymore. In *China Watch*, Fairbank defined the opium trade from India to China as "the longest-continued systematic international crime of modern times." Hong Kong remained a British colony until 1997, when it was handed back to China.

During the war, China tea, the item that had served as initial justification for the British position, continued to flow into Great Britain for the benefit of every Victorian parlor and the indispensable five o'clock. Imports slowed down somewhat during intensified hostilities and recouped during the many lulls between battles. China had been the sole supplier of tea to the world, but even this was not to last. After flooding the country with opium, the British were intent on cutting out China from the tea trade altogether. It was not long before tea would become a British empire product.

The Tea Spy Who Came from the West

Eastern learning has spirit as its point of departure;
Western learning has matter as its point of departure.

—Liang Ch'i-ch'ao, Chinese reform leader, 1873–1929

"*Fankwei! Fankwei!*" (Foreign devil!) the angry mob shouted. Dozens of Chinese boys and men were closing in on a tall figure walking along a road in the outskirts of Canton. Their hands were holding stones and bricks, ready to throw them at the slightest provocation. The figure moved rapidly toward the open gate of a cemetery, but the mob followed and attacked. A brick hit the *fankwei* in the back, cutting off his breath and causing him to lose control for a moment. The crowd took advantage. Someone seized his hat, another his umbrella, several hands were in his pockets, other hands immobilized his arms. Nothing but a desperate desire for survival helped him fight his way through the hostile crowd. With all his might he threw himself against them, stumbled out of the cemetery onto the open road, and by sheer speed and determination made it back to Canton, beaten but alive.

The year was 1848. The memory of the Opium War was still raw, the Chinese resentment against the British still raging. The tall figure in question was the Scotsman Robert Fortune, gentleman and botanist of the Royal Horticultural Society. While Europe was in turmoil with worker uprisings in Paris and revolutions in Vienna, Milan, and Berlin, Britain was concerning itself with tea and dispatched the gentleman-botanist to China with a singular mandate: to act as the empire's tea spy.

By midcentury, the British had built an empire on the tea trade. Tea was such an important item in the British economy that at one point tea and the industry around it represented as much as 5 percent of the entire gross domestic product. But destabilizing factors were now at work. China was not a reliable tea supplier, given the general dishevelment and hostility reigning in the country. The East India Company had lost its monopoly on the China tea trade, which was now open to competitors worldwide. As a result, it was most urgent to establish an independent tea supply. In addition, Company officials reasoned, why should Britain make Chinese merchants rich buying tea by the tons from them when it could just as well produce its own? India, on the other side of the hill, seemed to be the perfect colony waiting to be exploited for that purpose. Some experimenting was already going on there, but with mixed results. Britain needed Chinese tea seeds and Chinese expertise.

Setting the idea into practice was not as easy as it sounded. The Chinese had been able to maintain high secrecy around tea production. They had kept the plantations strictly off limits to foreigners and had spread false information regarding processing procedures. As a further deterrent, the giving away of any kind of secret and even the teaching of the Chinese language to a foreigner had been declared acts punishable by death. Some, like the Dutchman J. L. L. L. Jacobson, had still managed to smuggle seeds out of China and start a small plantation in Java, but the results had been disappointing; to this day, Java is known for coffee, not tea. The Englishman George Gordon had also been able to send plants to Calcutta, but the transplants were not successful. Why? What was missing, what went wrong?

Company officials believed Robert Fortune was the man who

might find the answers to those questions. By then, Fortune had become curator of the Chelsea Physic Garden. He was thirty-five years old and already had one China trip behind him. He had become somewhat of a celebrity in botanical circles for bringing back numerous exotic trees, shrubs, and ornamental plants that were unknown in the West and quickly became nursery favorites: the now famous Fortune's Double Yellow, a much-admired yellow climbing rose; azaleas, chrysanthemums, rhododendrons, tree peonies; the fan palm, the cypress tree, the plum yew, the kumquat, the holly grape, and many others still bearing his name today.

When Company officials asked Fortune to go on a tea-discovery mission to China, they did not need to do much convincing. Fortune's plant-hunter soul had been stirred. He set sail for China only two years after his first trip with unabated excitement. Whether he was aware of it or not, by signing on he became the main character in one of the first modern cases of international industrial espionage. He was to collect seeds and plants, observe cultivation and production techniques, keep a daily journal (considered Company property), and even hire specialized tea workers willing to immigrate to India. A faithful and efficient tool of the empire, Fortune did all this and later told his stories in several books, which read more like Victorian Indiana Jones adventures than the botanical treatises one would expect.

The Opium War had broken Chinese barriers. The "unequal" Treaty of Nanking had turned China into a humiliated, wounded dragon, forcing it to open its ports. People were flocking to Shanghai, Ningpo, or Canton from all over the world to take advantage of the dragon's weakness. Still, the dragon was weak but not dead. China had been at least able to negotiate that foreigners be denied access beyond the ports to the countryside farther inland. As a result, acquiring information on tea from the hill plantations was a challenging proposition. This did not stop Fortune, whose concept of sovereignty seemed to be applicable to Great Britain only. He considered the laws limiting access to foreigners "absurd laws of the Celestial Empire" and did not hesitate to venture into forbidden territory.

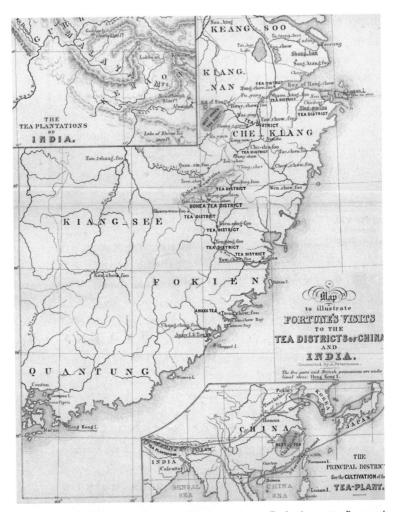

The principal districts for the cultivation of the tea plant, map, England, c. 1850s. Reprinted from Fortune, *Two Visits to the Tea Countries of China*, 1853.

To be able to travel undisturbed, Fortune disguised himself as a mandarin from the northern regions, where people's physical features were more Caucasian than Chinese. He called himself Sing Wa and chose the sedan chair as his main means of transportation. He wore

Chinese dress and shaved his head. The latter was an operation Fortune remembers as one of the most painful in all of his travels to China: "I suppose I must have been the first person upon whom he [the barber] had ever operated, and I am charitable enough to wish most sincerely that I may be the last." The inexperienced barber had not shaved but *scraped* Fortune's head, following which the fearless botanist found himself "with tears running down my cheeks and crying out in pain."

None of the life-threatening adventures he had on his previous China voyage ever provoked such a reaction. Not when he fell in a wild boar trap and would have slowly but surely died in it had it not been for an overhead branch with which he was able to lift himself up. Nor the time when he woke up in the middle of the night and found that robbers had looted his boat and set it adrift in the middle of the river. Nor when, sailing through the Formosa Channel during monsoon season, he was caught in a furious gale, in which frightening masses of water forced their way into the cabins and destroyed Fortune's carefully collected plants. The botanist in him mourned the plants; the man never even asked himself by what miracle he survived.

Fortune did not even lose his British aplomb on that famous occasion when five pirate ships full of armed men attacked the unarmed Chinese junk in which he lay shivering and sweating, struck down by a potent fever. The fearful sailors manning the junk disappeared belowdecks at the first sight of the pirate ships and left Fortune to deal with a desperate situation by himself. On that day he would certainly have had good reason to cry. Instead, he did what any tough Scotsman would do. He got his shotgun and his pistols, went on deck, waited until the enemy was within close range, and shot with precision, killing the helmsmen of two of the ships, which spread terror among the crews. This discouraged the remaining attackers, who sailed away swiftly. And only after this was accomplished did he allow himself to fall back into bed, exhausted.

This second trip was less adventurous but equally profitable from the botanical perspective. Fortune systematically collected seeds, plants, and information on tea. He was a spy with meticulous reconnoitering habits. He visited the most famous tea districts in southeast China, including the spectacular Bohea mountains in Fukien Province, which produced the black tea for European export; the Huichow district and the northern provinces where the best green tea originated; and the tea plantations in Chekiang Province, around Shanghai and Ningpo, and in the Chusan Islands. Patiently, Fortune observed and made notes about the quality of the soil, the pruning and plucking procedures, the manufacture of the dried leaves, even the particular mode of transportation of the tea chests from the plantations to the shipping ports.

In addition to providing answers to the big questions, Fortune also solved little mysteries, for example, the origins of the famous "blue tea," in high demand in Europe at the time. Blue tea, he determined, was nothing more than green tea colored with Prussian blue

Early Chinese apparatus for the manufacture of tea: 1. Stand and trays for sun-drying. 2. Rod for moving trays up or down. 3. Withering stand, set in the shade. 4. Cast-iron pan for steaming or "panning" the leaf. 5. Trolley transport. 6. Rolling by hand; 7. Basket-firing over charcoal fire. 8. Tray for dried or fired tea. 9. Hand-picking tray. Reprinted from Ukers, *All About Tea*, 1935.

and gypsum powder! The Chinese never drank dyed tea but only manufactured it for export to Europe. Concerning taste for dyed teas, Fortune definitely sided with the Chinese: "It seems perfectly ridiculous that a civilised people should prefer these dyed teas to those of a natural green. No wonder that the Chinese consider the natives of the west to be a race of 'barbarians.'" On the other hand, he realized that the epithet of *barbarian* could be equally applied to the Chinese when it came to solid food: "And yet, tell the drinkers of this coloured tea that the Chinese eat cats, dogs, and rats, and they will hold up their hands in amazement, and pity the poor celestials!"

Fortune spent three years crisscrossing the Chinese tea districts, amassing plants and knowledge. On a foggy spring morning in 1851, four vessels set sail from the port of Hong Kong in the direction of Calcutta. They carried two thousand plants, seventeen thousand seedlings, and a team of experienced tea workers. The secrets of tea, held in China for thousands of years, were sailing away on the South China Sea. Robert Fortune had accomplished his East India Company mission. Or so he thought. While he was busy collecting, a very different tea tale had been taking shape on the other side of the Himalayas. His tea knowledge would prove useful but, in an ironic twist, the Chinese tea seed would in part compromise, rather than foster, the nascent tea industry in India.

After his tea mission, Fortune took three more trips to the Orient and spent many years traveling mostly in China but also in Japan and India. He was on assignment for the American government on one of these trips. Perhaps inspired by the British success story, the Americans also hired Fortune to go to China to bring back the necessary goods to start tea plantations in America. Fortune obliged, but the tea industry, as we well know, never made it in the ex-colony. Only one small tea plantation in Charleston, South Carolina, survives to this day.

Fortune spent his retirement years farming in Scotland and later moved to London, living off the royalties of his books and the sale of Oriental antiques. He dedicated a lifetime to botanical study and exploration. He did not question the motives of the empire, which he

The Wilds of Assam

The position of the labourers in many tea-gardens is almost as bad, if it is not worse than the condition of the
American Negro slaves before their emancipation.

—Babu Dwarakanath Ganguli, assistant secretary of the
   Indian Association, sent to Assam to inquire into
   working conditions in the tea gardens, 1886

The Bisa Gaum, one of the chiefs of the Singpho tribe of Upper
Assam, was meeting with one of those white-skinned foreigners
who had been roaming the jungle as of late. The year was 1823, the
foreigner Robert Bruce, former major in the Bengal Artillery, at the
moment adventurer in search of opportunities. Long before Robert
Fortune's exploits in China, Bruce, a fellow Scotsman, was about to
extract a promise from the unsuspecting Singpho chief. The fulfill-
ment of the promise would mark the beginning of unparalleled economic gains for British enterprise along with unparalleled grief for
indigenous populations as well as for many of the less privileged Europeans who came to India in hopes of a better life.

The promise consisted of delivering tea seeds and plants to Bruce
on his next trip to Assam. While the whole Western world was convinced that the one and only source of tea was China, the Singpho
people—and other tribes indigenous to Southwest Asia including the
Shan and the Naga—had been making use of tea growing wild in
their lush jungle hills for centuries, perhaps millennia. They chewed

the leaves or pickled them, a practice still in use today in neighboring Myanmar (Burma), or they used them as a poultice for medicinal purposes. The Bisa Gaum must have thought it such a simple gesture to give Bruce some tea plants gathered from the nearby forest. Bruce, on the other hand, was a man of dubious allegiance whose main interest was of a pecuniary nature. He must have seen pure gold upon spying those precious tea leaves. He must have imagined himself as the first Westerner in history to break the impenetrable Chinese tea machine, living in inexhaustible wealth as a result of what he considered, from a quintessential colonial perspective, his "discovery."

If Bruce dreamed of it, the dream didn't last long. He died not long after the meeting. But another Bruce, Robert's younger brother Charles Alexander, picked up where Robert left off and became the recipient of the Singpho chief's gift. He planted the seeds in his garden in Rangpur, where he was stationed, and sent some to the Assam commissioner David Scott, suggesting the possibility of growing tea in India. Several others had done so before him. Joseph Banks, the English naturalist, had written about the subject as early as 1788. In 1815 the superintendent of the botanical gardens at Saharanpur recommended experimenting with tea planting in Bengal, while in that same year a Colonel Latter talked about wild tea in Assam. A year later, an Englishman residing in Bengal saw what he thought was a tea bush growing in Kathmandu and sent leaves to Calcutta for verification. But Dr. Nathaniel Wallich, the superintendent of the Royal Botanical Garden, determined that they were not tea leaves, but only an unknown camellia variety. All these and other signals fell on deaf ears. For as long as the East India Company was the holder of a monopoly on the tea trade with China, no competition was tolerated, and the Company was going to remain hard of hearing when it came to tea in any other place in the world.

Meanwhile, British expansionism in India continued undeterred. A fairly common technique among European colonial powers of the time was to help one tribe against another tribe and then take control of the winner's land in exchange for providing military support. Britain did exactly that in Assam in 1826. British forces helped the

Ahom, who had been the rulers of Assam since the thirteenth century, defeat the invading Burmese. The Ahom were grateful at first. But the next step the British took was to "annex" parts of Assam to British India. This meant that the Ahom's land was now the property of the British government. At first, the East India Company did not quite see what profit could be extracted from such a remote, treacherous, mosquito-infested jungle. British administrators contented themselves with selecting an amenable local rajah, twenty-five-year-old Purandar Singh, as the official ruler. In exchange, Singh was to pay the Company a yearly tribute of fifty thousand rupees—this at a time when a family of four lived on three rupees a month, and Assam's population had been decimated by the war with Burma, which made the collection of such a huge amount quite problematic.

What changed things was the Company's loss of the China trade monopoly in 1834, which prompted the urgent need of a new source of tea supply. After 1834, the East India Company was not a trading establishment anymore, but it was still India's governing entity. Now all those reports on the wild tea plant were pulled out of dusty drawers and reexamined. Lord Bentinck, then governor-general of India, requested the appointment of a tea committee to explore the possibility of growing tea in India. A scientific commission, which included the same Dr. Wallich who had rejected previous suggestions, was dispatched to explore Assam as a possible area for establishing tea plantations. There, Charles Alexander Bruce was waiting for the learned gentlemen and showed them around. This time Dr. Wallich nodded in agreement, and the committee sent a report back to Calcutta: "It is with feelings of the highest satisfaction that we are enabled to announce to his Lordship in Council that the tea shrub is beyond all doubt indigenous in Upper Assam. . . . We have no hesitation in declaring this discovery . . . to be by far the most important and valuable that has ever been made in matters connected with the agricultural or commercial resources of this empire." Eleven years after Robert Bruce's meeting with the Bisa Gaum, the tea committee report was the spark that set the colonial machine in motion.

Suddenly the East India Company knew what to do with the

mosquito-infested jungle land. Charles Bruce and the scientific committee members continued to search for areas rich in wild tea plants and prepared to set up experimental tea gardens. At the same time, the military-administrative arm of the operation set about stripping the tribal people of land rights and privileges they had enjoyed for centuries. The land that was already under British control was an easy catch. Purandar Singh was summarily deposed with the excuse that he had not paid his yearly tribute. For the land that was not under British control, the administration adopted what came to be known, according to economic historian Muhammed Abu Siddique, as the Policy of Gold and Steel: the tribes were offered cash for their land—the gold—and, if they refused to accept the "offer," armed soldiers would help persuade them they should—with the steel of their sabers and guns.

Once the land was under Company control, land grants were offered and rules established to regulate their distribution. One rule required the applicant to show proof of possessing a capital of three rupees per acre. The smallest land grant available was set at one hundred acres (later increased to five hundred acres). Not very many Assamese had thirty, let alone three hundred rupees available. Clearly, the rules existed to exclude them and attract European settlers instead. One exception was the wealthy aristocrat Maniram Dutta Baruah who, by some accounts, was responsible for introducing Bruce to the Singpho and therefore to the Assam tea plant. After applying for land grants and being refused, Maniram bought his own land and over time established tea gardens on it. But he would not be able to withstand the pressure and hostility of the European colonists for long.

The Company's objective was to develop tea cultivation to the point of commercial viability and then open the doors to private capital. Charles Bruce had become superintendent of tea culture for the Company but, aside from his knowledge of the wild tea plant, he did not know much about tea cultivation; he had arrived in Assam as a gunboat commander. His ignorance was compounded by the general belief, reinforced by two hundred years of China tea imports, that the Assam tea plant could not possibly be as good as its Chinese counterpart, and that Chinese tea workers were the only ones who really knew about tea. As a consequence, for many years the Company went to a great deal of trouble to smuggle tea seeds and tea workers out of China and bring them to India. Robert Fortune was one of the most successful men, although not the first, to be assigned this task. Of the two imports—seeds and men—the first came to be known in some circles as "the curse of the India tea industry," because, by cross-pollinating with the wild Indian variety, it forever compromised the purity of the latter. Bruce voiced his concern about this issue but was ignored. From the Chinese tea workers, on the other hand, Bruce learned a good deal. And so it was that, in 1838, the first eight chests of Assam tea were sold at auction in London.

The tea was not very good, but it was good enough to get a new industry going. A year later, the newly formed Assam Company, a private enterprise under the control of London investors with a board of directors in Calcutta, took over two-thirds of the experimental gardens developed by the British government. Although the Singpho were involved in the production of these first teas, the collaboration did not last long. Their lives were based on subsistence agriculture and barter. From their perspective, producing for a distant market was an odd idea, and money an abstract and fairly useless concept. Then there was the question of social hierarchy, both for the Singpho and for other Assamese who were asked to perform menial work for the Company.

For the colonizers, all indigenous Assamese were brown and primitive. But members of the middle and upper classes of the various tribes had no experience submitting to labor for someone else's benefit. In general, they worked only when it was necessary and were not prepared to allow women and children to suffer endless hours in the fields under a hot sun in exchange for a meager wage. For this the white settlers termed them "indolent" and "miserable opium-smoking Assamese." Bruce commented on the issue thus: "This alone ought to point out the utility of introducing a superior race of labourers, who would not only work themselves, but encourage their women and children to do the same;—in plucking and sorting leaves they might be profitably turned to account for both parties. This I have not been able to instil [sic] into the heads of the Assamese, who will not permit their women to come into the Tea gardens."

Indeed, tea cultivation is very labor intensive, a detail to which Bruce had alerted the Assam Company: "Unless more labourers can be furnished, a large amount of Tea must not be looked for at present. Last season it was with the greatest difficulty that I could get a sufficient number of hands to gather the leaves." With the growth of the tea industry and the Assamese unwilling to participate in what looked more and more like their own demise, labor shortage became a serious issue. One of the first measures the British administrators took in an effort to resolve the problem was to increase land taxation to such an extent that the locals would not be able to maintain their plots and would have to come to work at the tea gardens. When the results of this policy proved insufficient, the planters turned to importing labor from other parts of India. This was the beginning of one of the most wretched chapters of labor history, the repercussions of which are still felt in Assam today.

The system put in place was called indentured or bonded labor. Officially, there was a contract that the *arkati*, or recruiting agent, asked the mostly illiterate laborers to sign. Often the signature was nothing more than a fingerprint. The "official" paperwork could not hide the reality, which was frighteningly similar to slavery, perhaps even worse. The *arkatis* were sent out at first to neighboring Bengal and Bihar, but later also to Orissa and Madhya Pradesh. They canvassed overpopulated, rural areas and enticed the poorest among the people to immigrate to Assam with the promise of a good wage and a better life. Once the agents had assembled enough recruits, they took them to Calcutta, where they held them in "depots" under appalling conditions and then loaded them on a boat for the six- or eight-week trip up the treacherous Brahmaputra River under even more appalling conditions. Overcrowded, undernourished, ill accustomed to the swampy climate, many of them died from cholera, dysentery, malaria, or typhoid fever even before arriving at their destination. The ones who did survive the voyage were greeted by managers with whips in their hands and put to work clearing jungle land, hoeing hard soil, or plucking tea leaves, no matter how hungry, tired, or sick they were. At night they were escorted to their pitiful huts, from which they were not allowed to leave.

The "coolie," as the tea worker was called, was chronically underfed and underpaid, the wages on tea gardens were lower, not higher, than on other plantations elsewhere in the empire. Hunger and low pay were not the worst. Faced with the daily risk of physical violence; unable to protect his wife from the sexual advances of a manager or a foreman; hopelessly enmeshed in a vicious cycle of payments and debts sanctioned by a one-sided contract he was incapable of understanding; left on his own and without pay when ill to get well or die—if the coolie entertained the idea of escape, one look at the endless surrounding jungle, populated by tigers and king cobras, was enough to discourage even the bravest one. "Shoot away!" was the answer two of these brave ones gave one day when the pursuing guard threatened to shoot them if they did not return. A swift death was preferable to the misery of tea garden life.

Laborers suffered a very high mortality rate due to malnourishment and exposure to airborne and waterborne diseases. Historian J. C. Jha, who studied indentured labor in northeast India, wrote that between 1863 and 1866 32,000 of the 84,000 laborers brought to the tea plantations died. In his memoirs, the chief commissioner of Assam Henry Cotton gave a more graphic description of the situation: "I have seen dead and dying coolies lying in the ditch by the roadside and in the bazar." And tea laborers were not the only ones dying. In the 1860s, the years of the Tea Mania, when tea plantations started to turn a profit and everyone wanted to invest in tea, land speculators lured many Europeans to Assam with the offer of cheap land and the prospect of easy wealth. The men who undertook the voyage were mostly the ones for whom the doors of upward mobility were closed in England and who dreamed of being landowners one day, or at least having a nest egg for their old age. Alas, mosquitoes and bacteria are color-blind, and many of the dreams of the white man died on the shores of the Brahmaputra along with the coolie's dreams of a better life.

Nothing could stop Empire tea. By the turn of the century, almost 340,000 acres of Assamese jungle had been converted to tea gardens. Tens of thousands of additional acres were bought up by overzealous land speculators but were left fallow. Local tribes were not allowed to plant subsistence crops or gather firewood on this land. Of the converted acreage, 97 percent was under European ownership, which left less than ten thousand acres to Indians. Maniram Dutta Baruah, the Assamese aristocrat who started his own tea gardens, was not among them. His enemies used the turmoil of the 1857 Sepoy Mutiny that shook Britain's grip on India to accuse Maniram of conspiracy against the empire and hanged him after a mock trial in 1858.

Tea cultivation expanded to other parts of northwestern and southern India as well. Darjeeling emerged as the star of teas, and Ceylon (Sri Lanka) had a tea story of her own. British India became the main supplier of tea on the world market, displacing China, whose tea exports plummeted from 100 percent to a mere 10 percent of the market. In 1900 the north Indian plantations alone shipped nearly 140 million pounds of tea to England. As William Ukers said in *All About Tea*: "Indeed the far flung Kingdom of India tea extends to all the countries of the earth where tea is grown or is used as a beverage. . . . Verily, the sun never sets upon India tea's dominions."

In less than fifty years, British Empire tea reached the international status that it had taken China tea hundreds of years to attain. Though the newly acquired colonial wealth could be measured in pounds and acres, the human cost was incalculable. A measure has yet to be invented that can assign a numeric value to human grief.

Tea Tom and Mr. Taylor

They called him *sami dorai* (the master who is god).

—Referring to James Taylor, the true father of Ceylon tea

Scotsmen seem to be mysteriously attracted to tea. Robert Fortune, the tea spy in China, was a Scotsman. The Bruce brothers in Assam, who were the first to come into contact with the Indian tea plant, were Scotsmen. Now two more Scotsmen landed on the shores of that mesmerizing island, the teardrop of India—Sri Lanka, once called Ceylon. They covered its hills with acres and acres of lush, deep-green tea bushes. Within a few decades of their arrival, the word *Ceylon* would be a synonym for tea, recognized around the world. One Scotsman did the real work; the other raked in the profits. Predictably, history remembers the millionaire, not the genius.

The story of Ceylon tea starts with coffee. The *Hemileia vastatrix* is not an ancient Roman goddess of war and destruction, but something close to that. Also called coffee rust, *H. vastatrix* is a devastating fungus that takes the form of an orange powder. It attacks the bottom of coffee leaves and slowly chokes the plants to death by impairing photosynthesis. One of the most feared diseases among coffee growers, it appeared in Ceylon during the 1860s and—microscopic in size but relentless in scope—proceeded to destroy 250,000 acres of coffee plantations over a ten-year period. The coffee rust ruined not only plants but also the livelihoods of countless people involved in coffee plantations, whether pickers or investors, carriers or managers. Many of the Europeans who had come to Ceylon with great hopes were left penniless. A few were able to scrape together enough money for the passage back home. For the ones who stayed behind, the future looked just like their coffee bushes: sterile, dried out, hopeless.

One of the young men who stayed was James Taylor. He was the first Scotsman of our story, the one who did the work. Taylor arrived on the island in 1852 as a boy of sixteen. Encouraged by his cousin, he had left his small village in the Scottish Highlands and signed a three-year contract to work on a coffee plantation. Young James was inquisitive and interested in learning about everything. He worked hard, was persistent, and was good at whatever he did, be it building a road, constructing a bungalow, or solving problems large and small on the plantation. Experimenting was an activity that came naturally to Taylor. He planted some newly arrived China tea seeds along the roadside of the Loolecondera Estate where he was employed.

While *H. vastatrix* was spreading death and destruction, and people were abandoning the island like rats on a sinking ship, Taylor was busy focusing on a solution. At first he grew cinchona, the plant from which quinine is extracted and which helped the estate through the difficult years. Then he turned his attention to tea. He asked questions wherever he could, investigated soil characteristics, tested pruning techniques, learned how to pluck. In the beginning the results must have been somewhat disappointing, as Taylor himself recollected in a letter years later: "The first [tea] I made long ago was pretty nearly rank poison." But Scottish obstinacy has its advantages. For Taylor, giving up was not an option. He spent years testing, spoiling a batch, trying again with a new batch, transforming his little bungalow into a small tea factory. There he spread out tea leaves to dry and then moved batch after batch onto his dinner table, rolling leaves by hand, using wrist to elbow like a rolling pin.

It is unclear whether Taylor then pestered his bosses, D. G. B. Harrison and Martin Leake, about trying out tea on a plantation scale, or whether his bosses decided to import Assam tea seeds after hearing an encouraging report on growing tea in Ceylon. As true Victorian gentlemen, both Taylor and Leake later credited each other with the idea. And certainly, at least some of the credit must go to George Thwaites of the Peradeniya Botanical Gardens, whose warnings about the coffee rust went unheeded and who was instrumental in importing the precious Assam seed. Regardless of who first suggested the idea, the fact is that when the seed arrived in 1867 and was "entrusted to that watchful nurse, Mr. James Taylor," the watchful nurse was years ahead of everyone else. He knew how to handle every step of the process from seeding to serving tea. Oh, he may have been a little weak in this last step. It is said that he was somewhat lacking in social skills, particularly around tea-drinking ladies— a result perhaps of living the rough life on a plantation and consorting with other socially challenged, sometimes hard-drinking males, often also of Scottish descent. But he knew how to get the tea leaves ready, taking backstage when it came to afternoon tea and chinaware and scones.

Others had planted tea bushes in Ceylon before, including the Worms brothers—from the fabulously wealthy German banking family and cousins of the Rothschilds. One would never imagine Worms or Rothchilds roughing it in primitive tropical islands, but rather relaxing in evening attire, sipping champagne at intermission at the Berlin Opera. Yet, they were there, in Ceylon, and they got their hands dirty up-country on their seven-thousand-acre estate. But their focus was on coffee. The few tea bush cuttings Maurice Worms had brought back from China and planted on the estate never really acquired any significance in the brothers' eyes. They managed a model coffee plantation and sold it at an unprecedented profit just before the coffee rust arrived.

The nineteen acres Taylor cleared for tea in 1867—still known today as the famous "No. 7 field"—represented the first commercial tea plantation on the island of Ceylon. During the following few years, Taylor perfected the process, trained assistants and workers, and even invented a machine for rolling the leaves so his wrists and elbows

Packing Tea Chests, by John Abercromby Alexander, one in a series of twenty-four photographs on tea cultivation, England, c. 1920. Royal Commonwealth Society Collections, reprinted by permission of the Syndics of Cambridge University Library, Cambridge, UK.

could take a break. His tea was appreciated around the island, and small amounts were even sold in London and Melbourne. He was deeply dedicated to his work and only left the plantation once, and then only to travel to what was becoming the land of the queen of teas, Darjeeling, to study tea. Taylor also shared his knowledge freely with visiting planters keen on trying the new crop. In time, the tall, imposing man with a wild, flowing beard became a sort of patriarch of tea, loved by his workers and respected by his peers. One writer of the time called him "Mr. Taylor of Loolecondera, than whom a more intelligent, practical planter does not exist."

Soon what had started as a young man's experiment and could have chugged along as a small cottage operation became a national industry. Planters, eager for a chance to recover their losses from the coffee blight, converted their acreage to tea with lightning speed. By 1875, only eight years after the establishment of the No. 7 field, approximately a thousand acres had been converted to tea. Twenty years later the figure was 305,000 acres and, by the 1930s, almost half a million acres. In 1883 tea production had grown to such an extent that a tea auction house was set up in Colombo to sell the product worldwide. It is still in operation today.

Two things made the expansion possible, apart from Taylor's hard work: One was *H. vastatrix*, which literally cleared the stage. In his book on Ceylon tea, Denys Forrest significantly quotes: "It is in no small measure due to *Hemileia vastatrix* that the British are now a nation of tea drinkers." The other was the hardy Assam seed, which, from the northeastern jungles of the Indian subcontinent, bestowed its magnificent bounty around the world. It was brought to the Dutch Javanese tea plantations and helped raise Java tea, which had never distinguished itself, to a level that at least allowed it to be called tea without embarrassment. Later it was also used to start the African plantations. The introduction of the Assam seed led Ceylon tea to be known as one of the best teas in the world.

After most of the problems were solved and the Ceylon tea machine was well oiled and in motion, the second Scotsman of our story, the one who made the millions, appeared. As a rule, millionaires have a fine nose for smelling the chance to make more millions. Thomas Lipton was no exception to this rule. Another Scotsman who immigrated at the age of fifteen, Lipton left Glasgow not for the wilderness of the tropics but for America. There he learned the business practices and the advertising methods that made his fortune when he applied them to the chain of grocery stores he opened back in Scotland. When he arrived in Ceylon, he was already a millionaire and snapped up the remaining debilitated coffee plantations at throwaway prices. There he set up tea plantations with the official intent of eliminating the middleman and helping the working class buy tea at lower prices. His slogan was "Direct from the garden to the teapot."

Yet for all his touting the populist tune, Lipton did not own much land in Ceylon. His 5,500 acres represented only a small fraction of the supply to his worldwide distribution; the rest he bought from other tea planters. He had eliminated the middleman by becoming the middleman himself. Nor was Lipton the tea pioneer he professed to be. Taylor was—and to a lesser extent, so were Thwaites, Harrison, and Leake, and the other planters who took risks and put in the work twenty years earlier. But advertising has the power to turn fiction into reality. Soon the general population, writes Forrest, came to see "Ceylon as a Lipton rather than a British colony; they pictured the island as one great 'tea garden,' presided over by a father-figure with a goatee beard, a yachting cap and a blue-spotted bow tie. And that is exactly what 'Tommy' Lipton intended them to think."

Along with the popularization of Ceylon and Indian tea at the world fairs in London and Paris, Lipton's marketing gave the final touches to what, from the point of view of the British empire, had become the Indian tea success story. By the end of the nineteenth century, the mention of the word *tea* did not evoke secretive, elusive China anymore but the tropical lushness and the seductive heat of India and Ceylon. Now tea was not a product to be wrested from the hands of intractable Chinese merchants; it was instead a friendly product, a yield from "our" colonial plantations. For the Victorian bourgeoisie, drinking full-bodied black Indian or Ceylon tea was a satisfying experience, the tangible result of the hard work of bringing the "brown" people up to speed with the rest of the civilized world. Tea Tom, as

Tamil tea plucker, Ceylon, illustration from *The Graphic*, England, 1886. Courtesy of the Bramah Museum of Tea and Coffee, London.

Lipton was later nicknamed, was the perfect embodiment of the commercial accomplishments of the British empire.

Even though he did not witness the Lipton-Ceylon equation and subsequent international tea boom, James Taylor foresaw the developments of the tea industry. In his later years his youthful excitement turned to disillusionment as he watched big companies buy up small estates, while men with business suits, who stayed in the hotels in Colombo and never came up to the fields, displaced small planters. The same large-plantation scheme as in northern India, with the same unbearable conditions for tea workers, emigrating this time from the southern Indian states, was reproduced on the island. Taylor had kick-started a machine that had taken its own course. Once big capital was involved, it was unstoppable. His own attempts at reaping some small benefit from his work failed when his many applications for land grants to start his own plantation were turned down. For his entire working life he remained the superintendent of Loolecondera with a monthly salary. And even that didn't end well.

In a frenzy of property consolidation, Loolecondera changed hands several times until it was acquired by the Oriental Estates Company. This was an abstract entity, as far as Taylor was concerned, populated by individuals who didn't know anything about tea or life on a plantation, and even less about his own profound attachment to the sprawling fields of Loolecondera, on which he had lived and worked for forty years. However abstract, the entity had power to act. In 1892, according to a report by Taylor's neighbor, the company asked Taylor to take a six-month leave. Taylor interpreted the request as an attempt to get rid of him. He replied he was in perfect health and refused to leave. In response, the company asked him to resign. The denouement of the story brings to mind the end Herman Melville chose for his Bartleby the Scrivener, that unique character of English-language literature whose quiet resistance against the powers to be is epitomized in his unwavering response: "I would prefer not to."

James Taylor "preferred not to." He contracted dysentery and died within a few days, still on the grounds of Loolecondera. Twenty-four of his men took turns carrying their *sami dorai* (the master who is god) for eighteen miles to the cemetery in Kandy. There James Taylor lies buried, without ever having seen his native Scotland again, amidst rolling hills covered with his beloved tea plants. Sri Lanka is today one of the leading tea-exporting countries in the world.

Tea Clippers:
A Race to the End

The old Clipper days are over, and the white-winged fleets no more,
With their snowy sails unfolded, fly along the ocean floor;
Where their house-flags used to flutter in the ocean winds unfurled,
Now the kettle-bellied cargo tubs go reeling around the world.

—*Some Merchants and Sea Captains of Old Boston,* 1918

For nearly two hundred years the East Indiamen, the large, wide-bowed, and ponderous merchant ships of the East India Company, crossed the oceans and rounded the capes, faithfully supplying England with its beloved China tea. Cargo capacity being the main consideration, East Indiamen were built with huge holds and manned by large crews. They docked at the Whampoa anchorage in the Canton estuary—the only port open to foreigners before the Opium Wars—loaded up thousands upon thousands of tea chests, and sailed homeward at a leisurely, complacent pace, taking a year or more for the round-trip journey. Why hurry when one is the uncontested master of trade as the East India Company was then? Yet change was in the air at the beginning of the 1800s. Change that came in stages, each one dealing a blow to the all-powerful Company. Change that also gave birth, among other things, to one of the most exuberant times in the world of seamanship.

The Company began to die a slow death even before 1834 when it lost its China trade privileges. In 1813 it lost its India trade monopoly, following protest and lobbying by merchants who had long resented being excluded from the trade. India was finally opened to private enterprise from all across Great Britain—Glasgow to Manchester, Liverpool to Birmingham. The Company continued to administer India in trust for Great Britain, but it could not trade it in anymore. Twenty years later, amid much clamor about the Company's enormous long-standing and growing debt, which had earlier played its part in the loss of the American colonies, the China monopoly ended also. After 1834, the East India Company, which had started as a joint-stock trade enterprise and had become the largest commercial trading venture in the world, was restricted to being the Crown's colonial administrator, fulfilling nothing more than civil servant duties in India.

Along with these changes came other major changes in the world order. The Opium War had forced China to open five treaty ports—one of them, Foochow, had become the largest tea-exporting center in the world before Indian tea took over—and the China trade was open to any seafaring nation or enterprise that chose to enter it. In addition, the British Navigation Acts, designed to favor the British merchant marine in the international cargo transport business, were repealed in 1849. This meant that not only British ships but any vessel from any nation could carry goods to and from Great Britain. India was open, China was open, British ports were open, and the East India Company was out of the way. Trading channels and opportunities that had been sealed and inaccessible for centuries were available to anyone. Provided they move fast.

"Fast" became an element of crucial importance in the trading world of the first half of the nineteenth century. Now the focus was on who could get there and back first rather than who could carry the most. And America, the new and enterprising nation of the West, was ready. Up until the 1840s, vessels were either large but slow or fast but small. The small fast ones had been used for smuggling tea and other goods in colonial times, for stealth maneuvers around the British frigates during the War of Independence, or for short coastal passages. The large slow ships, such as the East Indiamen, were commonly used for transatlantic cargo transport. An alternative to the two was nonexistent and unimaginable. So when the shippers Howland and Aspinwall of New York saw that a fortune could be made in the China tea trade and decided to commission the building of a ship that was both large and fast, people thought they were mad and called the ship "Aspinwall's folly."

But the *Rainbow*, as she was called, was not a folly, although her innovative lines did revolutionize the commonly accepted navigation design principles of the time. She was the first of what came to be known as true clipper ships—sleek, fast vessels with sharp bows and tall masts carrying an exceptional spread of sails. The true clippers were built for speed, but unlike their smaller predecessors, known as the Baltimore clippers, they also functioned as transoceanic transport vessels with large, ingeniously planned holds for light cargo. In 1844–45, the *Rainbow*, as well as the *Houqua*, another clipper conceived later but launched before the *Rainbow*, were the first American clippers to be sent off to China to fetch tea.

Before long, shipyards along the New England coast and in New York were busy building clipper ships. The increasing demand for vessels was due to the lucrative China trade but also to other equally, if not more, lucrative endeavors requiring speed. One was the opium trade, which made the fortune of a few Boston Brahmins and prominent New York clans. The other was the California gold rush, which turned San Francisco from a forgotten Mexican settlement to one of the most crowded harbors in the world; the number of ships requesting dockage went from just a few in 1848 to 775 in 1849. Tea, opium, and gold sparked a construction frenzy among American shipbuilders—not only in the sheer quantity of ships being built, but also in the daring design of faster and faster vessels, known as extreme clippers. One of them, the *Lightning*, "flew" on the water, logging 436 nautical miles in a day, astonishing the nineteenth-century world in the same way the first spaceships did the twentieth-century one.

The East Indiamen with their jolly paunches sat helplessly in their docks while the American speed machines were whizzing back and forth. The days of the old "tea waggons" were numbered. One of these speed machines, the *Oriental*, jolted the British out of their torpor by being the first American ship to deliver a load of tea to a London dock on December 3, 1850. This took place only a year after the repeal of the Navigation Acts, which the Americans had long resented. It took the *Oriental* ninety-one days to sail from Hong Kong to London, half of what it took an East Indiaman. As Ralph D. Paine reported in his 1921 book on the American merchant marine, *The London Times* registered the dismay: "We must run a race with our gigantic and unshackled rival. We must set our long-practised skill, our steady industry, and our dogged determination against his youth, ingenuity, and ardor. Let our shipbuilders and employers take warning in time. There will always be an abundant supply of vessels good enough and fast enough for short voyages. But we want fast vessels for the long voyages which otherwise will fall into American hands."

And a race it became. British shipbuilders did not waste time copying American designs and sending off their own speed machines to China. In a matter of a few years, British clippers were as elegant and fast as their American counterparts. Soon what started as commercial transport operations turned into international sports events: the Tea Races, in which clippers, now aptly called tea clippers, would race one another from England to China and back to be the first to deliver fresh tea at the London auctions. The journeys were really transatlantic regattas, complete with fan clubs, betting agents, and premiums for the winner. Captain and crew had the preparation and discipline of a professional racing team and kept an eye not on the day calendar but on the stopwatch. Clippers that had sailed for eighty or ninety days often arrived at their destination within minutes of one another, with half of London cheering them on along the docks. In fashionable society, securing an order of fresh tea from the newly arrived tea clippers became the snobbery of the moment. The Tea Races were great fun, and being the first to taste the new crop was the Beaujolais nouveau event of nineteenth-century London.

The era of the tea clippers was exciting and beautiful and perhaps the most innocent and romantic aspect of the Western contribution to the tea story. But it was very short-lived. The world was moving faster and faster. The greyhounds of the sea, as the clippers were called, could not keep up. Mr. Watt's invention, the steam engine, was conquering land and sea. Even the most extreme clippers could not compete—in speed or cargo capacity—with the new transatlantic steam liners. As if this were not enough, in 1869 the Suez Canal opened, too narrow for sailing ships to negotiate but perfect for

A tea label advertising the novelty of tea transported via the Suez Canal, England, late nineteenth century. Courtesy of the Bramah Museum of Tea and Coffee, London.

steamers. Gone were the days in which the dazzling *Fiery Cross*, the *Flying Spur*, or the *Spindrift* would fly down the Atlantic, round the Cape of Good Hope, sail up along Madagascar and cross the Indian Ocean and the South China Sea to pick up the season's new crop of Gunpowder or Bohea. Now the *Achilles*, the *Ajax*, and the *Agamemnon* chugged through the Mediterranean and the Suez Canal and were back in half the time it took clippers, which only a couple of decades earlier had been half the time it took the East Indiamen. In the span of a generation a trip that took a year or more was cut down to three months. By comparison, it is as if today we could fly from London to Los Angeles in two and a half hours instead of ten.

The clippers completed their last tea voyages in the late 1870s. After that, some were dismantled, others were used as passenger ships, and a few were put to work in other trades. The only survivor of this era is the famous *Cutty Sark*, an extreme clipper and one of the last ones to be built. She was launched in 1869, the year the Suez

Canal was opened, and she bankrupted her owners. After a few years in the China tea trade and several others in the Australian wool trade, the *Cutty Sark* was sold to a Portuguese company and then bought back by a British captain who restored her. Today the *Cutty Sark* is dry-docked in Greenwich, England, not far from the Greenwich Meridian Line, and she functions as a maritime museum.

The demise of the tea clippers marked the end of an era in more ways than one. China tea was finished. British Empire tea, mass produced with the large plantation system, displaced myriad small Chinese tea producers. Venture capitalists across the globe controlled production and distribution. The tea from the Indian territories hardly even made it on the clippers, but was transported on steamers for reasons of speed and profitability. In the passage from East to West, tea underwent a profound transformation. From object of reverence at the center of literary endeavors, artistic achievements, and spiritual quests, tea was relegated to the anonymity of an international mass commodity along with all the other colonial products that made the wealth of the Western nations. The image of the gargantuan steamship, the cold, lifeless, mechanized "kettle-bellied cargo tub," transporting goods in never-before-seen quantities, was emblematic of the transition.

Along with the tea clippers and China tea, the East India Company was finished, too. The curious irony was that the faster tea traveled from East to West, the more it was removed from the control of the Company. The very institution that had once been the initiator and the powerhouse of the tea trade, the corporate mastodon that had held the reins of the entire Orient trade on the basis of tea for two and a half centuries, had now nothing whatsoever to do with tea. After losing the India and China monopolies and descending to the lower realms of administration, the East India Company was dealt the fatal blow in 1858, after the Indian Sepoy Mutiny—the Sepoys were Indian soldiers employed by the Company—and the subsequent atrocities that rattled India and the empire.

The Company was accused of ineptitude in governing India in general and inability to control its own army in particular; after all, it was her own soldiers that had mutinied. The public had long resented the Company's favored status. First, as holder of a monopoly it had, for two hundred years, eliminated competition and unilaterally imposed high prices, against which the public had no recourse. Second, corruption, rapacious behavior, nepotism, and general conflicts of interest were widespread and well-known practices among Company management. Third, its stockholders (in 1836 there were only 3,590 of them) were seen as the privileged few, particularly since after the Company ceased trade in 1834, the stockholders continued to be guaranteed the 10.5 percent fixed dividend they had been enjoying since 1793 and would continue to receive for the subsequent forty years. Even though there was no trade to produce dividends, payment was secured against the territorial revenues of India, which meant that Indian taxpayers supported Company stockholders. Later, after the final dissolution of the Company, stockholders were offered government annuities or two hundred pounds for every one hundred pounds of nominal stock in their possession. An unending succession of sweet deals. Rancor toward the Company was a feeling almost too easy to come by.

In tune with the general critical atmosphere, Queen Victoria noted that most Englishmen felt "that India should belong to me." And so it was that the Company lost the administration of India, too. The government of India was transferred to the Crown on September 1, 1858. In an effort to preserve some vestige of dignity, the Company directors issued one last official commentary on the day of the transfer: "Let Her Majesty appreciate the gift, let Her take the vast country and the teeming millions of India under Her direct control; but let Her not forget the great corporation from which She received them, nor the lesson to be learnt from their success." The Crown also assumed the Company's by now disconcerting debt of 100 million pounds, which was transferred to the government of India, and thus, again, to Indian taxpayers.

The grand East India House on Leadenhall Street, Company headquarters for more than two centuries, was demolished. A secretary and a clerk were housed in more modest quarters until 1874 when dividend payments ran out and the Company was definitively dissolved. With that, an entity that had ruled the tea trade and the business world for 275 years, owned its own armies, coined its own currency, shaped the relations between East and West, and in one way or another determined the fate of populations across the globe, ended, in T. S. Eliot's famous words, "not with a bang but a whimper."

Slogan and logo for the Ceylon Tea Bureau, c. 1920s. Reprinted from Ukers, *All About Tea*, 1935.

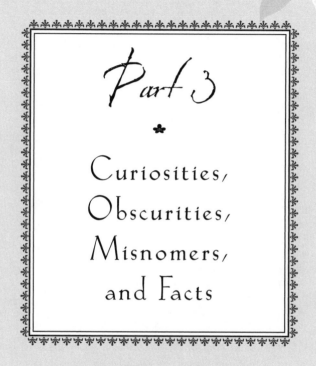

Part 3

❧

Curiosities,
Obscurities,
Misnomers,
and Facts

Tea and Tay,
Ch'a and Chai

That excellent and by all Physicians approved China
drink, called by the Chineans Tcha, by other nations,
Tay, alias Tee, is sold at the Sultaness Head Cophee
House in Sweeting Rents, by the Royal Exchange,
London.

—First newspaper tea ad, already reflecting an awareness
 of lexicographic issues—September 30, 1658,
 in the *Mercurius Politicus*

Words travel through time and space on odd routes. This is why
etymological dictionaries can be fascinating portholes into the
meanderings of history. The origin of the word *tea*—and its European
variations, such as the Italian *tè*, the German *Tee*, or the French *thé*—is
really Chinese. In other countries around the world—Iran, Russia, India, Japan, Arabic countries and, surprisingly, Portugal—the word for
tea is *cha* or *chai*. The latter, now a very popular drink in the West,
refers to the way Indians commonly take their tea: a mixture of black
tea, rich milk, sugar, and spices such as cardamom, cinnamon, pep-
percorn, cloves, or ginger. Yet the origin of the word *cha* is also Chinese. Why does the Chinese language have two words for the same
thing, and why do most Asian and Arabic countries use one word

The *ch'a* character in seal script is composed of two prominent elements. At the top is the Chinese word *radical*, which means "herb," while the radical of the lower part means "tree." The two elements refer to the tea plant as both tree and leafy herb. The term *seal script* refers to a style of Chinese calligraphy used on stone and metal seals. Image and explanation courtesy of Steven D. Owyoung.

while Western European countries use the other? And why is Portugal the only Western European country that doesn't fit the pattern?

Trade routes sometimes determine more than just what goods get transported where. To begin with, China had more than two words for tea. In the *Ch'a-ching*, the eighth-century Chinese treatise on tea, Lu Yü mentions five: *ch'a, chia, she, ming,* and *ch'uan*. And there were even more in the numerous regional dialects spoken around China. While *ch'a*, and later *cha*, emerged as the main word for tea in both Cantonese and Mandarin, the Amoy dialect in Fukien Province continued to refer to it as *t'e*, pronounced "tay." This is where the trade routes come in. Arab traders who reached China with camel caravans along the northern land routes brought back with them, along with the actual leaf, the Mandarin word *ch'a*. But the first Western seafaring traders who popularized tea in northern Europe at the beginning of the seventeenth century were the Dutch. And they traded with Amoy merchants in the beginning. First impressions are everlasting; *t'e* stuck and was introduced and forever adopted by England and the rest of Europe. The word was variously spelled *thea, tey, tay,* and *tee,* before it became *tea* around the middle of the eighteenth century.

Except for the Portuguese. They did indeed reach China before the Dutch, and Queen Catherine of Braganza was acquainted with tea long before her English consort. But the Portuguese docked in Macao and Canton, not Amoy, and therefore they incorporated the

Cantonese *ch'a*. And whatever "ch'a" they brought back was consumed locally, not exported. Had the Portuguese merchant marine controlled the European trade at the time, the way the Dutch did, the Western world might be saying *ch'a* today, and *t'e* would be an obscure word in an obscure regional dialect in China. Instead, all the Portuguese managed to do was to disseminate the word *ch'a* among European sailors working on their ships, which is the reason why the word survives as *char* in English and Irish slang.

Today, if you ask for *ch'a*, or *cha*, in Russia, you'll get a steaming cup of thick, smoky black tea. In Iran they will bring you a small glass of scented tea with a few sugar cubes on the side, which you'll bite into with each sip of tea. In Morocco you'll be awed by the precision with which green tea mixed with mint is poured from a metal pot several feet away into your glass. In Japan you'll be handed a bowl of bright green whipped *matcha* or delicate *sencha*. But you won't get the sweet, spicy, milky Indian chai listed on the menus of our urban coffee shops along with lattes and espressos. That particular chai is the result of a new trade route, only about a dozen years old, that went from India directly to the marketing departments of American coffee chains. Portuguese caravels are not involved.

The Enigma of the Camellia

From what enchanted Eden came thy leaves
That hide such subtle spirits of perfume?
Did eyes preadamite first see the bloom,
Luscious Nepenthe of the soul that grieves?

—Francis S. Saltus, "Tea," nineteenth century

Walking into a tea shop can be an overwhelming experience these days. Green tea, black tea, white tea, scented tea, smoked tea, compressed tea, Silver Needle, Gunpowder, Sencha, first flush, second flush, Yunnan, Keemun, Assam, Nilgiri . . . the choices are nearly endless. The countries of origin span the globe, from India and China to Argentina or Kenya, from Turkey to Taiwan to Indonesia. The actual tea leaves vary widely in size and shape—long and skinny, short and broken, powdered, twisted, compressed. And the color ranges anywhere from a pale gray-white to different shades of green, to reddish browns, dark browns, and almost black.

Consequently, it might not seem unreasonable to ask how many different plants, growing in such varied parts of the world, produce all these teas. And the answer would be: one. Just one, and it is a type of camellia, *Camellia sinensis*, closely related to the camellias we have in our gardens. *Sinensis* means "Chinese" in Latin, and the word *camellia* honors the Moravian Jesuit and pioneer botanist George Joseph Kamel (Latin *Camellius*) whose work on plants from the Far East was well-known in seventeenth-century Europe. That the *Camellia sinensis* is the one and only plant to yield every single one of all the teas around the world, except for mostly caffeine-free herbal infusions, has been common knowledge in China for thousands of years. But in Europe the information was acquired after much effort, confusion, quasicomical twists and turns, and only fairly recently.

During the second half of the seventeenth century, Europeans learned to appreciate tea as a beverage but had no idea what it was, other than an exotic herb from China. Doctors, the German Simon Paulli and the Dutch Cornelius Bonteköe, for example, or pharmacists, like the French Philippe Sylvestre Dufour, wrote treatises on tea but were not much better informed about tea's botany than the general public. The Dutch physician Willem ten Rhyn and the German naturalist Engelbert Kämpfer both traveled to Japan and published descriptive and historical accounts of the tea plant—Rhyn in 1678

Branches of the tea plant, by Engelbert Kämpfer, engraving, Germany, 1692. Reprinted from Kämpfer, *Geschichte und Beschreibung von Japan*, 1712.

and Kämpfer in 1712. They called it "thea" but did not recognize its botanical origin, nor its relation to the camellia. Kämpfer gave the tea plant an impossibly long-winded Latin name: *Thea frutex folio cerasi flore rosae sylvestris, fructu unicocco, bicocco & ut plurimum tricocco.*

Then the celebrated Swedish naturalist Carolus Linnaeus came along and brought order to the living world by reviving the forgotten system of binomial nomenclature—using two Latin words to identify genus and species—which is still in use today. In 1753 he published the *Species Plantarum,* in which he classified plants according to this system, though he defined the tea plant as *Thea sinensis* in one volume and as *Camellia* in another. In the same year, the English writer John Hill added to the confusion. He decided that, since most of the tea that arrived in Europe during the eighteenth century was either black or green, there should be two types of tea plants: *Thea bohea,* after the Chinese Bohea mountain range where most of the black tea imports originated, and *Thea viridis* (*viridis* means "green" in Latin). Linnaeus later adopted this view, but he wanted to observe things firsthand and decided to import the actual tea plant to Sweden.

Linnaeus asked one of his students, Peter Osbeck, to bring back a tea plant from China. Osbeck performed successfully until the ship reached the Cape of Good Hope, where sudden gusts of wind blew Osbeck's plant overboard. Linnaeus then passed the assignment to Magnus von Lagerstrom, who brought back two plants to Uppsala. The plants were cared for over a period of one or two years before it was discovered that they were only decorative garden camellias. Sometime after that, a tea bush finally reached Göteborg. Since it was such a special plant, it was immediately discharged from the ship and stored in a safe place with limited access—except for a party of rats that devoured the plant, apparently delighting in the taste, before Linnaeus could get to it.

Linnaeus would not give up. He asked Captain Ekeberg, who was in the China trade, to try one more time. This time the captain did not carry mature plants. Instead, he planted seeds, which germinated during the voyage back to Sweden. Upon arrival in Göteborg, half

Cat Merchants and Tea Dealers at Tong Chow, by Thomas Allom, engraving, England, c. 1840s. Reprinted from Wright, *The Chinese Empire: Historical and Descriptive,* 1843.

the seedlings were sent to Uppsala and perished during transport. Perhaps they were from damaged seeds; travelers to China had noted that Chinese merchants, in an effort to protect their trade, often boiled seeds before selling them so that the plants would either not germinate or be diseased. Nevertheless, Captain Ekeberg delivered the other half of the seedlings himself, and this time the operation was finally successful. Specimens of these very plants are preserved at the Swedish Museum of Natural History. Linnaeus studied these plants carefully and was even able to make them flower, but he did not clarify the confusion in the classification.

Despite Chinese resistance, others succeeded in importing the tea plant into Europe a few years later. In 1768 the English Kew Gardens shows a *Thea bohea* in its records, and some tea plants also reached the Jardin des Plantes in Paris. Observations all across Europe were fruitless until 1818, when the English botanist Robert Sweet determined that *Thea and Camellia* were of the same genus. The tea plant was finally recognized as belonging to the camellia family, but confusion continued to reign about the different plant varieties. When the British came in contact with wild tea trees in Assam a few years later, the question was whether Assam and China tea plants belonged to the same genus. Green or black, Indian or Chinese, camellia or not camellia—botanists disagreed, sometimes vehemently. Not until the 1905 International Botanical Congress was the debate definitively settled. From then on the International Code of Botanical Nomenclature decreed that the tea plant is one and it is called *Camellia sinensis*, no matter where it grows and no matter what type of tea is made from it. The enigma was solved, but it took 250 years from tea's first arrival in Europe.

Today we recognize two main varieties. The first—*Camellia sinensis* var. *sinensis*, the China plant—is a sturdy shrub, with multiple stems and small, firm leaves, that can grow up to ten feet in the wild. Able to withstand cold winters, the China variety is a long-lived and very productive plant: one and the same bush can give tea for a hundred years. Some ancient specimens, allegedly up to 1,700 years old, survive in the wild in Yunnan Province in southwest China. The other is the *Camellia sinensis* var. *assamica*—the Assam variety, a treelike plant with one single stem and larger, softer leaves. The *assamica* is shorter lived, about forty years, and more delicate than the *sinensis*, but it can grow sixty to eighty feet high. This variety may also have been growing wild in the southern Chinese jungles and may be the one Lu Yü was thinking about when he wrote in the *Ch'a-ching*: "Tea is from a grand tree in the South." The *Camellia sinensis* var. *parvifolia* is sometimes recognized as a third, Cambodian, variety and sometimes as a subspecies of the Assam plant. From these, hundreds of hybrids and varieties have been developed for different commercial purposes, but they are all *Camellia sinensis*.

The tea tree, from which so many soaps, shampoos, ointments, and cosmetics are made these days, has nothing whatsoever to do with the *Camellia sinensis*. The plant from which all these products originate is the Australian *Melaleuca alternifolia*, a tall, bushy tree with thin leaves related to the eucalyptus tree. The *Melaleuca* has powerful antiseptic and fungicidal properties, well known by Australian aborigines who brew the leaves for a variety of healing purposes. Captain Cook named it "tea tree" after he learned of its value from them and brewed strong tea for his crew to prevent scurvy.

I Say High Tea, You Say Low Tea

Our trouble is that we drink too much tea. I see in this
the slow revenge of the Orient, which has diverted the
Yellow River down our throats.

—John Boynton Priestley,
British novelist and playwright, 1894–1984

High tea is really low tea. But low tea originated with the so-called higher classes, the aristocracy, and high tea with the so-called lower classes, the ones who work for a living. Confusing? Yet history does suggest an explanation.

The practice of afternoon tea was established in European aristocratic circles during the second half of the seventeenth century. William Ukers in *All About Tea* quotes Madame de Sevigné (1626–96) referring to the *"thé de cinq heures"* in her letters. The Dutch and also the English, who had acquired the habit from their Portuguese Queen Catherine, commonly drank tea in the afternoon. By the beginning of the 1700s, tea etiquette was in place. Among the many details: extending the little finger while raising the cup was a sign of elegance; the spoon was placed over the cup when one had had enough tea; tea was often drunk out of the saucer, not the cup, and "audible sipping and sniffing, in the expression of gratification, were considered polite rewards to the hostess for a 'nice tea,'" so Ukers states.

Lady and Gentleman Sitting at a Table, Drinking Tea, Under a Grape Arbor, needlework chair-back, linen embroidered with wool and silk threads, England, early eighteenth century. Philadelphia Museum of Art. Gift of Sarah McLean Williams in memory of Mrs. William L. McLean, 1942.

Questionable etiquette aside, Lady Anna the Duchess of Bedford, who lived at the turn of the following century (1783–1857), is somehow credited with the invention of afternoon tea. Hunger pangs between lunch and dinner supposedly prompted her to add small crustless sandwiches, toast, and cakes to the afternoon tea she enjoyed in the company of her friends. The leisure classes of those times kept strange hours and had dinner so late that "the meal was now in danger of being entirely confounded and lost in Breakfast," as one commentator remarked. The hunger pangs may have been justified, although Lady Anna was certainly not the first to have the idea of eating something with the tea. The practice of afternoon tea as a light meal with snacks and finger foods—which we know today as high tea—was referred to as "low" tea. Some say it acquired the "low" attribute because it was served in the drawing rooms at the lower, and smaller, tea tables; others because it was served during the low part of the afternoon.

High tea, on the other hand, was a serious affair. The working classes had no time to dillydally with finger sandwiches in the afternoon. They had an economy to support and were busy in the factories, the mines, or the fields until sundown. When they came home, they were ready for their main meal of the day: high tea, also called meat tea. This was a hearty evening meal that included meats, ham, bacon, potatoes, eggs, cheese, bread and butter, anything substantial— and hot tea. It was reportedly called high tea because it was served at the main meal tables, which were higher than the coffee tables. Of course, not everyone could afford such a substantial meal. Even if only a piece of bacon and a potato were available, the name of the meal didn't change, and the ubiquitous teapot reigned over the table. A remnant of high tea as the main evening meal is found in the northern parts of the United Kingdom, Australia, and New Zealand, where the word *tea* is still sometimes used to indicate dinner.

In time, the names of meals fluctuated. Dinner, which was originally the meal in the middle of the day, slid up toward evening and meshed with supper, which had been a late-evening meal. Dispossessed of its place, high tea slid back down toward the afternoon and became the finger food entertainment that we know today. Once established, these names, definitions, and practices traveled from Britain to the rest of the English-speaking world. There, afternoon or evening, tea never stopped flowing, and for some throughout the day. Ukers says that New Zealanders, for example, have "bedside tea, a large cup served on arising. . . . At breakfast another large cup is consumed. At eleven o-clock comes the morning tea. . . . At lunch, at least ninety percent of the population drinks tea. At four o'clock tea again. . . . At dinner time there is more tea drinking, and about nine or nine-thirty, New Zealanders indulge in the meal they term supper; and tea may be said to be the main reason for partaking of this last repast of the day." Priestley, as stated in the epigram above, was right: Britain or Commonwealth, high or low, entirely too much tea was being poured down Western throats.

Milk in First?

I was recently the guest of Baron Alfred de Rothschild in his Seamore Place. Early in the morning, a liveried servant entered my room pushing a huge table on wheels. He asked, "Would you like tea or a peach, sir?" I chose tea, which immediately provoked another question. "China, India, or Ceylon, sir?" When I asked for India tea, he enquired, "With lemon, cream, or milk, sir?" I opted for milk, but he wanted to know which breed of cow I preferred: "Jersey, Hereford or Short-horn, sir?" Never had I drunk such a good cup of tea.

—Cecil Roth, British historian, 1899–1970

MIF, please. Yes, there is an acronym that stands for Milk in First, the mere existence of which may give a measure of the vastness of the argument. Does one pour milk into the cup first and *then* add the tea, or vice versa? It is a distinctly human skill to develop topics of disagreement, and the MIF affair is an excellent example of the levels of sophistication our species is capable of reaching in this area.

Historically, the argument most often given in favor of MIF is that milk softens the impact of boiling hot tea on delicate china and avoids possible cracking. MIFs, as supporters of Milk in First are often called, also assert that pouring milk first is a sign of good breeding and that, in any case, the tea tastes better. In addition, they believe that hot tea poured over cold milk serves the double purpose of warming up the milk nicely and avoiding cup stains from the tea. For

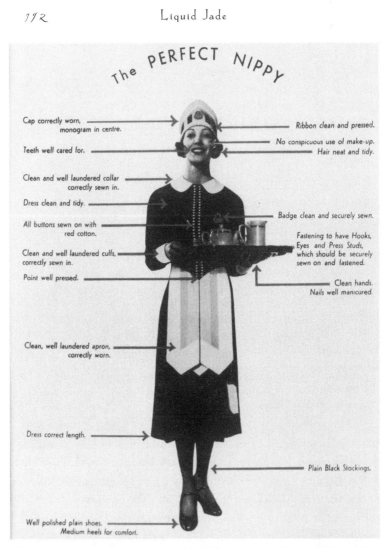

The PERFECT NIPPY

Cap correctly worn, monogram in centre.

Teeth well cared for.

Clean and well laundered collar correctly sewn in.

Dress clean and tidy.

All buttons sewn on with red cotton.

Clean and well laundered cuffs, correctly sewn in.

Point well pressed.

Clean, well laundered apron, correctly worn.

Dress correct length.

Well polished plain shoes. Medium heels for comfort.

Ribbon clean and pressed.

No conspicuous use of make-up. Hair neat and tidy.

Badge clean and securely sewn.

Fastening to have Hooks, Eyes and Press Studs, which should be securely sewn on and fastened.

Clean hands. Nails well manicured.

Plain Black Stockings.

The nippy—the black-dress and white-apron uniform—became a trademark of the Lyons Corner Houses, the tearoom chain popular in England during the first half of the twentieth century.

The Perfect Nippy, England, c. 1930s. Courtesy of the Bramah Museum of Tea and Coffee, London.

minimum-exertion types, yet one more benefit is that MIF saves the bother of stirring, as the tea poured over the milk does the mixing job by gravity. The practical-minded say that if you MIF and the milk is bad you will see it or smell it before you waste good tea in it.

TIFs (advocates of Tea in First, of course), on the other hand, ignore all the MIF advantages and argue simply that one must pour the milk in after the tea in order to be able to control the tea-to-milk ratio. Eric Arthur Blair, better known by the pen name George Orwell, whose genius defines twentieth-century literature and whose historical and political foresight resonates darkly in the world events of our day, was an unswerving TIF and was not beneath writing about it. In a delightful 1946 article, he lists eleven points on how to prepare the perfect cup of tea. Among others, he suggests to use Indian or Ceylonese tea, to warm the pot beforehand, to make sure the water is in full boil, to not use strainers, bags, "or other devices to imprison the tea," to avoid the use of sugar—"How can you call yourself a true tea-lover if you destroy the flavour of tea by putting sugar in it? It would be equally reasonable to put pepper or salt"—and, what he considers "one of the most controversial points of all," to put tea in first "and stirring as one pours," by which "one can exactly regulate the amount of milk whereas one is liable to put in too much milk if one does it the other way round." He adds, "I maintain that my own argument is unanswerable." So there.

In Great Britain the argument is of such magnitude that in 2003, for the commemoration of the centenary of Orwell's birth, none less than the Royal Society of Chemistry (RSC) issued a press release on how to make the perfect cup of tea, which included the scientific pros and cons of MIF. "Half the population of Britain will take this as a declaration of war," commented the British daily *The Guardian* in response to the press release. "After months of research the Royal Society of Chemistry has announced the answer to a question that for generations has shattered households, sundered friendships, splintered relationships: the milk should go in first." According to the RSC, the milk proteins are more likely to suffer "denaturation" if the milk is added after the tea. But the RSC also suggested warming the teapot in the microwave and, alas, adding sugar to the tea. This surely must have lowered its credibility in the eyes of scores of tea lovers. At the end of the day, TIFs will most likely continue to be TIFs, and the debate that has been going on for a hundred years or more will continue to raise tempers, or at least eyebrows, on both sides of the tea world.

As to when and how the practice of adding milk to tea came about in the first place, opinions also differ. Some say it is a French habit started by the Marquise de la Sablière around 1680. Others believe that, after the newly imported China black teas became popular, Europeans began adding milk to them in order to soften the tannin taste. As a result, the increasing consumption of black tea reinvigorated the dairy industry, particularly in England, where tea with milk quickly became second nature. In the tea-growing regions of China, on the other hand, milk always was anathema to tea drinkers, and everyone knows that to this day the Chinese do not add milk to tea. However, there are some rare recorded exceptions, such as Johannes Nieuhof's 1665 report of the Dutch East India Company's visit to Canton:

> At the beginning of the Dinner, there were served several bottles of the *The* or *Tea*, served to the Table, whereof they drank to the Embassadors, biding them welcom: This drink is made of the Herb *The* or *Cha*, after this manner: they infuse half a handful of the Herb *The* or *Cha* in fair water, which afterwards they boil till a third part be consumed, to which they adde warm milk about a fourth part, with a little salt, and then drink it as hot as they can well endure.

This may be explained by the fact that over time certain areas of China adopted the northern nomadic tribes' habit of adding dairy products to tea, particularly after the northern Manchus became the ruling dynasty in China in 1644. The first Westerners then observed the rare practice and brought it to Europe. It may be a stretch but not entirely inconceivable to think that we may have learned our milk-in-tea practice from our nomadic central Asian brothers.

Whatever the origin may be, it is a good idea to limit the use of milk or cream to hearty black teas, such as Assam and Ceylon or African teas. Lighter teas lose their delicate aroma if milk is added. As for green teas: no MIF, no TIF, no dairy products of any kind should go near them, lest the wrath of the tea gods should descend upon you.

The Accidental Inventors
Part 1: The Tea Bag

Lichilai, a Sung poet, has sadly remarked that there were three most deplorable things in the world: the spoiling of fine youths through false education, the degradation of fine art through vulgar admiration, and the utter waste of fine tea through incompetent manipulation.

—Kakuzo Okakura, *The Book of Tea*, 1906

A las, it was a Yankee who invented the pouch that ruined the art of tea drinking in the West. Thomas Sullivan was a tea merchant operating in New York at the turn of the twentieth century. His marketing strategy included, among other things, sending tin boxes with different tea samples to prospective clients. One fine day in 1908, Mr. Sullivan realized that these samples were costing him good money. So he came up with the idea of putting single servings of tea leaves in tiny silk pouches. He would send these out, instead of the tin boxes, at a fraction of the cost.

Sometime later he was surprised to receive requests from his customers, particularly public establishments, for more of those little pouches. Well, what could be so good about tea in pouches, he wondered. And he soon discovered that his clients, assuming that it was their supplier's intention, were dropping the whole pouch, with the tea inside, into the teapot. They found that preparing the tea this way was hassle free, and the subsequent cleaning of the pot effortless. Thus, the tea bag, object of chagrin for tea lovers around the world, was born. Before long, this accidental invention took over the mass market, both in the United States and Europe. At first, tea bags were made of cotton gauze or muslin, but around the 1950s the paper tea bag was developed. This greatly encouraged tea bag consumption in the United Kingdom, which

Woman holding tea bag above cup, a tea advertisement, photographic print, USA, 1929. Prints and Photographs Division, Library of Congress, Washington, D.C.

had initially been sluggish. Edward Bramah, the director of the Museum of Tea and Coffee in London, theorizes that the development and increasing popularity of fast-brewing and disposable tea bags was a result of competition from the new instant-coffee products. Today, the majority of the tea consumed in the United Kingdom is brewed using tea bags.

One might ask why the tea bag is such an undesirable item after all. One of the reasons is that standard commercial tea bags are filled with lower-grade tea. This tea is designed to give the water a brown color very quickly, but the taste of the loose leaf is not there. As the market for specialty teas widens and the public's palate becomes more discerning, an increasing number of tea companies have begun marketing loose-leaf-quality teas in tea bags. This offers the option of drinking good tea while enjoying the convenience of the bag, but choices are still limited. The second reason discerning tea drinkers shun the standard tea bags is that the manufacturing involves the use of paper bleached with chlorine, a process that creates a dioxin residue. To solve this problem, tea companies, especially organic and specialty dealers, are now using oxygen-bleached or unbleached paper instead, but the practice has not become commonplace yet.

For people who insist on having the tea leaves contained, there are alternatives to the bag. One of them is the tea infuser, or tea ball, a wire mesh or perforated metal container designed to hold a certain amount of loose-leaf tea. Many tea drinkers are not partial to the tea infuser, because it does not leave enough room for the tea leaves to expand and fully release their flavor; in some teas, the size of the leaves increases fivefold when infused. Tea filters, made of organic cotton or biodegradable paper, are often considered preferable to the tea ball, because they don't interfere chemically and they give the tea leaves enough space to expand and properly mix with the water. Yet the ultimate tea drinker will always want the leaves to "agonize" freely in the teapot. The so-called agony of the leaves is the poetic and somewhat disquieting trade expression used to describe the unfurling of the rolled or twisted leaves during steeping time. It takes time and space and patience but, tea experts insist, the agony alone releases the full character of the tea.

The Accidental Inventors
Part 2: Iced Tea

Tea should be drunk when hot. Cold tea will aid the
accumulation of phlegm. It is better to drink less of it,
rather than more. Better yet! Don't drink it at all.

—Chia Ming, *Yin-shih hsü-chih*, fourteenth century

From the perspective of the tea purist, iced tea is yet another compromising, if not altogether degrading, development in the tea
story. According to the commonly accepted lore, the invention of
iced tea takes place in the year 1904 at the St. Louis World's Fair. It
was a sweltering summer day, and Mr. Richard Blechynden, in charge
of the East Indian Pavilion, was worried. He was offering free samples
of the newly arrived India black teas. They were still relatively unknown in the United States, where China green tea was the norm,
and the fair was a great opportunity to acquaint the public with them.
But the teas were being served hot. Who would even want to go near
them in such weather? This being one of the cases in which necessity
became the mother of invention, Mr. Blechynden tried something
new. He filled glasses with ice and poured hot tea over them. And, lo
and behold, iced tea was born, or so the story goes. Exposition visitors flocked to Mr. Blechynden's stand and passed on the word about
the new sensational drink.

Other food historians state that iced tea existed long before 1904

Poster for the U.S. market promoting the consumption of hot and cold tea, India Tea Bureau, c. 1920s. Reprinted from Ukers, *All About Tea*, 1935.

and cite as proof an 1890 newspaper article—describing a mass event where no less than 880 gallons of the beverage were served—as well as various iced tea and tea punch recipes from early-nineteenth-century cookbooks. This evidence indicates that Mr. Blechynden popularized rather than invented iced tea. Either way, the United States is clearly the home of iced tea. And popularize it Mr. Blechynden certainly did. Today, iced tea makes up 80 percent of the entire tea consumption in the United States, a trend not followed anywhere else in the world. Yet, today's commercial iced teas are not made with the Assams and Darjeelings Mr. Blechynden was trying to market in 1904. Instead, companies manufacture canned or bottled iced tea with lower-quality teas, liquid tea extracts, or sometimes only food coloring and no tea at all. Some commercial iced teas contain significant amounts of sweeteners, of which cane and beet sugars are the least harmful, and high fructose corn syrup one of the most insidious. Buying a bottle of iced tea instead of a soft drink with the intent of making a healthy decision is therefore often not the solution to the problem. A few health-conscious companies produce better-quality iced teas, but these still represent a small portion of the market. The best way to drink iced tea is still to make it at home with quality teas and little or no sweetener. Or, as the Chinese said seven hundred years ago, in the epigram above: "Better yet! Don't drink it at all."

What Color Is Your Tea?

Tea has countless forms. To speak in vulgar terms, there are tea cakes that resemble a barbarian's boot, wrinkled and shriveled. There are cakes that look like the dewlap of an ox, folded and draped. There are those like floating clouds appearing from among mountains, round as wheels and mushrooms. There are tea cakes that appear to swell and ripple, like water ruffled by a light whirlwind. And there are those that look like a smooth clay slurry that the potter's son purifies and clarifies with water. There are also cakes like newly laid fields in a sudden heavy rain, flowing and flooding in rivulets.

—Lu Yü, *Ch'a-ching—The Classic of Tea* (Owyoung translation)

Colors are very important in the tea world, although the inclusion of some of them in tea names can be misleading. Orange pekoe (pronounced "peck-oh"), for example, is not linked to the color or the fruit. Some say that a long time ago in China orange blossoms were added to the tea as a scent, but the most likely explanation is that the word *orange* was given in honor of the Dutch royal family of Orange-Nassau, the ruling house at the time the Dutch first brought tea to Europe and still the ruling house today. Gray is another color that has nothing to do with the hue of the tea infusion and everything to do with a family name. In fact, gray in tea happens to be a rather undesirable color, the result of putting milk in a type of tea

that should be drunk without it. A fashionable Victorian tea blend—
black tea scented with oil of bergamot, the still very popular Earl
Grey tea—was named after Charles Grey, second Earl Grey of How-
ick, a respected Whig M.P. and British prime minister. Grey fought
for the introduction of the one-man–one-vote principle in the British
parliamentary election system, for the abolition of slavery in the
British dominions, and, ironically, for the end of the East India Company monopoly of the Eastern trade.

Family names aside, colors are used in the tea world as a system of
categorizing the various teas in existence. In the West we are mostly
familiar with what we call black tea, which accounts for three-
quarters of world tea production. In the last dozen or so years, green
tea—which was the very first tea introduced to Europe in the 1600s
and was subsequently pushed into obscurity by Chinese blacks and
by the mass-produced Indian black teas—has made a grand come-
back in Europe and North America and represents about 20 percent

Board of tea experts during a tea tasting, photographic print, USA, 1954. Prints and
Phototgraphs Division, Library of Congress, Washington, D.C.

of world production. More recently, we are being introduced to some of the rarest and most expensive teas: white teas. Three colors—black, green, white—sounds simple. Yet white teas are a type of green tea, according to some. What we call black teas are considered red teas in China. And the Chinese oolong (or *wu-long*) tea, a category the West is least familiar with, is not a recognizable color in Western languages, although in Chinese *wu* means "dark, black"; the pictograph for *wu* is a crow. Yet oolongs are not considered black teas, but form a separate category, albeit a very small one, as they make up only 2 percent of world production.

Yet why such wide color variation in the first place, if all these teas come from one and the same plant, the *Camellia sinensis?* Small distinctions in hue, as in a light amber Darjeeling versus a rich, malty Assam, may be the result of using different plant varieties. What creates the main color differences is determined during the actual tea manufacture, specifically the oxidation process: how long, if at all, the leaves are allowed to oxidize after they are plucked. During oxidation the leaves turn from green to varying shades of brown by being exposed to the oxygen in the air. We can observe oxidation at home if we cut an apple or an avocado and leave it sitting on the counter, where it will soon turn brown. For the apple this is undesirable, but for many teas oxidation is an essential part of production. In the case of black tea, the leaves are allowed to fully oxidize and, when brewed, the tea has a reddish brown hue and a definite, sometimes quite robust aroma. For green tea, on the other hand, the leaves are steamed or pan fired after plucking to keep the oxidation process from even starting. This is why the leaves stay green, and the brewed tea is light green to yellow with a mild, natural, grassy, and sometimes nutty aroma. Oolong tea is somewhere between the two: the leaves are left to oxidize for varying amounts of time, depending on the type of tea desired, but not as long as for black tea. Oolong leaves can be anywhere from dark green with a bluish tint to brown, depending on oxidation time. The color of oolong infusions is light yellow to light brown, and the fragrance is often subtler and more complex than black teas.

Black, green, and oolong are the three generally accepted main categories, but the Chinese classification is a bit more specific: there are white, yellow, and green in the nonoxidized category, oolong in the semioxidized, and red and black in the fully oxidized. White and yellow teas are placed in the same group as green tea, because in all three teas the leaves are not oxidized, but the processing for white and yellow tea is slightly different. White tea is rare and expensive because the harvest takes place only a few days a year and the processing requires delicate manual labor. Only the youngest, top leaf buds are plucked—they are still covered with the white hairy down of young shoots that gives the tea its name—and only under certain climatic conditions. It is one of the least processed teas in that the leaves are simply plucked and air dried, but those simple steps require great skill and attention to detail. Brewed white tea is a very pale yellow and yields an extremely delicate aroma that an untrained palate can easily miss. Yellow tea is also a rare tea. The processing of the leaf is similar to white tea but the leaves are stacked and dried more slowly. This allows time to develop a more distinctive fragrance and a brighter yellow hue of the brewed tea.

What we call black tea in the West the Chinese call red tea on account of the warm reddish brown color of the infusion. Most of the Chinese red tea is produced for export to the West. The other red tea that is becoming increasingly popular in Europe and the United States is not at all related to Chinese red tea and is not derived from *Camellia sinensis*. It is a caffeine-free, antioxidant-rich herbal infusion produced from the needle-shaped leaves and stems of the South African *rooibos*, the red bush. When the Chinese talk about black tea, they are mostly referring to teas that have been processed as green teas but that undergo a further transitional phase that changes them into other kinds of tea by a variety of different processes. They can also be compressed into tea bricks, the format preferred by northwestern Chinese populations, Mongolians, and inhabitants of the Himalayan countries. *Pu-erh* teas, increasingly popular in the West, are also often compressed. They are sometimes processed as black teas, sometimes as green, but are more often than not considered in a class of their own. True *pu-erh*

Telling Fortunes by Tea Leaves, by William H. Rau, USA, stereograph, c. 1897. Prints and Photographs Division, Library of Congress, Washington, D.C.

teas are different from all other teas in that the leaves are withered but not fired, although sometimes they are sun dried. They are essentially a raw tea that is processed in many different ways but does not undergo the final stage the way other teas do. However, all *pu-erh* teas are aged, sometimes up to fifty years, which can make them quite expensive. *Pu-erh* teas take many different forms: rounds, cakes, squares, nuggets, balls, baskets, disks, wafers, and even mushroom shapes.

No one knows exactly how many types of *Camellia sinensis* teas exist in the world. Some say a few hundred, some a thousand, others claim even two thousand or more. Color covers only the main differences among them, beyond which each culture has its own complex tea categories, substrata, and distinctions, the result of variations in centuries-old local practices or historical oddities. Japan has a system of classification for the many types of green tea based on the growing method, the types of leaf and/or stem used, and the final manufacturing techniques. In China, teas are often named after the region of provenance or by describing the shape of the loose leaf. Sometimes, the further processing determines the category, as in the case of *pu-erh* teas. Other times, it is what's added to the teas that singles them out as yet another separate group, as with scented teas such as jasmine or peach tea or any other tea to which flower petals, fruits, essential oils, or fragrances have been added. A mesmerizing landscape of teas, indeed, but a delicious one in which to get lost.

The Mystery of Acronyms

Tea is naught but this:
First you heat the water.
Then you make the tea.
Then you drink it properly.
That is all you need to know.

—Sen no Rikyū

Drinking tea should be as easy as Zen tea master Rikyū suggests. And yet, no two worlds are more distant from each other than the limpidity of Zen tea and the stratified complexities of today's commercial tea industry. Ever notice an "FOP" or a "BOP" on your tea package next to the name of the tea? Or an "FTGFOP"? Or even an "SFTGFOP"? And what does "CTC" mean? "First flush," "second flush"? Just a few letters and terms, but those acronyms contain a world of information regarding the tea inside the package.

First, all these terms and acronyms apply only to black tea, not green or oolong. All black tea on the market today is either orthodox—the specialty tea found in tea shops—or CTC—the machine-processed tea used mostly for tea bags—and is further classified into four main grades: whole leaf, broken leaf, fannings, and dust. The term *orthodox* refers to a processing technique that is similar to the traditional hand-produced method and yields mostly high-quality whole-leaf and broken-leaf tea. The quality is determined by the processing but also by which leaves are used. Tea leaves have their own classification method according to size and where they are

PER FIRST STEAMER

SUPERBLY CHOICE
SPECIALLY SELECTED
NEW SEASON'S
KEE MUN

LEE PAH LEE

C H I N A

Label from a crate of Chinese tea transported by steamer, England, late nineteenth century. Courtesy of the Bramah Museum of Tea and Coffee, London.

placed on the branch. In tea terminology, the preferred leaf size is not described with a size or placement number but with a name: orange pekoe, or OP. *Orange*, as we know, is a historical leftover in homage to the Dutch royal house of Orange-Nassau, and *pekoe* is a Westernization of the Chinese word *pai hao* that refers to the white hairy down on the young leaves. The smaller and younger leaves and buds growing above the orange pekoe leaf are considered of even finer quality and are variously called "flowery" (F), which does not refer to the flower but only to the leaf tips or buds; "golden" (G), when the young leaves are still opening up and golden or yellowish in color; or "tippy" (T), as in just the tips of the leaves.

Thus, a flowery orange pekoe, or FOP, is a good-quality whole-leaf tea that is a mixture of orange pekoe leaves and some of the tips.

A higher grade would be GFOP, or golden flowery orange pekoe, which would include some of the younger, more delicate golden tips. Above that is TGFOP, or tippy golden flowery orange pekoe, with a larger ratio of golden tips. The next grade up is FTGFOP, or finest tippy golden flowery orange pekoe, with an even higher ratio of tips. For this grade the inside joke is that "FTGFOP" actually stands for "Far Too Good for Ordinary People." And, in a world of superlatives, beyond ordinary people and insider elitist jokes, the top grade is defined as special finest tippy golden flowery orange pekoe, or SFTG-FOP, mostly composed of buds and golden tips. The northeastern Indian region of Darjeeling produces a large part of these top-quality teas, which is why Darjeeling is often referred to as "the champagne of teas."

Darjeeling and other northern (Assam, Dooars) teas are also classified according to "flushes," or harvests, of which there are generally four a year. During the winter, the tea plants in the northern hemisphere go dormant and tea production stops, while in tropical regions like Sri Lanka and Kerala in South India there is no hibernation, and harvesting takes place throughout the year. First flush is from mid-March to May, while second flush begins toward the end of May until June-July. In Darjeeling and in the Dooars, first flush tea is often considered the best, while in Assam the richer and more mature second flush is the harvest of choice. Then there are the monsoon flushes, or rain teas, plucked during August and September; they are stronger and often used for blends. And, finally, there are the autumnal teas, harvested in October and early November. These are again more delicate than the rain teas and have a very different taste from the spring teas.

Yet tea preferences are very personal, and teas with big acronyms are not the only teas of good quality. Tippier teas, as teas with a large percentage of tips are called, may be fashionable and expensive, but many people prefer coarser teas with more body. "S" is another meaningful letter in the family of tea acronyms and stands for "Souchong." This is the name of a larger, more mature leaf that grows below the orange pekoe and is used in some Chinese teas, such as the famous smoked Lapsang Souchong. Daring a comparison to the world of wines, if a top Darjeeling is equated with a champagne, a Lapsang Souchong could be thought of as a good Cabernet Sauvignon. Even when we leave the domain of whole-leaf tea, excellent teas are produced with broken leaves. These are still considered orthodox teas even though the leaves are not whole. The acronyms are the same as above but with the addition of a "B" for "Broken." BOP would signify broken orange pekoe, FBOP flowery broken orange pekoe, GFBOP golden flowery broken orange pekoe, and so on. Broken leaves infuse faster than whole leaves. Fannings (F—leaves that are broken in even smaller particles, thus called because they are small enough to be "fanned" away) and dust (D—the term speaks for itself) are generally considered of lower quality. Even fannings and dust have acronyms: BOPF would be broken orange pekoe fannings, for example; PD would be pekoe dust, SFD would be super fine dust, GD golden dust. These don't have much left of the delicate aroma of the top-quality teas, but they infuse very quickly.

Poster promoting consumption of India Tea, France, c. 1920s. Reprinted from Ukers, *All About Tea*, 1935.

Most orthodox teas are produced in China, Sri Lanka, Darjeeling, and Assam. They represent about 31 percent of world tea production. An additional 25 percent is green and oolong tea. The remaining 44 percent is CTC tea. CTC stands for "Crush, Tear, Curl" and describes a machine process invented in the 1930s to optimize yield and packaging. The CTC machine does not discriminate among leaf sizes; it crushes, tears, and curls all sorts of leaves and stems down to a certain size, mostly fannings and dust. Indians are great consumers of loose CTC, with which they prepare their ubiquitous sweet chai. In the West CTC tea is rarely used. Sometimes, only sometimes, a good CTC tea may be better than a badly processed orthodox tea. But most tea connoisseurs consider CTC tea beneath their dignity.

The Tea Taster

Connoisseurs of the lowest level are those who praise the degree of smoothness, darkness, and flatness of tea leaves. Connoisseurs of the next level are those who commend the degree of wrinkled-ness, of yellowness in the hollows and mounds of leaves. Superior connoisseurs are those who speak of good leaves and bad leaves. What are the reasons for the differences in tea leaves? Those from which their juices have been expressed are smooth. Leaves that contain their juices are wrinkled. Those processed overnight are dark in color. Those finished within a day are yellow. Leaves steamed and pressed are flat. Those that are loose, have hollows and mounds. The characteristics of the tea leaf are the same as the leaves of other plants. The connoisseurship of tea is preserved through oral transmission from one connoisseur to another.

—Lu Yü, *Ch'a-ching—The Classic of Tea* (Owyoung translation)

Everyone knows the wine industry relies on wine tasters to assess quality. Few are aware that a similar figure exists also in the world of tea. Before tea is served in a cozy tearoom or brewed at home on a misty morning, several people in different parts of the world will have evaluated and tasted it at various stages of the production and distribution process.

Large plantations have their own tasters for quality control. Brokers in the producing countries taste the tea in order to choose sam-

Inspecting and tasting tea, stereograph, Japan, 1926. Prints and Photographs Division, Library of Congress, Washington, D.C.

ples to send to their foreign importers. Tea is tasted when sold at international auctions. After making their selections, large buyers and blenders taste the tea upon arrival at their warehouses to make sure quality has been maintained after shipment. Then they taste it again to choose the teas to include in their blends; like wines, most commercial teas are blends of different varieties, sometimes up to thirty or thirty-five. The blenders' priority is to maintain the same recognizable taste for a particular tea year after year. Small specialty tea dealers, who offer mostly individual, whole-leaf teas, also taste but for opposite reasons. They are looking for characteristics that will make a tea stand out and be worth listing in their catalogs or serving in their tea shops. In these cases, the owner of the tea company is often also the passionate master taster. And lately, a new type of taster has emerged on the scene of high-end restaurants and hotels or fashionable tearooms: the tea sommelier, who tastes in order to select types and vintages for the menu and also to counsel patrons about how to best match teas with foods.

"It has been said that a tea taster, like a poet, is born, not made," writes William Ukers in *All About Tea*. Tea tasting certainly requires a variety of skills and talents and has often been termed an art rather than a science. An art in which the actual tasting, the sipping of the brewed tea—called liquor in the tea-tasting world—is only the last in a series of steps that include looking, smelling, and touching. Compiling all the sensations, variables, and impressions into a fine-tuned judgment seems to be more the result of a creative, intuitive process than a scientific one. Accordingly, a tea taster's definitions are evocative rather than quantitative, and yet surprisingly precise. A tea is brassy when it is incorrectly withered and has an unpleasant metallic quality to it. It is muddy when the infusion is dull and lacks transparency. It is bakey when it is overfired, but biscuity when the firing was just right and the infusion produces a well-rounded aroma. A self-drinking tea is a tea that tastes well by itself and does not need blending. Full-bodied Assams are malty; delicate Darjeelings are muscatlike; the roasty aroma of some Japanese greens is nutty; smoky Chinese Lapsang Souchongs can be tarry.

Colorful glossaries aside, the tea taster's day starts early, when their taste buds are at their best and most alert. Waiting in the commercial tasting room, also called cupping room, are: a long table set up with a line of lidded tea mugs and corresponding tasting bowls; shallow pans to hold the dry tea sample behind each mug and a scale to weigh each sample; a tea kettle, often made of copper, to boil the water; a timer or an hourglass; a tasting spoon; and, yes, a spittoon. Where wine tasters must avoid excessive intakes of alcohol, tea tasters use spittoons to avoid caffeine. Once everything is set up, the first thing the taster does is examine the dry leaf. First visually: Are the leaves well sorted and graded? Is the color even, and is it appropriate to the tea type being examined? Do the leaves look fresh? Are they well twisted and properly withered? Is there a good balance of tips present? Or, on the other hand: Do the leaves look gray and dusty? Are they blistered? Is there too much stem? Does the tea look underwithered? Overwithered? Then comes the olfactory test. The taster warms up some leaves in the cupped hand and inhales. A great deal of information is released from their aroma. An expert taster can often tell from the smell alone whether a particular black tea is from Sri Lanka, Indonesia, Africa, or India, among other things. In addition to evaluating aromas, some tasters also use touch to determine the freshness of the tea by gently pressing it in their hand. New tea is somewhat pliable and springy, whereas old tea crumbles more easily and shows dust.

The second step consists of preparing the liquor. A small amount of dry leaf is taken from each sample, weighed (generally around two or three grams, but it varies depending on the tasting purpose), and put in the lidded mug. When all the mugs are ready, boiling water is poured over the leaves, the mugs are covered with the lids, the timer is set, and the tea begins to brew. Standard brewing time for black tea is five minutes, but some tasters brew at four, others at six. Other types of tea are brewed only one or two minutes. When the infusion time is up, the tea is poured from the mug into the tasting bowl. The infused leaves, now wet and expanded, are placed on the lid of the mug, ready for inspection. They, too, tell some of the story. Again, the taster looks at how the color of the leaves has changed now that they are wet, how they have expanded, how they hold the liquid, and also what kind of aroma they release, which can be considerably stronger than that of the dry leaf. The taster then examines the color of the liquor. Is it bright and rich, or is it dull and grayish? Is it clear or cloudy? The ideal color varies greatly, depending on the type of tea being evaluated: a reddish copper for a hearty Assam, a bright greenish yellow for a certain type of green tea, a pale tender yellow for a delicate white. Because so much of the tasting process is visual, it is important to have good lighting in the tasting room. Windows exposed to northern lighting, also preferred in artists' studios because of their brightness and neutrality, are ideal because they don't influence and distract the senses. This is also why, in the standard cupping room, mugs and tasting bowls are invariably made of white porcelain.

Finally, it is time for the third and last step, the actual tasting of the liquor. If black tea is being tasted in a tea-with-milk market, as in the United Kingdom, the taster stirs a spoonful of milk into the liquor. In most producing countries, however, tea is tasted without milk. The tea has now cooled enough so that the taste buds won't be desensitized by the heat. The taster fills the tasting spoon with some of the liquor, brings it to the mouth, and makes a most surprising, loud sucking noise, beyond standard acceptable table manners. The reason for this procedure is that the liquid has to be sucked in with sufficient speed and force to reach all the taste buds and to be sprayed all around the palate and to the back of the mouth. There, the olfactory nerves transmit the sensations through the nasal passage for a complete experience. When we drink the tea we experience all these sensations naturally because we swallow the liquid, but tasters do not have that luxury. The liquid is briefly swished around the mouth to assess fullness and body, astringency and pungency, in addition to taste, and then it is released into the spittoon.

The whole operation sounds like a lengthy procedure, but in practice, preparation and brewing is what takes the longest. The actual assessments are performed within a matter of seconds. Tea tasting is different from wine tasting in that it is very much an instant judgment operation. All of the elements collected through the preliminary examinations—color, aroma, appearance, feel—are held in balance and are very quickly confirmed or refuted by the final test, the actual tasting. The assessment sequence—look, touch, slurp, spit—is repeated two or three dozen times per tasting session. Then there is a break, during which it may become necessary to eat a banana or an apple to clean out the taste buds. After this, the taster is ready for a new session. Tasters who work for blenders are known to go through several hundred teas a day. For them, all tea tasting is a comparative exercise, in which a tea or a batch of teas is always measured up against another tea or another batch, never evaluated on its own. Buyers of individual whole-leaf teas are more similar to wine tasters in that they taste a much smaller amount of teas at a time, perhaps twenty or thirty, and they dedicate more attention to each one.

Hizen porcelain bowls from Arita, Japan, Edo period. Reprinted from Audsley and Bowes, *Keramic Art of Japan*, 1875.

Tea tasting varies a great deal depending on the objective. Is the tea to be selected for a popular blend, or is a new blend being developed? Is the tea meant to add a specific flavor? Should it add body and character to an already flavorful but thin mixture? Is the tea meant for a high-end market where trendy tip content is more important than actual taste? Is it destined for areas with particularly hard water? Or for a public that favors fast-brewing tea? Is the market strictly a tea-with-milk one? Or is the taster's job to select unusual teas from a specific production area? The market requirements dictate the tea taster's evaluations. A tea taster may therefore be an expert in one area and a complete beginner in another. Someone who has spent twenty years tasting for a black tea blender specializing in the tea bag market may be very inexperienced when it comes to grades of green tea; and a specialist of Chinese *pu-erhs* may be lost if asked to evaluate CTC teas from Kenya.

Considering the complexities of tea tasting and the technological advances of modern society, it is surprising that tea tasting is still very much a métier, with skills and knowledge acquired in an artisanal environment. Tea associations in various countries now offer certification programs, but they generally provide fairly basic information, often geared to people who want to open a tearoom. The best way to become a tea taster is still by the old method: get a job in a tea company and quietly learn from the greats while performing menial tasks. Apprenticeship is long, five to seven years. Master tea tasters insist that nothing beats decades of experience tasting and comparing hundreds of thousands of teas, using that most wonderful of advanced measuring equipments—the five human senses—and elaborating the information in that most wonderful of advanced computers—the human brain.

For all the associations of tea with the feminine—dainty cups, afternoon tea gossip, Victorian tea parties—tea is still very much a man's world. Corporate executives are male, as are plantation managers. Tea brokers are male. So are directors of tea boards, certifying inspectors, and importers. Tea tasters are also often male, even though a sensitive palate, intuition, patience, comparison skills, multitasking, and the ability to be receptive to subtle differences and to capture immediate impressions are all qualities that suggest feminine participation. Conversely, women represent the majority of the workforce when it comes to the humble tasks. In Asia, where most of the tea in the world is grown, more than half of all tea pluckers are women. Some encouraging signs are beginning to show in India, where a few courageous women are venturing into plantation management. And in England, where the tea industry is substantial, women are increasingly choosing tea tasting as a profession. In the United States, the tea taster, male or female, is a relatively rare figure. With tea drinking experiencing a powerful renaissance in the last decade, a different kind of tea taster is being bred: the tea enthusiast who travels to the East and becomes a tea expert, bringing back delightful and unusual teas, educating the public about the endless array of surprises and possibilities the taste of tea can offer.

Like Water for Tea

When you hear the splash
Of the water drops that fall
Into the stone bowl,
You will feel that all the dust
Of your mind is washed away.

—Sen no Rikyū

Since water is the main ingredient in a cup of tea, it deserves a proportionate amount of attention. Most people prepare a pot of tea
by simply boiling tap water and pouring it over the tea leaves. Others, sadly, fill a cup with tap water, heat it in the microwave, and
dump a tea bag in the lukewarm water for a few fleeting seconds until
the water turns brown. Used this way, water is an item taken for
granted, a mere carrier of the final result, the restorative cup of tea.
Yet water varies greatly in character and history, depending on
source, mineral and chemical composition, or treatment process, and
it can make a significant difference in the taste of tea.

In T'ang China, when tea was an object of great reverence, knowledge of water quality was considered an essential element of proper
tea preparation. Writes tea master Lu Yü in his tea treatise, the
Ch'a-ching:

> Of water, the water from the mountains is superior; river water is
> of moderate quality; well water is inferior. . . . Of mountain water,

gently flowing waters selected from stalactite springs and rock pools is superior. Do not drink rushing water that cascades and gushes or turbulent water that scours and erodes. Over time, such water causes disease of the throat. Of the many different waters flowing amid the mountains and valleys, there are those that run clear, pure, and full, unabsorbed by the ground. However, from the season of heat until just before the first frost is the time when secluded dragons accumulate poisons; those who taste the affected water can judge. Use the gently flowing waters of a new spring to flush out the toxins. Of river water, it should be fetched far away from people. Of well water, it must be drawn from a well that is frequently used.

Over the centuries, Chinese medical tracts classified different types of water. These were discussed and evaluated by tea-loving emperors and poets. Tea connoisseurs claimed the ability to identify the water used in a particular tea. And special teas were traditionally matched with preferred water sources for best results, such as Dragon Well tea with the Tiger Run Spring water near Hangchow. Subtle differences in water were culturally significant enough to be included even in fiction, as in the Chinese novel *Dream of the Red Chamber* by Tsao Hsüeh-chin, set in eighteenth-century China:

> The nun poured tea . . . and presented it to the Matriarch. . . . The Matriarch asked her what water she used, and the nun answered that it was rain water saved from the year before. . . . [The nun then also offered tea to Black Jade] "Is this also last year's rain water?" Black Jade asked, sipping her tea. "I am surprised to hear you say that," the nun said. "Can't you tell the difference? This water was snow that I gathered from the plum trees five years ago. It filled that blue jar there, and I have saved it all this time. It was buried under the earth and was opened only this last summer. This is the second time I have used it. How could you expect rain water to possess such lightness and clarity?"

The *mizusashi* is a fresh-water storage jar, an essential element in the Japanese tea ceremony. Water is ladled out of the jar and poured into the kettle to prepare the tea.

Tea Ceremony Water Jar (mizusashi), by Eiraku Hozen, ceramics, Japan, c. 1825–50. Freer Gallery of Art, Smithsonian Institution, Washington, D.C. Gift of Charles Lang Freer.

These days, most of us do not have the choice of melted snow over well water or rainwater. Our rivers are polluted; our busy schedules certainly do not allow us to store waters by type and year; and our neighbors might suspect subversive activity or mental instability if they saw us bury water jars underground. Our most common choice is tap water, also called source water in the trade. But knowing a little more about this type of water will give us the option of preparing a better cup of tea, or, at least, help us understand why sometimes our tea may have a disappointing taste even though we spent good money on the leaf.

The main factors in evaluating water for tea are: how hard or how soft it is, which has to do with calcium and magnesium content; what the general mineral composition is, which accounts for part of the taste; what chemicals are added to the water, most commonly chlorine and sulfur compounds, which also affect the taste and odor; and, of course, pesticide content and any other undesirable contaminants. This all sounds complicated, but it is, in fact, very easy to get information on water quality. Public water companies throughout the United States are required to publish an annual water quality report, which is sent home to customers and often also available online. If the report is obscure, a phone call to the local company's water quality department should offer clarification. Such information is useful not just for tea but for general health issues.

But how do we decide what kind of water is good for tea? As a general rule, whatever constituents, taste, and odors are in the tap water will pass into the tea, so the idea is to keep what's good and eliminate what's bad. Very hard water is generally not good for tea. Yet, water that is completely devoid of calcium and magnesium—too soft—is not necessarily the best for tea, either. Water hardness is measured in grains per gallon, or GPG. As a guideline, soft water is below 6 GPG, medium is between 6 and 9 GPG, and hard water is above 9 GPG. Of course, it is always possible to find a bottled water with the right taste and constituents and use it to brew tea; if we like the water, we'll like the tea. But the choice is not for all budgets, and the environmental pollution from plastic bottles is a growing issue.

Some parts of the world are blessed with natural soft water, for example, the north of England or the city of New York, where the range is 1–5 GPG. In some hard-water areas, public water is softened at the treatment plants. If you live in an area that has neither natural nor artificially softened water and your water is excessively hard, you may want to consider an ion exchange water softener, which would be beneficial not just for tea but for all your appliances, your water lines, as well as your skin. On the other hand, some studies state that soft water is too high in sodium and that consuming moderately hard water as daily drinking water is, in fact, good for your health, on account of all the precious minerals in it. The controversy is ongoing in terms of general well-being. But as far as tea is concerned, soft water—but not 0 GPG—is preferable, not only for the taste but also because it produces a clear liquor, pleasing to the eye. All tea tasters agree that the visual component plays an important role in a good cup of tea.

The mineral content is what gives water its characteristic taste, color, and odor, and it varies widely from one area to another. It is measured in total dissolved solids (TDS) and considered a secondary, aesthetic standard in the water trade. The federal standard for TDS is 500 parts per million (ppm). For comparison, seawater contains an average of 10,000 to 35,000 TDS; groundwater ranges from 500 to 2,500 ppm; and rainwater has only 10 to 30 ppm TDS. Some tea gourmets think that the TDS in municipal water is generally too high and that the ideal TDS for a good cup of tea should not be higher than 30–50 ppm, much lower than the federal standard. Others consider that a TDS content of up to 200 ppm is acceptable, and even necessary for tea not to taste flat.

To a certain extent, choices in water taste are a matter of personal preference, but as a whole it is advisable to keep some of the good taste from the minerals in the water destined for tea. This is why distilled water is not a preferred choice for tea, unless the objective is to test a certain tea without being distracted by any other taste in the water. And this is also why reverse osmosis (RO) filters are not usually the best choice for tea water, as they remove almost everything from the tap water and produce a type of water that is very similar to

Tea advertisement for Horniman's tea, England, late nineteenth century. Courtesy of the Bramah Museum of Tea and Coffee, London.

distilled water—unless, of course, TDS levels are excessively high and create such objectionable taste that it is preferable to have no taste at all, in which case RO filters may have to be used. Chlorine and other undesirable elements, such as lead and arsenic and any pesticide residuals, should be removed. An activated carbon filter is an ideal choice for this, because it does remove organic compounds and unpleasant odors and colors, yet retains some of the minerals and, therefore, taste.

With the exception of substantive health hazard issues such as waterborne bacteria and the like, chlorine is by far the biggest general complaint in public water quality, which has prompted some water companies to switch to chloramine. This compound lasts longer than chlorine, has less of chlorine's annoying taste and odor, and does not generate dangerous by-products. Public water quality continues to improve and, in a desirable future, we may get perfect water from our tap. For high-end tea and coffee shops this is not happening fast enough. In order to have total control of the quality and consistency of their water, these businesses use processing equipment capable of essentially taking everything—good *and* bad—out of the water and putting back into it carefully selected constituents designed to achieve the ideal combination for the perfect cup. For the rest of us, awareness of the issues and a good filter choice may be our best bet for home-brewed tea.

Once good water quality is achieved—soft enough but not too soft; with a good balance of minerals; free of toxic elements and bad taste, color, and odor—there is the question of heating the water. Lu Yü had precise ideas about the various stages of boiling water for tea, which he explained in the *Ch'a-ching:*

> When bubbles appear like fish eyes and there is a faint sound, that is the first boil. When bubbles climb the sides of the cauldron like strung pearls in a gushing spring, that is the second boil. When appearing like mounting and swelling waves, that is the third and last boil. Boiled any more, and the water is old and spent and undrinkable indeed.

Most of us won't be able to see fish eyes and pearls innumerable in the water, but in time we will be able to identify the different sounds of water heating up, water preparing to boil, and water boiling. This is important because different teas require different water temperatures. Just as it is very easy to destroy a good leaf tea with overchlorinated or hard water, it is equally easy to ruin it by brewing it with the wrong water temperature. The only teas that should be brewed with water at a full, rolling boil (212 degrees Fahrenheit or 100 degrees Celsius) are black teas and some compressed brick teas. The water should not be left to boil for any amount of time, but should be poured into the teapot as soon as it comes to a full boil. The Chinese say that overboiling takes the chi, the life force, out of the water. More scientifically minded Westerners say that overboiling reduces oxygen content and increases mineral concentration. Whatever the explanation, freshly boiled water is best.

Oolong teas should be brewed with water that is close to boiling but not quite (180 to 195 degrees Fahrenheit or 80 to 90 degrees Celsius). Steaming but not boiling water should be used for green and white teas (160 to 170 degrees Fahrenheit or 70 to 75 degrees Celsius). For these teas, if the water doesn't get turned off early enough and is boiling already, it is best to let it sit and cool off for several minutes before brewing the tea. The delicate aromas of green and white teas are very easily ruined by boiling water. General guidelines for brewing times are three to five minutes for black tea, three to seven minutes for oolong, and two to three minutes for green or white tea. But these are only guidelines; some green teas steep for only a minute, some black teas for up to seven or eight minutes, and some whites for twelve to fifteen minutes. An increasing number of tea companies and specialty tea shops include brewing instructions and steeping times on their packages.

Yet within certain limits, brewing styles are also a matter of personal preference. Suggested brewing times, as well as tea leaf quantities, are designed to avoid bitterness and astringency, among other things, but some people do like the astringent and bitter taste. Experimenting freely is the best way to discover personal preferences.

Adding knowledge and awareness of water to the experimentation can be surprisingly rewarding. Unlike alchemists, who never did manage to transform lead into gold, adventurous tea enthusiasts can make wonders with just a few leaves, the right brewing time, and, of course, the right water.

Tea Buzz

If this is coffee, please bring me some tea; but if this is tea, please bring me some coffee.

—Abraham Lincoln

Tackling the issue of caffeine content in tea brings to mind the story of the five hundred hats of Bartholomew Cubbins: underneath each hat Bartholomew took off from his head there was always another one. So the opinions about caffeine in tea. Some say the amount of caffeine varies according to the type of tea. Others maintain that it is exactly the same in all teas. Many believe that black tea has the most caffeine, green tea about half of black tea, and oolong about two-thirds. Some claim that green and white teas have the same amount; others say that green and black have the same amount, but white has less. Some say that white tea has almost no caffeine, whereas others contend that it has double the amount of black. Most everyone seems to agree, however, that tea has less caffeine than coffee. But even that can be true or untrue, depending on how it is measured. And so on ad infinitum.

What follows seems to be the prevailing wisdom, gleaned from the multitude of data. Surely someone will disagree. Caffeine—the chemical term is *methylxanthine*—is the world's favorite legal psychoactive substance, the beneficial effects of which have been touted throughout the ages and by people on all continents. It is an alkaloid found in the seeds, leaves, and fruit of more than sixty plants, the best-known sources being coffee, cocoa, the Argentinean maté, and, of course, tea. The caffeine in tea used to be called "theine" until it was determined, in the 1830s, that caffeine and theine were the same compound. The *Camellia sinensis*, the tea bush, grows at different altitudes, latitudes, and under different climatic conditions. Sunshine, rain, soil quality, age of the leaf, plant varieties, pruning techniques,

Frontispiece art for one of the first manuscripts on caffeinated beverages, a novelty in seventeenth-century Europe. Reprinted from *Traités Noveaux & Curieux du Café, du Thé et du Chocolat* (New and Curious Treatises on Coffee, Tea, and Chocolate), by Philippe Sylvestre Dufour, engraving, France, 1685. Bitting Collection, Rare Books, Library of Congress, Washington, D.C.

harvest time, and even the type and amount of pests the plant has to combat—all play a role in determining the amount of caffeine in the tea leaf, which varies between 2 and 5 percent.

Once this variation is taken into account, the actual processing of the tea, which turns the leaves into black, green, or oolong, does not significantly increase or decrease the amount of caffeine in the tea. This means that the generally accepted notion that black tea has the most caffeine, green very little, and oolong an amount between the two is not as clear cut as we think. On the other hand, it is also not true that all three teas have exactly the same amount of caffeine. Studies of caffeine levels in various types of tea show that some green teas may be low in caffeine, but others may surpass both oolong and black teas in their caffeine values. A first-flush Darjeeling may very well have less caffeine than a China green, for example. And the same studies show that oolongs often have less caffeine than greens. White teas, which are often classified as a lighter type of green tea, are commonly believed to be very low in caffeine. The opposite is true if we consider that young leaves contain more caffeine than old ones, and white teas are made up mostly of young leaves and buds.

Gone is the notion, therefore, that one should drink strong black tea only in the morning and choose green or white tea, as if they were almost soothing herbals, for the evening. That "strong" taste in black teas often has more to do with the darkness of the liquor and the fullness of the body than with caffeine content. What does make a difference is the actual quantity of tea used to brew a cup. Since green and white teas tend to be brewed with less leaf than black tea, sometimes just a pinch, they do indeed have less caffeine, but only in relative terms due to a different leaf-to-cup ratio. A shorter brewing time may also diminish the amount of caffeine released into the infusion. Since caffeine is an issue for many consumers, a few companies have begun to add caffeine percentages on their tea containers, even though the U.S. Food and Drug Administration does not require it. On the whole, specific data on caffeine levels in various teas are not easily available in the industry, and imprecise information is often passed along to the public.

As a general rule, it is safe to assume that:

1. All nonherbal teas, whether black, white, green, or oolong, in the bag or loose, compressed, in bricks or balls, have a variable amount of caffeine in them.
2. The average range of caffeine content in an eight-ounce teacup is around 20 to 60 mg.
3. Certain classes of green tea tend to be lower in caffeine than blacks or oolongs—as low as 10 mg—but many others hover around 25 mg, and some can reach up to 50 mg.
4. Oolongs are often lower than greens, with an average of 18 to 20 mg.
5. Only the strongest blacks reach the 50 to 60 mg levels, while many are closer to 30 to 40 mg.

When it comes to the comparison with coffee, things are a little clearer. On a dry-weight basis, a pound of tea has more caffeine than a pound of coffee beans. However, a pound of coffee beans yields only around 40 to 60 cups, while up to 180 to 200 cups can be brewed with a pound of tea. Because, on a weight basis, more bean is necessary to brew coffee than tea leaf to brew tea, the caffeine concentration in coffee is higher: a standard eight-ounce cup of drip coffee—we are not measuring that hair-raising triple *venti* at your local coffee chain—tends to have 80 to 120 mg of caffeine. Compared to the 20 to 60 mg in tea, this explains the rule of thumb that tea has about half to one-third less caffeine than coffee.

Because of this, a cup of tea is often seen as the gentler alternative to coffee. Naturally, there are extremes and, as toxicologists like to say, the dose is the poison: a Wall Street stockbroker drinking one cup of coffee in the morning would fit the "gentler alternative" profile a great deal more than a wired-up Irish farmer downing sixteen cups of tea throughout the day. But, as a whole, tea suggests an undeniable sense of peaceable moderation while coffee evokes vivid images of road rage. After all, there is no Japanese coffee ceremony.

The 22,000 Virtues of Tea

Tea has the blessing of all deities

Tea promotes filial piety

Tea drives away all evil spirits

Tea banishes drowsiness

Tea keeps the five internal organs in harmony

Tea wards off disease

Tea strengthens friendship

Tea disciplines body and mind

Tea destroys the passions

Tea grants a peaceful death

—Attributed to Japanese Buddhist priest Myoe
  (1173–1232), who had it inscribed on a
  teakettle

Thousands of years ago in China, tea was renowned for its many medicinal properties. An ancient Taoist story tells about an old herbalist who knew the benefits of 84,000 medicinal herbs and, over time, had been teaching his son about them. He died before he could finish, and the son was left with knowledge of only 62,000 of them. The son feared he would never find out about the rest, when one night he had a dream, in which his father told him to come visit his grave. There he would find knowledge about the remaining 22,000. The next day the son went to the grave and found not 22,000 plants, but only one: the tea plant. And he understood that this one marvelous plant contained all the 22,000 virtues.

In the eighth-century *Ch'a-ching*, Lu Yü also mentions tea's benefits for a variety of ailments: "If hot and thirsty, feeling melancholy, suffering from headache, strained eyes, troubles in the four limbs, constrictions in the hundred joints, then one must take four to five drafts of tea. Tea is comparable to butter-rich koumiss or sweet dew." Lu Yü also quotes from other sources with more specific remedies that include tea as an ingredient. Take chronic ulcers, for instance. It is recorded in *Prescriptions from the Pillow* that "to heal chronic boils and ulcers, take bitter tea and centipedes and roast together until fragrant and cooked, divide into doses, and then pound and sift into powder. Boil sweet herbs into a draught to wash the wound. Finally, use the powder to cover the sore." To cure small children of anxiety and dizzy spells, the *Prescriptions for Children* suggests to "treat with a dose of boiled bitter tea and onion roots." For excitable children the Pillow Book prescribes bitter tea and onion beards. In another Chinese book of remedies of the Ming (1368–1644) period, the *Pen-ts'ao kang-mu*, a recipe is given for a "Noise in the Head: Take white Ants of the largest sort dry'd, with some Seed of Tea, reduce them to a Powder and blow them up the Nostrils. This Remedy has a good Effect."

When Buddhist priests introduced tea to Japan, tea's fame as a health remedy traveled with it and spread from the monasteries to the imperial court and to the general population. Tea became an item of everyday use, with which monks cured the poor. In the thirteenth century, the Buddhist monk Eisai recorded tea's health benefits in the *Kissa Yojo Ki*, or "The Book of Tea Sanitation." When tea was imported to the West, one of the first documents to advertise tea's health "vertues" was Garway's broadside, which the great China scholar Joseph Needham considers a derivation of a Ming tea book. The fame of tea as a health remedy has survived the test of time, traveling over continents and spreading through cultures for two thousand years or more.

Minus the roasted centipedes, Western science has been catching up with Eastern tea pharmacopoeia only recently. Over the last fifteen years, tea's effects have been studied in connection with cardiovascular disease, cancer prevention, oral health, bone density, the immune system, and weight loss. The healthful properties of tea are

Frontispiece art for an early manuscript on the medical benefits of the fashionable beverages of tea, coffee, and chocolate. Reprinted from *Le bon usage du thé, du caffé et du chocolat pour la preservation & pour la guerison des Maladies* (The Good Use of Tea, Coffee, and Chocolate for Preserving Health and for Treatment of Maladies), by Nicolas de Blegny, engraving, France, 1687. Bitting Collection, Rare Books, Library of Congress, Washington, D.C.

mainly attributed to its high levels of flavonoids, particularly catechins, which are compounds present also in other vegetables, fruits, and flowers. The main one in tea is epigallocatechin gallate, or

EGCG. The acronym sounds like a fashion brand or a robot in a science fiction series, but it is actually a polyphenol with high antioxidant power. The polyphenols in tea appear to be much more effective than vitamins C or E, considered the antioxidants par excellence. All *Camellia sinensis* teas are rich in polyphenols, but the less processed green and white teas contain a higher percentage of them than black or oolong teas.

Antioxidants are an essential tool for maintaining healthy cells. They are powerful scavengers of free radicals, which are produced by our cellular metabolism and are responsible for the aging process in our bodies. The well-known French paradox—the rate of heart disease for French people is only 40 percent that of Americans, even though they eat saturated fats and don't exercise as much—has been explained by the French habit of accompanying meals regularly with a *coup de rouge,* one or two glasses of red wine containing antioxidant-rich polyphenols. Tea contains much higher levels of polyphenols than red wine, which has prompted several researchers to explore the possible effect of tea on cardiovascular disease. According to a paper published by the Linus Pauling Institute reviewing several population studies, consumption of at least three cups of black tea a day may be associated with a modest (11 percent) decrease in the risk of heart attack. A Boston University study also reports a favorable influence of black tea on vascular health but suggests that it may be due to other flavonoids and polyphenols, not the antioxidant catechins.

Black, green, and white teas' potential cancer-preventive properties are also being studied, but the mechanisms of action are still not clearly understood. Earlier animal studies found tea to have a protective effect against certain types of cancer and attributed the results to EGCG's antioxidant activity. A recent University of Rochester study on green tea and cancers linked with dioxin exposure suggests instead that EGCG inhibits cancer-cell growth by binding with and blocking Hsp90, a protein that makes cancer cells grow. Other experimental studies have been investigating the connection between antioxidants in tea and enzyme activity; still others have explored antimutagenic properties of tea and DNA protection.

In addition to cancer and cardiovascular disease, the leading killers in the United States, tea's beneficial effects have been studied in connection with oral health, due to both the antibacterial activity of flavonoids and the anticavity effect of the fluoride in tea leaves. Fluoride analysis showed that the tea leaves with the highest fluoride content are the older, more mature leaves, used for brick tea and lower-quality teas. This property was recognized with great precision a thousand years ago in China without lab analyses or chromatography: "I have found it advantageous to rinse my mouth with strong tea after each meal. . . . The teeth will be strengthened. Dental disease will be reduced. The effect is achieved with teas of low and medium quality," writes Su Tung-p'o in 1083 C.E.

The roles of tea in suppressing appetite, helping to burn calories, and stimulating insulin production are also being studied, potentially addressing diabetes and obesity, two of the most urgent health problems today. In addition, European population studies found that those who drank tea had greater bone mineral density than those who did not drink tea. Research is ongoing in several other areas of human health, such as the immune system, kidney stones, and cognitive function. Tea's benefits seem endless. Given the furious research activity going on at the present time, the 22,000 benefits claimed by the old Chinese story don't seem too outlandish after all.

Naturally, the tea companies and herbal supplement producers are eager to take advantage of any pronouncement on tea and health, particularly those relating to weight loss. But the U.S. Food and Drug Administration and the scientific community are cautious. Many of the studies sound promising but the results are still inconclusive, they say. There are several reasons for this. Epidemiological studies are difficult to evaluate, because extraneous confounding factors in the population and environmental influences cannot be excluded. In animal studies researchers can control these factors by carefully designing the study. But the results on animals cannot be automatically extrapolated to humans. Also, there is the issue of bioavailability, which is the extent to which a chemical can be absorbed and used by the body. The fact that a chemical studied in vitro acts in a certain way is

Newspaper advertisement for Empire tea, England, c. 1930s. Reprinted from Ukers, *All About Tea*, 1935.

not a guarantee that it will act in the same way in a human body. Nevertheless, it seems that these days people are drinking tea more than ever. We are a long way from that Austrian Jesuit Martino Martini who, in the 1600s, thought that tea was responsible for the "yellow, desiccated appearance of the Chinese." Nowadays we are more likely to hear about the yellow, desiccated appearance of Westerners for *not* drinking the magical brew. And why not? It is undeniable that antioxidants are great allies in our care of body and mind and that tea is a magnificent source of antioxidants.

Much research needs to be done still; a scientific exploration of 22,000 virtues takes time. Yet in its own way, with animal experiments and clinical trials, modern Western science is offering its own contribution to the slow but steady growth of human knowledge. Western researchers are coming full circle back to the beginnings of tea, to Shen Nung's tea experiments in his transparent stomach, and to the Taoist concept of tea as an elixir of immortality. In yet another of the many permutations in history, tea as an object of scientific observation is helping bring together the strengths of two cultures: the East's ancient empirical integrative wisdom, collected over millennia, and the West's systematic, analytical approach to understanding the complexities of nature.

Part 4

*

Tea Today:
The People and
the Earth

Two Leaves and a Bud

European imperialism, which does not disdain to raise
the absurd cry of the Yellow Peril, fails to realise that
Asia may also awaken to the cruel sense of the White
Disaster.

—Kakuzo Okakura, *The Book of Tea,* 1906

The world of tea has come a long way from that mythical afternoon, thousands of years ago, on which Shen Nung—revered
emperor, divine husbandman, and intrepid herbalist—sipped the pri-
mal cup of tea while resting among the gentle hills of South China.
From there, the cultivation of tea spread to three dozen other countries. Because tea likes heavy rainfall and acid soil, it grows mostly in
tropical and subtropical regions. Whether on the verdant hills of
Kenya, in lush tropical Sri Lanka, on large Indian plantations on the
misty hills of Darjeeling and the plains of Assam, or on Chinese
smallholder family farms, endless expanses of tea bushes cover the
earth like soft velvet and regale the world with breathtaking scenery.
Worldwide tea acreage amounts to 6.2 million acres (2.5 million
hectares), of which 89 percent is located in Asian countries and the
rest in Africa and South America.

Today the main players in tea are India and China, which together produce half of all the world's tea, and Kenya and Sri Lanka,
which are major exporters. India is the world's largest producer of

black tea, but it consumes most of it domestically and exports only about 20 percent of its production. More than half of all Indian tea is cultivated in the northeastern region of Assam, the largest tea-growing area in the world. The other main Indian tea-growing regions are West Bengal in the north, where the famous Darjeeling is grown, and Kerala in the south. Over the last few decades, China has been recouping the commercial terrain it lost so dramatically with the onset of the British tea enterprise during the 1800s. Chinese tea production, mostly green, is closing in on Indian output, although China exports a great deal more, around 35 percent of its production. This is not surprising, since China has been increasing overall export output on a massive scale and is set to become the world's biggest exporter and fourth largest economy by 2010. In terms of total figures, Sri Lanka and Kenya grow less tea than China and India, but since nearly all of their production is put on the international market, they are the world's largest exporters. In Sri Lanka, tea represents 70 percent of all agricultural exports—a figure Ceylon tea pioneer James Taylor could not have imagined in his wildest dreams.

In 2004 world tea production reached 3.2 million metric tons (one metric ton equals 1,000 kg, or 2,200 pounds), three times as much as forty years ago. Provided all the tea produced is actually consumed, this figure translates to an astounding 3.8 billion cups of tea drunk every day around the world. For tea drinkers, pouring tea into a cup is such a pleasant, effortless act, even when it's done 3.8 billion times a day. Yet most of us are unaware of how much work needs to be completed before we can enjoy our tea, how difficult and sometimes unbearable the working and living conditions are, and how many millions of workers' hands are necessary to accomplish the daily tasks. In India alone, the tea industry is the second largest national employer, after Indian Railways: 1.2 million permanent tea workers and around 1 million temporary day laborers work in India's 1,600 large estates and 126,000 small tea gardens.

Manufacturing tea after the harvest is the least labor-intensive task. Only about 10 percent of the labor force is dedicated to factory work. Most tea goes through five stages of production: withering,

rolling, oxidation or fermentation, drying, and last, sorting and grad-
ing. As soon as the tea leaves are plucked, they start to wither and
continue to do so for varying amounts of time after they are spread on
long troughs inside the tea factory. When they have lost some of the
moisture and become flaccid, the leaves are ready for the next stage,
in which they are gently twisted and rolled until the cell tissue rup-
tures and releases the juices that spread around and coat the surface of
the leaves. This operation was once done by hand for all teas. Today
hand rolling is limited to expensive varieties, and most commercial
whole-leaf tea is machine rolled. In the third stage—commonly but
erroneously called fermentation because of an enzyme being involved in the chemical reaction—the leaves are placed on flat racks
and undergo an oxidation process, during which the leaves turn
color. This process is carefully monitored under controlled temperatures. The leaves are then dried, to inactivate the enzymes and stop
the oxidation process, but also to eliminate most, but not all, of the
moisture; processed tea leaves still have 2 to 3 percent moisture. The
drying is followed by the fifth and last stage of tea manufacture, in
which teas are sorted and graded according to leaf size. This whole
process takes place in the tea factory, which is located on the plantation itself. Unlike other plantation crops, tea is harvested and processed on the premises because the leaves are quite perishable and
need to be treated as soon as possible after plucking.

The remaining 90 percent of the tea labor force is employed on
the fields. Some of the workers, often males, are dedicated to the ongoing tasks of pruning, weeding, spraying, hoeing, fertilizing, draining the soil, and taking care of seedlings in the nursery. The vast
majority of the workforce is needed for plucking the tea leaves, a job
that must be done by hand to produce good-quality tea. Machine
harvesting is too indiscriminate, breaking off young and old leaves as
well as stems, and it generally yields low-grade teas. In Asia, the large
majority of tea pluckers are women. Every morning, after taking care
of household and children, they walk into the fields with a basket on
their backs and begin their work. This consists of walking along the
tea bushes, which are kept pruned at a height of three or four feet,

northeast of India, while Sri Lanka brought in workers from the south Indian state of Tamil Nadu. Because tea plantations are generally located in remote regions, today's immigrant tea workers, the descendants of those first laborers a hundred and fifty years ago, live not only far away from their family origins, but also isolated from neighboring towns or villages. In addition to isolation, they are discriminated against because they are seen as foreigners who don't belong. Yet where *do* they belong?

Generation after generation, tea workers are born and die on the plantation. Here, they are marginalized as intruders, and, because as unskilled laborers they are considered inferior, they are relegated to the bottom of

The Bud and First Leaf, by John Abercromby Alexander, one in a series of twenty-four photographs on tea cultivation, England, c. 1920. Royal Commonwealth Society Collections, reprinted by permission of the Syndics of Cambridge University Library, Cambridge, UK.

the social scale. But they are too distant, physically and emotionally, from the places their fathers and grandfathers came from and don't have much of a chance of ever going back there. Therefore, they don't belong there, either. In Sri Lanka, for example, this state of things escalated into a social and administrative impasse that was brought to closure only recently. There, the immigrant Indian Tamils, also called Tea Tamils, were—and still are—looked down upon, not only by the majority Sinhalese, but also by the Sri Lankan Tamils. In the reassessment after Indian and Sri Lankan independence in 1947–48, the Tea Tamils, living in the limbo of the tea plantation reality, lost their civil rights and even their Sri Lankan citizenship. Considered to be neither Sri Lankan nor Indian, tens of thousands of them were left in stateless suspension until, after half a century of struggle, they reacquired their legal Sri Lankan status in 2003. In northeastern India, and particularly in Assam, discriminatory behavior toward immigrant laborers has taken the form of violent attacks by extremist groups, sometimes ending with deaths.

Aside from historical displacement and social marginalization, the working and living conditions of the average tea laborer are appalling. The daily wage for a tea worker who has met his or her daily plucking quota varies from 60 cents to $1.50. Work is not guaranteed during the slow season. Workers get paid less if they are sick or not at all if there is no work. Sundays are not paid. Chronic back pain from the heavy plucking baskets, exposure to chemical pesticides, and the danger of snakebites are common hazards in the life of the plucker. Leeches are a common nuisance in the hot, moist environment of the tea gardens during the rainy season. Families live in small, cramped quarters that are often unsanitary and in disrepair. Electricity and running water are rare luxuries. Health facilities are often lacking in personnel, equipment, and medication. Communicable diseases such as tuberculosis and malaria are common, as are gastroenteritis, dysentery, and other illnesses due to contaminated water sources. Anemia and malnutrition are widespread. Alcohol dependency is a growing problem within the context of the social isolation in the plantation communities, particularly among men. Plantations are required to offer children primary education, but not secondary. Plucker families not only cannot afford to send their children off to school for more advanced studies, but also need them as pluckers during harvesting season to help the family make ends meet. Without an education, young men and women have no prospects for better employment. Thus the cycle is perpetuated, and one generation of underprivileged pluckers follows the next.

To make matters worse, the price of tea on the world markets has remained stagnant. This is in good part due to a worldwide production increase and competition among the traditional tea suppliers— India, China, Kenya, and Sri Lanka—and smaller tea producers such as Vietnam, Bangladesh, or Indonesia. The result has been a vicious circle of oversupply that keeps prices depressed, which in turn leads to increased production in a desperate attempt to maintain the level of cash flow. Some analysts argue that low tea prices may be due to more than just oversupply. The less-than-transparent auction system used for tea sales in the producing countries is seen as open to abuse, allowing the possibility of collusion among big buyers and manipulation of the bidding process to keep the prices low. It doesn't help that

Coolie Children Picking Tea at Talawakele, Near Nuwara Eliya, stereograph, Ceylon, 1903. Prints and Photographs Division, Library of Congress, Washington, D.C.

ownership of the tea industry is concentrated in the hands of a few major transnational corporations, some of which control all the steps of the supply chain from tea bush to teapot. Critics also claim that while auction prices are low—FAO's (the United Nations' Food and Agriculture Organization) composite price for tea averaged a mere $1.65 per kg in 2004—retail prices for tea continue to grow. Yet producing countries are squeezed out of the larger profit scheme, which goes mostly to the transnationals that control the blending, packaging, and marketing end of the business. Whichever the triggering factors and conditions, the generalized industry reaction to price stagnation is to direct efforts toward cutting production costs on the plantation. And this has increased the pressure on farmers and laborers and further exasperated their already meager living conditions.

Over the last few decades, a general pattern of conflict between labor and management has developed, particularly in India where the economic contrast between workers and large tea plantation operations is most evident. Tea workers have been asked to take lower wages or work longer hours for the same wage. Permanent workers have been let go, while hiring of casual day laborers has increased in order to cut benefit costs. A fairly common practice on some Indian plantations has been to hold back pay for several months, which has triggered protests and episodes of violence. In some extreme cases, plantation managers have held back pay as long as possible and finally abandoned the plantations altogether, with catastrophic results for the workers, who are entirely dependent on the plantation infrastructure for housing, food rations, health care, or schooling.

In the summer of 2005, 350,000 tea workers went on strike during peak harvest season, demanding higher wages and better conditions. What they were accorded was a day rate increase of two rupees (less than five cents) for the next two years, without the requested retroactive pay. Critics found the results profoundly inadequate. But some negotiators argued that at least the workers got something. From their perspective, given the glut on the tea market, it's only too easy for large corporations to leave India altogether and look for alternative tea sources in countries without "labor unrest." Not too long ago, that is exactly what the British did. Sensing that it was only a matter of time before India would gain independence, British planters began to set up large tea plantations in Africa, and today more than half of British tea imports come from Kenya, Malawi, and Zimbabwe.

This is the reality on the other side of those 3.2 million metric tons of worldwide annual tea production. Tea, this most refreshing, most consoling, most reassuring of beverages, whose leaf grows in idyllic surroundings, is borne from struggle and hard labor. And yet, millions and millions of patient and agile hands, plucking two leaves and a bud, two leaves and a bud, two leaves and a bud, continue to ensure our access to this great source of enjoyment. They have done so for hundreds of years, without reaping much of the benefits. As the world becomes increasingly aware of these conditions, more and more people are asking: What to do? Over the last few decades, a whole movement has developed around this question, with encouraging signs of success on a global scale.

A Fair Cup

A sense of powerlessness often overcomes us when we read bad news or hear descriptions of desperate circumstances. Given the relentlessness of the global powers at work, it is not difficult to succumb to such feelings. What difference could our small, individual actions make in the context of such widespread and firmly entrenched problems? And yet, sometimes what can make a difference is something as small as drinking the right cup of tea. Fair trade tea.

What is fair trade tea? What do we accomplish when we buy fair trade products? And what does fair trade mean, exactly? The idea started after World War II when, in an effort to help alleviate extreme poverty, various Western relief organizations, religious groups, and individual companies began buying handicrafts from developing countries and selling them in Europe and North America. These Alternative Trade Organizations (ATOs) sought to establish equitable, long-term relationships with their trading partners and spread the "trade not aid" message around the world. The goal was to stop pouring indiscriminate funding into developing countries and instead strengthen direct, fair-minded commercial ties with them. Over the years, the ATOs expanded to other commodities, particularly coffee and tea, but also cocoa, bananas, rice, sugar, and other products. Today, the general fair trade movement in its various forms has grown to such an extent that when socially conscious consumers choose to buy fair trade products, the accrued benefits are enjoyed by an estimated 5 million people around the world—growers, laborers, and their family members. Eight hundred thousand fair trade producers supply products to fair trade partnerships in fifty-eight developing countries. Overall yearly fair trade sales are nearing 1 billion dollars and are growing by about 40 percent a year.

During the Victorian era, colorfully decorated trade cards were a popular way of advertising goods and products, and collecting and trading these advertisements, often issued in series and limited quantities, was a popular pastime. Trade cards saw their peak of popularity during the 1880s and 1890s when color lithography was at its height. They ceased to be produced after 1900 when magazine advertising proved more cost effective.

Teacup trade card (front and back), The Great Atlantic & Pacific Tea Company, USA, late nineteenth century. Private collection, Los Angeles.

When we, as consumers, choose fair trade tea, our fair trade dollars set in motion a complex yet efficient mechanism supported by a network of national and international organizations operating in all three areas of activity: production, import, and retail sales. On the production end, the Fairtrade Labelling Organizations International (FLO), a German-based umbrella organization that regulates fair trade throughout the world, has established fair trade criteria and inspects and certifies tea plantations to ensure compliance in the areas of wages and working conditions, child labor, schooling and housing, health and safety, and environmental standards. National organizations in the consumer countries then supervise and coordinate the import and retail sales of tea produced on plantations that meet the fair trade criteria. They collect the fair trade premium importers are required to pay and send it back to the fair trade plantations. There, a joint body of workers and managers meets and decides how best to invest the accrued premium for the benefit of the community.

The fair trade premium is reflected in the final retail price of fair trade tea, which is the reason why we pay a little more for it. How little is little? The fair trade premium and registration add up to a grand total of 72 cents per pound of tea. A pound of tea makes two hundred cups. This means that it costs about a third of a cent to enjoy a cup of fair trade whole-leaf orthodox tea. For CTC tea it's a fifth of a cent, since the premium is lower. In Oslo, Paris, Chicago, or Frankfurt, where people don't bother to pick up change on the street anymore, a third of a cent is not even a comprehensible notion. But in Africa, India, or Sri Lanka—suppliers of most of the fair trade tea to the world— it stretches far.

What does the fair trade premium accomplish on a practical basis? The priorities vary according to specific community needs. On a Stassen estate in Sri Lanka, for example, the funds were used for scholarships awarded to children of tea workers who wished to pursue their studies. At the Ambootia tea garden in Darjeeling, workers decided to use the funds for a reforestation program to combat soil erosion after a major landslide destroyed three hundred of their homes. In Tanzania, on the Herkuku estate, workers were able to purchase new roofs for their homes. In some cases, funds are used to acquire skills that will enable workers to earn additional income. In others, a road is built so that workers have better access to services. On one estate, funds were used for an ambulance to facilitate an otherwise slow and difficult access to emergency services. On another, a retirement fund was established to help provide for elderly former tea workers without other means of assistance. Whichever way the premium is used, there is no question that it not only contributes to substantial improvements in people's lives, but also offers workers an excellent empowerment model in the decision-making process on how funds are allocated. With a roof over their head, a better education, a fair wage, and a strong sense of themselves as productive and respected members of a community, tea workers on a fair trade estate are able to offer their children a better future, and at least the option to break away from the cycle that has kept generations tied to the plantation. That's how far that third of a cent stretches.

Support for what is nowadays called "ethical consumption" is clearly on the increase among Western consumers. In the United Kingdom alone, where according to the Fairtrade Foundation one in two adults recognizes the fair trade label, consumers spend $3.6 million a week on fair trade products. British cities strive to be awarded "fair trade city" status by committing to offer a wide variety of fair trade goods in coffee shops, businesses, supermarkets, schools, and public and private institutions. In 2004, Cardiff was the first in the world to become fair trade capital. New York and San Francisco are following in the their footsteps. In 2005 both the New York City Council and the city and county of San Francisco passed resolutions that require city and county agencies to purchase fair trade products.

Religious groups in various countries are also increasingly serving fair trade tea and coffee in their offices and at their functions. Massachusetts-based Equal Exchange, a 100 percent fair trade company, is a pioneer in bringing fair trade products and faith-based organizations together. Dunkin' Donuts, the largest coffee and baked goods chain in the world, switched to fair trade coffee for its espresso cups in 2003; they were the first national brand to do so. *Time* maga-

act of choosing it is a powerful transformative tool. It begins to address the accumulated wrongs of hundreds of years of colonial abuse and its modern correspondent, today euphemistically called the "free" market. But fair trade is not only a bridge that shortens the economic distance between marginalized producers and consumers with disposable income. It is also a meaningful act of human connection, the possibility of sending a grateful smile across the globe, a little sign of hope. In our divisive and finger-pointing world, such a connection among people seems not so much a choice as a necessity for survival. As a hopeful Raymond C. Offenheiser, president of Oxfam America, said: "Together we can change the world one cup at a time." He meant it for coffee, but it works just as well with tea.

Where the Birds Sing

The burden of responsibility is placed on the wrong
people: the non-organic companies should be the ones
required to list on their tea packages all the pesticides,
herbicides, and chemicals they use. The organic, sustainable growers shouldn't be the ones who, in addition
to making the effort of doing the right thing, also have
to jump through hoops to prove they are doing it correctly.

—David Lee Hoffmann, a tea expert who has been working
with Chinese tea farmers on sustainable practices for the
last three decades

How many of us would buy that beautifully decorated tea tin sitting on the shelf if the label said: "The tea bushes that produced
this excellent tea were sprayed with dicofol, endosulfan, ethion, pro-
pargite, tetradifon as well as chlorpyrifos-methyl, cypermethrin, delta-
methrin, fenitrothion, flucythrinate, methidathion, and permethrin.
Enjoy your tea!" And yet, the chemicals listed here are only a few of
the many regularly used on what is generically called "conventional"
tea, which is still the large majority of all tea consumed in the world.

A variety of government agencies in various countries do regulate
maximum residue levels (MRLs) for pesticides, herbicides, and other
chemicals in tea. Some years ago, for example, Germany threatened
to stop importing tea from Darjeeling because it considered the

MRLs unacceptably high and unsafe for consumption. But possible food toxicity is only one of the dangers of the widespread use of chemicals in agricultural practices. As consumers at the end of the line, mostly living in large urban areas far removed from daily farmwork, we often do not think about other consequences affecting people and the environment in the producing areas. Tea workers spraying pesticides are exposed to substantial health hazards when they are not provided with adequate protection gear. Contaminated water is sometimes the only source of drinking water for local populations, who then develop long-term health problems. Ecosystems are disrupted. Beneficial insects are killed along with the damaging ones. When the air is filled with sprayed chemicals, the birds disappear. Pollution of rivers with leaked wastewater kills fish and wildlife and triggers disease and gene mutation. Worst of all, the soil is pumped with chemical fertilizers and force-fed to increase crop yields. Within this artificial setup, a strained and depleted soil is reduced to a mere sterile medium for chemicals to flow through. And when the soil is not viable, vibrant, and replenished, its fruits are also not alive, healthy, and nutritious. Or, as David Hoffmann says with regard to growing tea, if the soil is dead, the tea is dead.

The fair trade movement focuses on giving back to the people, addressing social and economic disparities. This is important work. But what good is having happier people if the Earth, from where all our sustenance derives, is dying? Contributing to a more balanced distribution of energy and resources is a two-pronged process directed to both people and the Earth, if the planet is to survive. Western countries are in a privileged position to do so, with technology, information capabilities, and material resources. Eastern countries hold the knowledge and wisdom of millennia of sustainable agricultural practices—a knowledge and wisdom that have been marginalized only in recent history with the changed priorities of quantity yields and profit margins of big agribusiness. It is in China and India, and not Germany or England, that the roots of the modern organic movement are to be found. Farsighted observers went to those countries and learned and brought back to Europe and North America

Progress, as most of us know, is excruciatingly slow and erratic, while manmade destruction can take place with the swiftness of a beheading. It takes minutes to destroy a soil by pouring a toxic chemical in it. It can take years of hard and systematic work to restore it to health. The world is still dominated by conventional, chemical-based agriculture. In California alone, one of the largest agricultural areas in the world, nearly five hundred thousand pounds of pesticides are sprayed on agricultural crops every day, according to the California Department of Pesticide Regulation. Yet F. H. King and Sir Albert's messages have been heard and increasingly put into practice during the last century. As the public becomes more aware of the downside of chemical farming, organic alternatives become more commercially viable, more visible, and more available, which in turn increases the demand. In the world of tea, organic is still small compared to conventional in terms of total volume, but it is clearly a growth area. The FAO estimated that between 1998 and 2005 organic tea production grew by nearly 12 percent yearly. The demand for organic tea is particularly strong in Europe and Japan. India is the largest producer of organic tea in the world, but it may soon be surpassed by China. According to an FAO projection, China will be providing the world with 56 percent of all organic tea by 2010.

Yet for all the increased interest and awareness, ask ten people to give you a definition of *organic* and you shall receive ten different answers. What is organic tea really? What goes—or doesn't go—into a cup of organic tea that makes the difference? For many, organic simply means that no chemical pesticides are used, but there is much more than that behind a true organic cup of tea. The general concept of organic is holistic and relies on nature's self-renewal. An organic grower creates a system of soil nutrition and pest and disease prevention by recognizing and using biological processes and by adapting the crops to natural cycles. In the same way we know that strengthening our immune system is by far a healthier choice than taking antibiotics, so the organic grower works to create an environment in which plants will thrive and be healthy and will not need help from external agents such as chemical fertilizers or pesticides.

In the organic tea world, it is understood that tea is a healthy drink only when it is grown in healthy soil. The first thing that happens on a tea plantation converting to organic practices, therefore, is that it goes through a three-year process—sometimes it takes four or five years—during which the chemical residues in the soil are neutralized and the nutrients are reestablished. If leaves are harvested during this period, the tea is labeled "organic in conversion." At the same time, several other elements are put in place in the areas of biodiversity (large monoculture tea plantations are known to disrupt ecobalance), beneficial insects, alternative pest control, and composting. Indigenous trees are grown along and around the tea bushes to offer shade, to contribute to biodiversity and better air quality, and to prevent soil erosion, as well as for fuel wood. Certain trees, such as the native Indian neem tree, known for its antimicrobial and insecticidal properties, also provide the raw material for the production of natural, plant-based insecticides. Pests are also controlled by reestablishing a balance between them and their natural predators. As an example of this, organic gardeners in our own temperate climates use ladybugs to eliminate aphids. It's difficult to imagine lovely ladybugs as predators, and yet they are, and very efficient ones at that.

On an organic tea plantation, everything that has nutrient value is put back into the soil and participates in the self-sustaining cycle. Mulching, manuring, composting, and vermicomposting—as opposed to synthetic fertilization—are the backbone of organic soil treatment. They provide a wholesome way to feed the soil, but they also build humus and thereby allow the soil to drain and aerate properly. Livestock is raised to help with manuring but also to provide milk for nutrition and additional income for the workers. On the most advanced organic tea plantations, biodynamic principles are applied. According to these, the entire farm is seen and treated as a self-sustaining interrelated whole in harmony with nature. Renewable sources of energy are used. Lunar cycles are respected and activities planned accordingly. Special vitalizing preparations—made with healing plants such as yarrow, valerian, chamomile, stinging nettle, oak bark, or dandelion—are used to improve the compost fermentation process. On these plantations it is believed that the dynamic forces of nature, the soil, and the sun, moon, and planets are a source of physical as well as spiritual sustenance. At the Ambootia Tea Estate in Darjeeling, one of the best-known biodynamic tea plantations, it is said that by drinking their tea one experiences "the subtlety and the hues of the universe."

What comes to mind when observing organic processes is that each step in the sequence is designed to regenerate, to reinforce, to invigorate. At each stage, one thinks of life, more life, and more life being created. In conventional processes, the chemical shortcuts produce artificial, forced growth of nutrient-poor crops, but at each stage degeneration, depletion, and ecological imbalance are created instead. Ultimately, land managed with such systems resembles a body at the last stages of life in a hospital's intensive care unit: it isn't clinically dead, but can it really be called alive if it is kept going only by the machines? From this perspective, choosing to drink organic tea is more than something we do for the benefit of our own health. It is an act of restoration, a contribution to life, an act of consciousness to support an ailing Earth.

Of course, organic tea growing has its own set of issues. There is the problem of lack of income during the conversion period, the difficulty accessing reliable and updated information, the high fees for inspection and organic certification that effectively cut out small growers from the process. Development projects with good intentions lose momentum once they enter the bureaucratic labyrinths of international support organizations. Organic growers are mostly left to take commercial risks alone, in a market that is unforgiving, particularly for small growers with few resources. On a larger scale, there is also the concern that, under pressure of big agribusiness wanting a share of the organic market but not the costs, organic standards are being lowered and, as a result, what is called organic will not be produced according to reliable organic principles. Grassroots organizations are constantly monitoring the situation and requesting updates of safeguards and policies to maintain valid organic agriculture standards.

Stages of Tea Cultivation, fourth of a series of twelve images depicting the Chinese tea industry from planting to shipping, attributed to Tinqua, watercolor and gouache, China, c. 1850. © Mystic Seaport Museum, G. W. Blunt Library Collection, Mystic, Conn.

Nevertheless, growers who have gone through the process are finding that, once the conversion period is over, organic crop yields are higher, not lower, than with conventional practices. Even though some production costs are higher, profit margins for organic tea growers are good. This is true for other organic crops beside tea. According to IFOAM (International Federation of Organic Agriculture Movements), the general organic market is in strong growth and in 2005 was valued at $28 billion worldwide. Total world organic land surface is 64 million acres (26 million hectares), run by almost six hundred thousand farms. Australia and Argentina are leaders in organic grazing land, while Europe has the highest proportion of organic versus conventionally managed land. In the European Union Italy is the country with the highest number of organic farms as well as the largest acreage. With only 0.3 percent of total agricultural area, North America's percentage of organic land is lower than in the EU. However, on the consumer side, the North American market for organic products is showing the fastest and highest growth world-wide.

With such trends and figures, the day might arrive in which organic, biodynamic, and fair trade practices will be the rule and chemical agriculture the exception. Then the term *conventional tea* would come to mean something entirely more wholesome. While ethical and environmentally conscious consumers are waiting for corporations, institutions, and governments to catch up with the wisdom of long-term views on trade justice and environmental protection on a grander scale, they have at least one consistent power: the power to support the growers who are putting that wisdom in practice every day. The power to choose tea grown on those plantations where mulch and earthworms and compost bring true health and vitality and sustenance to the tea bushes and to the soil itself. The power to contribute to the restoration of a balanced ecosystem. The power to bring the birds back—on organic and biodynamic plantations, the birds are sitting on the branches of the neem tree and they are singing again.

Singpho Tea

Where there is tea there is hope.

—Sir Arthur Pinero,
British playwright, 1855–1934

Long ago, two Singpho brothers went hunting deep in the forest in Assam. Wandering through the jungle a long time, they could not find any animals to hunt and ran out of food and water. Tired, hungry, and thirsty, they had no more strength to walk and decided to rest in a tree. Their hunger gnawed at them. In desperation, they reached out to the leaves of the tree and ate them. To their great surprise and delight, they started to feel better shortly after. They were not hungry or thirsty anymore. One of the brothers asked the reasonable question: *"Phalap?" Pha* means "what" and *lap* means "leaf" in the Singpho language. They plucked the seed and planted it at home. Soon, every Singpho learned the value of those leaves, and *phalap* became the word for "tea."

This is how Rajesh Gudung (also known as Rajesh Singpho) tells the story of the beginnings of tea among the Singpho tribes of Upper Assam. Rajesh is a descendant of the Bisa Gaum, the Singpho chief who gave Robert Bruce the tea plant gift in 1823. Almost two hundred years have passed since that fateful day in which tea changed from Singpho tribal to British imperial hands. Never in his wildest dreams could the Bisa have imagined that from that one little botanical transaction Assam would grow into the largest tea cultivation region in the world and that Assam tea would become a specialty item, with its own logo recognizable across the globe—the profile of the one-horned rhinoceros, an animal that exists only in the wilderness of the Assamese jungles. He could not have imagined that Upper Assam would become one infinite succession of tea garden upon tea garden, largely controlled by foreign corporations or wealthy Indian owners, but rarely by Assamese and hardly at all by Singpho tribes.

With its lush valleys and forests, blessed by the waters of the majestic Brahmaputra River and protected by the Himalayan range, Assam is a very fertile region in India's extreme northeastern corner, rich in natural resources, including oil, coal, and natural gas—a spectacular part of the world, but not a peaceful one. What the British left behind in Assam after India's independence is a jumble of ethnicities, with different languages, religious beliefs, cultural propensities, and contrasting political affiliations, all forced together within the artificial boundaries established according to British colonial priorities—a common profile of the ticking-bomb scenario left over by the waning British empire in various continents. A complex network of armed insurgents' groups fights a variety of causes. Separatist groups, some allegedly backed by foreign governments, seek political independence from India, which they see as nothing more than yet another colonial power. Other smaller groups seek independence not only from India but from the state of Assam itself and want to establish their own sovereign state within the state. Many resent the economic exploitation of foreign-owned corporations—and by *foreign* they mean not only European or American but also any non-Assamese companies—that reap profits but do not participate in the building of the state's infrastructure. Some groups take out their frustrations on underprivileged, immigrant laborers from other states, claiming they take away local jobs. And then there is the well-known Hindu-Muslim tension, ubiquitous in India.

Some rebel groups have forgotten their initial political objectives. What started as a legitimate request for social justice a couple of decades ago has developed into full-fledged criminal activity today.

Since tea plantations are Assam's main industry and generate a large cash flow, they are targets of violent actions, including kidnappings and ransom requests, which in some cases have ended in murder. Some groups have extended their extortion rackets beyond the tea industry to other businesses or professionals with any meaningful income. This situation has prompted the Indian government to declare any payment to insurgents illegal and to mount brutal counterinsurgency operations with massive military presence. Large corporate tea plantations have hired small armies of security guards to protect themselves. Smaller garden owners and managers quietly pay the ransom hoping that government authorities will not find out. If they do, chances are that local authorities will also require a "fee" in order to ensure that the information will not reach central government authorities and create real trouble for the tea garden owners. On account of this instability, relief operations, nongovernmental organizations, and international labor and agricultural support groups active in other parts of India do not feel it's safe to send their people to Assam. The general confusion and lack of monitoring mechanisms play into the hands of those companies whose business, environmental, and labor practices are well below international standards.

Amid such pervasive strife, something is growing again on the land around the Singpho jungle villages of Upper Assam. It is *phalap*, Singpho tea. After the British colonial operations disrupted their lives, after adjusting to Indian independence and to being a Buddhist tribal minority, and in spite of the unrest and intimidations around them, the Singpho are bringing back traditional tea-growing practices. Led by community leaders like Rajesh and other enlightened and determined growers, they are working hard to incorporate the principles of sustainability and organic agriculture into their practices, not only for tea but also for other crops. Most important, while they are interested in creating a viable commercial connection with Western markets, they are also promoting and encouraging consumption of organic products at a local level. Large segments of the populations in developing countries produce organic foods for affluent Western markets but cannot afford them for themselves, and eat cheap, toxic, pesticide-laden foods instead.

The Singpho effort is supported and facilitated by a mild-mannered yet single-minded woman named Peggy Carswell. A Canadian community development organizer and environmentalist with a smile in her eyes, Peggy belongs to that class of people who never lose their patience, never raise their voice, and never ever give up, no matter how big the obstacle. In 1998, Peggy traveled to Upper Assam in search of a source for organic, fair trade tea and found the area lacking in sustainable agricultural practices. With minimal financial resources, but with the determination and faith that comes to people who do what they believe in, Peggy founded Fertile Ground—East-West Sustainability Network, an organization dedicated to assisting motivated small growers in the implementation of organic principles.

Beginnings were not easy: conducting research into tea production; raising awareness about the expanded alternative market possibilities for organic and fair trade tea; establishing links between growers and researchers, brokers, and specialists in other parts of India; adapting the knowledge acquired from other parts of India to the different climate conditions of Assam; bringing people together and building community in a climate not particularly favorable to cooperation. All this hard work was accomplished with little or no budget. Peggy was able to identify the substantial challenges facing Singpho and other small tea growers in Assam. They may not have had to face British colonials with whips anymore, but their problems now included understanding and learning how to operate within international markets, competing with giant corporations with unlimited research and development resources, or accessing information on cultivation techniques in a language they could comprehend.

Peggy noticed a pervasive lack of information about alternatives to costly and toxic chemical pesticides and fertilizers. To address this, Fertile Ground set up an arrangement with Duliajan College, an agricultural extension of Dibrugarh University serving the northeastern districts of Assam, to collaborate in bringing the appropriate information to the farmers. Resource and educational materials are translated into Assamese; most farmers don't speak English and sometimes not even Hindi, an often overlooked but crucial detail. Books, videos, and audiovisual presentations are collected to help develop a regional resource center for sustainable agriculture. Two demonstration sites, one on college grounds and the other in the nearby town of Digboi, have been set up for a hands-on illustration of the different phases and treatments of plants and soil according to sustainable and biodiversity principles. If funding becomes available, a mobile educational unit will be purchased to help disseminate information to more remote villages. Ultimately, intensive training programs will be set up for growers to become proficient. When they return to their communities, they will become trainers themselves, helping to spread sustainable practices until they become commonplace.

During the last few years, Rajesh and Pabitra Ningda, the pioneers of Singpho tea, were able to learn, experiment, and incorporate more and more of this knowledge into their tea-growing practices. In 2005 they added an important element, essential for acquiring much-needed market access: they were able to purchase a small-scale tea-processing unit. Before that, all they could do was grow their tea bushes and sell the harvested green leaves without processing. The only sales outlets for green leaves are the bought-leaf factories. These establishments pay small growers a few rupees per kilogram for their green leaves, which they either process or resell to large tea companies. Both full-scale tea plantations and bought-leaf factories are able to draw profit margins from their operations, albeit not large ones. The most profitable stages in the tea production chain are packaging, blending, and marketing, which are mostly performed in the consuming countries. Small growers simply selling green leaf are at the bottom of the food chain with minimal or sometimes nonexistent profit margins. Without further resources they are effectively kept out of the tea market. Rajesh and Pabitra are trying to change that. Yet not all Singpho growers have the ability to buy processing units. Some of them only own a few acres of land; others don't own any acreage at all and grow their tea on public land. This is why one of Fertile

Ground's goals is to buy a small-scale tea-processing unit and set it up at Duliajan College for the most underprivileged small growers.

The other issue facing small growers with a desire to produce organic, fair trade tea is the problem of certification fees. Organic and fair trade certifications work well for medium and large tea growers. When it comes to small growers, the systems are still in need of fine-tuning. To be a certified grower means that an inspector has visited the tea plantation, evaluated the conditions, and given a stamp of approval. This inspection has to be paid for. The lowest initial certification fee for fair trade is two thousand euro. Subsequent inspections are less expensive but need to be scheduled yearly. The organic certification fee varies, depending on the size of the plantation, the time it takes the inspector to monitor the various areas, and what the travel costs are, to name a few variables. Organic certification can easily be more expensive than the fair trade certification and also requires on-going inspections. If a grower wants to be certified for both, two fees must be paid to two separate organizations. Though medium-sized and large tea plantations can absorb fees into their operating costs, such figures can be out of reach for small growers—and again, they are cut out of the market. Some small growers, particularly in Africa, have solved the problem by forming cooperatives and paying one fee for the cooperative. This is not always possible, particularly in Assam where, with insurgencies and a debilitated infrastructure, logistics are challenging, to say the least.

As if difficult market access and intimidations and small profit margins and high certification fees and generalized social unrest were not enough, the Singpho are also hounded by a persistent drug problem. An excessively high percentage—some say 60 percent—of their youth are addicted to opium, which is readily available just across the border from Myanmar's Golden Triangle, one of the largest opium cultivation areas in the world. Opium-eradication projects are under way in the neighboring state of Arunachal Pradesh, where consumption is also rampant. In spite of increasing community awareness efforts, the state of Assam does not seem to be taking steps in a similar direction. The work of local law enforcement agencies is made even more difficult by the activities of the various insurgency groups.

Much more work remains to be done. Peggy Carswell's three-year plan turned into a five-year plan, and her five-year plan expanded into a ten-year one. The balance to be achieved among the various social, economic, and cultural components is fragile. While one of Peggy's goals is to assist Assamese growers with Western experience and market access, she is also cautious about introducing any elements that might disrupt indigenous lifestyles, traditions, and practices. The future is uncertain. World tea prices remain depressed and profit margins are slim. Anything can break down at any moment in a context as volatile as Assam's. Help from outside institutions is not forthcoming. Small issues of small growers are easily forgotten in the larger scheme of world market outputs and composite price indexes. And funding is the eternal challenge. Yet Peggy's work is enduring because it is *hridayangam*—"from the heart" in Assamese. And any *hridayangam* work is worthwhile—not only for the concrete results it may bring, but even more so for that intangible and profound, caring energy that accompanies anything done from the heart and that makes people remember the best part of being human.

Within the larger context of the story of tea and the ravages of Western colonialism in Asia, the Singpho are a symbol of survival—however small their effort may be, compared to the large-scale operations that surround them. They are the historical initiators of British empire tea and, as such, the unwitting trigger of tea labor's sad destiny. But they are also the revivers of traditional tea-growing practices and patient implementers of sustainability. Perhaps encouraged by Peggy's *hridayangam*, perhaps because they are persistent by nature, the Singpho won't give up. They continue to make *phalap* and hope that their ways, enriched and improved with organic and sustainable methods, will be recognized and valued in the end.

One of their most unusual teas, little known in the West but fairly common in southwest China, is bamboo tea. The leaves are plucked and steamed in a pan until the green color fades, and then they are dried in the sun or over a fire if it is rainy. The dried leaves are broken into small pieces by hand and pressed tightly into the hollow tube of a bamboo shoot. There the tea sits and ages and acquires its distinctive taste. Whenever it is used, a small pile is scraped out of the bamboo cylinder and steeped. The compressed and airtight storage system allows the tea to be kept for years without losing flavor. The Singpho add a few new leaves to the already brewed ones and pour fresh, boiling water on all of them. They do this over and over again, sometimes until the pot is full of leaves. Then, the elders of the clan eat the spent leaves.

Contrary to the Chinese, who conceived a very precise date for their beginnings of tea—2732 B.C.E.—the Singpho are a jungle tribe that relies on oral tradition. They do not know how old their practices are, for how many centuries or even millennia their elders have been eating spent tea leaves. In the remote peace of their thatched-roof bamboo-and-mud houses, while the monsoons are raging around them, they enjoy the pure taste of their *phalap* and, even more, its sweet aftertaste. If the Singpho choose to ride the tiger of global marketing, some of that sweetness may soon spill out of Assam and reach our own Western cups. Where there is tea there is hope.

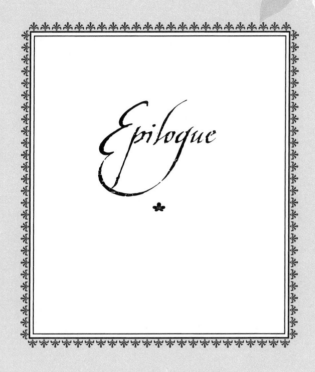

Epilogue

Tea Meditation with Friends

Ichigo ichie—one time one meeting.

—One of the guiding principles of *chado*,
the Way of Tea

The Japanese concept of *ichigo ichie* is a profound expression of Zen thought: every moment only happens once. Applied to the practice of tea, when host and guests come together they experience the uniqueness of that encounter. They treasure the moment as an opportunity to become conscious of their togetherness and of how they are enriched by it. Another meeting will bring a different awareness. This is mindfulness practice, the awareness of transience, the importance of being in the present. "What is happening in the present moment is life," writes Buddhist monk and Nobel Peace Prize nominee Thich Nhat Hanh. The following is his exhortation to use tea as mindfulness practice:

> You can organize a tea meditation to provide an opportunity for your friends to practice being truly present in order to enjoy a cup of tea and each other's presence. Tea meditation is a practice. It is a practice to help us be free. If you are still bound and haunted by the past, if you are still afraid of the future, if you are

carried away by your projects, your fear, your anxiety, and your anger, you are not a free person. You are not fully present in the here and the now, so life is not really available to you. . . . In order to be really alive, in order to touch life deeply, you have to become a free person. Cultivating mindfulness can help you to be free. . . . When you drink tea in mindfulness, your body and your mind are perfectly united. You are real, and the tea you drink also becomes real. . . . This is genuine tea drinking.

Just as the practice of Zen is deceivingly simple, a single sweeping act the expression of centuries of wisdom and infinite depth, so tea. In its many permutations from medicinal remedy to social beverage to fashion statement to object of religious ritual and then on to strategic tool, global commodity, and cause for labor strife, spanning five thousand years of myth, legend, history, and politics, tea, the heavenly brew, embodies the quintessential contradictions of human nature: profound spirituality and limitless greed, supreme artistic beauty and treacherous abuse and violence, exquisite kindness and hospitality, and ruthless dealings in the name of material profit.

In this light, the act suggested by Thich Nhat Hanh—genuine tea drinking—is also deceivingly simple. How much darkness to be metabolized before arriving at the clear, sparkling "genuine" in the full presence of the here and now. And yet what other choice do we have but to strive daily to be tenaciously "genuine," in tea drinking as in life? Whether we do it the Tibetan way and mix yak butter and *tsampa* (barley

The inscription reads: "In tranquility, the universe is great."

Tea Bowl with Design of Mountain Retreat, by Ogata Ihachi (Kyoto Kenzan II, act. 1720–60), stoneware, Japan, Edo period. Freer Gallery of Art, Smithsonian Institution, Washington, D.C. Gift of Charles Lang Freer.

flour) into our tea, or the North African way, pouring green and mint tea from high up into our little glasses, or the Irish way, with strong black tea "thick enough for a mouse to trot on," or the Japanese way, with a few sips of the bright green, frothy *matcha*, or any other way of tea from around this versatile world of ours—only when we practice genuine tea drinking, Thich Nhat Hanh says, are we real; only then is life truly available to us. A great gift in a cup of tea.

Appendix A

Chinese Dynasties and Japanese Chronological Periods

Major Chinese dynasties significant for the story of tea:

Han (Western and Eastern)	202 B.C.E.–220 C.E.
Pre-T'ang	220–618 C.E.
T'ang	618–907 C.E.
Sung (Northern and Southern)	960–1279 C.E.
Yüan (Mongol)	1264–1368 C.E.
Ming	1368–1644 C.E.
Ch'ing (Manchu)	1644–1912 C.E.

Major chronological periods of Japanese history significant for the story of tea:

Nara	710–784 C.E
Heian	794–1185 C.E
Kamakura	1192–1333 C.E.
Muromachi	1338–1573 C.E.
Momoyama	1573–1600 C.E.
Edo (Tokugawa)	1603–1867 C.E.

Appendix B

Chinese Romanization— Wade-Giles to Pinyin Table

Because *Liquid Jade* is mostly a historical book, I decided to use the older Wade-Giles system of romanization of Chinese characters. Although the more modern pinyin romanization is in use today, many names and places are still better known by the Wade-Giles version, for example, Canton versus Guangzhou.

Yet on a modern map, you might not find Canton and if you don't know that today it is called Guangzhou, you'll never know where it is. . . . To clarify possible confusions, what follows is a correspondence table between the Wade-Giles and the pinyin versions of names and places that appear in the text. If you see a name in the text but not in this table, it means that there is no difference between the two versions.

Places—Wade-Giles	Pinyin
Amoy	Xiamen
Canton	Guangzhou
Chekiang	Zhejiang
Ch'in	Qin
Ching-te-chen	Jingdezhen
Chusan	Jusan
Foochow	Fuzhou
Fukien, also Fo-Kien	Fujian
Hangchow	Hangzhou
Honan	Henan
Huichow	Huizhou
Hupeh	Hubei
Kaoling	Gaoling
Kowloon	Jiulong
Loyang	Luoyang
Meng-ting	Mengding
Nanking	Nanjing
Ningpo	Ningbo
Shansi	Shanxi
Sinkiang	Xinjiang
Szechwan	Sichuan
Wu-i shan, also Woo-e-shan (Bohea)	Wuyi Shan
Yangtze	Yangzi

Names—Wade-Giles	Pinyin
ch'a	cha
Ch'a-ching	Chajing
Ch'a-lu	Chalu
Ch'an	Chan
Ch'ang Ch'ü	Chang Qu
Ch'a-shu	Chashu
Ch'ien-lung	Qianlong

Names—Wade-Giles	Pinyin
Ch'in	Qin
Ch'ing	Qing
Ch'uan	Chuan
Chang	Zhang
Cheng Ho	Zheng He
Chi Ch'an	Ji Chan
Chia	Jia
Chin	Jin
Chou	Zhou
Chou Mi	Zhou Mi
Erh-ya	Erya
Fang-yen	Fangyan
fankwei, also fan-kuei	fangui
Hsü Tz'u-shu	Xu Cishu
Hua T'o	Hua Tuo
Hui-ti	Huidi
Hui-tsung	Huizong
Kan-lu	Ganlu
kung-fu	gongfu
Kung-hsi	Kongxi
Lao-tzu	Laozi
Liang Ch'i-ch'ao	Liang Qichao
Lin Tse-hsü	Lin Zexu
Lu T'ung	Lu Tong
Lu Yü	Lu Yu
oolong	wulong
P'eng-lai	Penglai
Pen-ts'ao ching	Bencaojing
Pen-ts'ao kang-mu	Benzaogangmu
Pu-erh	Puer
Pu-ti ta-mo, or Ta-mo	Budidamo, or Damo
Shen Nung	Shen Nong, also Shennong
Shih-shuo	Shishuo

Names—Wade-Giles	Pinyin
Su Tung-p'o	Su Dongpo
Sung	Song
T'ang	Tang
Ta-chin	Dajin
Ta-kuan ch'a-lun	Daguan chalun
Tao	Dao
Tao-kuang	Daoguang
Tao-te ching	Daodejing
Ts'ai Hsiang	Cai Xiang
Tsao Hsüeh-chin	Zao Xuejin
Tu Yü	Du Yu
Wen Chen-heng	Wen Zhenheng
Wen Tsung	Wen Zong
wu-wei	wuwei
Yang Hsiung	Yang Xiong
Yang-hsien	Yangxian
Yin Hsi	Yin Xi
Yin-shih hsü-chih	Yinshi xuzhi
Yüan	Yuan
Yüan-ti	Yuandi

Notes

Behind the Veils of Legend and Myth

Page 3: *"On the peaks of Mount Ling"* . . . Steven D. Owyoung, an art historian with a special interest in the art and culture of tea in ancient China, kindly made this translation available for publication. Owyoung was assistant curator of Asian art at the Fogg Art Museum, Harvard University. He then joined the staff of the Saint Louis Art Museum where he was curator of the Asian collections for more than twenty years until his retirement in 2005. Owyoung is currently working on an illustrated, annotated translation of Lu Yü's *Ch'a-ching—The Classic of Tea*, the first book devoted to tea. I am also thankful to Steven for all his help with the Chinese romanization.

Page 4: *The ancient Chinese healers believed* . . . Mackenzie, *China and Japan*, 159.

Page 4: *Some say Shen Nung had a transparent stomach* . . . Stevens, *Chinese Mythological Gods*, 37. Regarding Shen Nung's popularity Stevens adds that: "In Shanxi [Wade-Giles, Shansi] province, the home of Shen Nong, where anecdotes about him and his life circulated widely as recently as 1949, as though he had died only a few decades before, herbal doctors there referred to their 'Shen Nong Treatment,' much as in the West we might speak of Fleming or Pasteur."

Page 6: *"Tea is better than wine"* . . . As quoted in Ukers, *All About Tea*, 1: 21.

Page 6: *According to French ethnobotanist* . . . Métailié, *Manger en Chine*, 319.

Page 6: *By the third and fourth centuries C.E.* . . . . Information and quotes from Ukers, *All About Tea*, 1: 3.

The Tao of Tea

Page 9: *Attain the climax of emptiness . . .* From *The Spirit of Tao*, translated and edited by Thomas Cleary, © 1991, 1993, 15.

Page 10: *"Teaism is Taoism in disguise" . . .* Okakura, *The Book of Tea*, 18.

Page 11: *According to an old Taoist story . . .* Most historians agree that Lao-tzu ("old master") is not a real but a legendary figure, and that not he but a group of scholars in the third century B.C.E. wrote the *Tao-te ching*.

Lu Yü, the Tea Sage

Page 12: *"Tea may be the oldest, as it is surely" . . .* Carpenter, introduction to *The Classic of Tea—Origins and Rituals* by Lu Yü, 3. Until Steven D. Owyoung's new translation of the *Ch'a-ching* is available in print, Francis Ross Carpenter's 1974 version is the only one available to non-Chinese speakers.

Page 12: *Dragon Cloud, a Taoist monastery, . . .* I learned much about Lu Yü from the late John Blofeld and his *The Chinese Art of Tea*.

Page 13: *What we do know is that the* Ch'a-ching . . . Steven D. Owyoung (see note on p. 283) says the *Ch'a-ching* was written earlier, around 758 C.E. Owyoung's translation includes a biography of Lu Yü and an introduction to tea from mythological times through the T'ang dynasty. The biography and introduction attempt to provide the cultural background, that is to say, the artistic, literary, philosophical, historical, and archaeological contexts, for understanding the early development of tea as a beverage and as an aesthetic pursuit. I am indebted to Steven for kindly making parts of his yet unpublished translation available and for graciously offering explanations of several passages.

Page 13: *Divided into three volumes . . .* The quote in this sentence is from Carpenter, *The Classic of Tea*, 152.

Page 14: *"To brew tea with spring onions" . . .* Owyoung, trans. of *Ch'a-ching*, by Lu Yü, vol. 3, pt. 6.

Page 15: *In T'ang China (618–907 C.E.), the use of tea . . .* This was the first universal tax on tea, imposed from 782 C.E. on, and the rate was 10 percent ad valorem.

Page 15: *Steeped in Taoist and Confucian thought . . .* Carpenter explains this well in his introduction to *The Classic of Tea*, by Lu Yü, 8 and on.

Page 16: *Aside from his spiritual growth . . .* This story is told by Blofeld, *The Chinese Art of Tea*, 7.

I Care Not a Jot for Immortal Life, but Only for the Taste of Tea

Page 20: *Ironically, he met a tragic . . .* Blofeld, *The Chinese Art of Tea*, 14.

Page 20: I am indebted to Stephen D. Owyoung for taking time out of his busy schedule and offering this new translation of Lu T'ung's poem "Writing Thanks to Censor Meng for Sending New Tea."

Gloved Virgins at Dawn

Page 22: *"Among the kind of teas"* . . . Some of the most beautiful of the thirty stanzas that compose the long ballad are selected below:

Our household dwells amidst ten thousand hills,
Where the tea, north and south of the village, abundantly grows;
From *chinshé* to *kubyü*, unceasingly hurried,
Every morning I must early rise to do my task of tea . . .

The sky is thick, and the dusky twilight hides the hill-tops;
The dewy leaves and cloudy buds cannot be easily plucked.
We know not for whom, their thirst to quench,
We're caused to toil and labor, and daily two by two to go. . . .

The sweet and fragrant perfume's like that from the Aglaia;
In goodness and appearance, my tea'll be the best in Wuyen,
When all are picked, the new buds, by next term, will again burst forth,
And this morning, the last third gathering is quite done.

Each picking is with toilsome labor, but yet I shun it not,
My maiden curls are all askew, my pearly fingers all benumbed;
But I only wish our tea to be of a superfine kind,
To have it equal his "sparrow's tongue," and their "dragon's pellet." . . .

The yellow birds, perched on the boughs, warble their sweetest songs;
The weather most grateful is when the sky's half cloud half clear,
While pulling down the twigs, each vents her troubled thoughts,
We talk till our hearts are wounded, and tears are not restrained.

Our task is done, but our baskets are not half filled;
On the north the twigs are searched, we think we'll see the south
Just then I snapp's a twig, whose leaves were all in pairs,
And with my taper fingers, I fastened it upon my curls.

Among the kind of teas, the bitter still exceeds the sweet,
But among them all, these tastes can both be found;
We know not indeed for whom they may be sweet or bitter;
We've picked till the ends of our pearly fingers are quite marred. . . .

—Williams, *Middle Kingdom*, 577–81.

Page 23: *Art historian Steven D. Owyoung* ... Owyoung, "Connoisseurship of Tea," 27.

Page 24: *"In the first ten days of mid Spring"* ... Ibid, 28.

Tea Bricks, Ox Blood, Horses, and Cash

Page 28: *The leaves were dried in the sun* ... As described in Ukers, *All About Tea*, 1:294, 305.

Page 29: *According to at least one source* ... In a paper presented in 2001 at the International Primitive Money Society, Ken Bressett quotes Mosher, *Story of Money*, 42.

In Siberia, Mongolia, Thibet and Chinese-Asian marts, cakes of compressed tea resembling mud-bricks circulate as money. This "money" which is manufactured in Southern China, is made of the leaves and stalks of the tea plant, aromatic herbs and ox blood. It is sometimes bound together with yak dung.

The tea is compressed into bricks of various sizes and stamped with a value that varies depending upon the quality of the tea. It usually increases as the bricks circulate farther from the tea producing country. The natives of Siberia prefer tea-money to metallic coins because catarrhal conditions and lung diseases prevail in their severe climate, and they regard brick tea not only as a refreshing beverage but also as a medicine against coughs and colds.

The Guessing Game

Page 31: *"In idle moments/when bored with poetry"* ... From *The Chinese Art of Tea*, by John Blofeld, © 1985. Reprinted by arrangement with Shambhala Publications, Inc. www.shambhala.com, 41–2.

Page 34: *On one famous occasion he was even able* ... As told by Blofeld, *The Chinese Art of Tea*, 19 and on.

The Eyelids of Bodhidharma

Page 36: *Bodhidharma was a Brahman prince* ... Werner, *Dictionary of Chinese Mythology*, 359.

Page 36: *After the exchange reported above* ... The great Zen scholar Daisetz T. Suzuki reports the exchange in a more complete form:

The Emperor Wu of Liang asked Dharma [Bodhidharma]:
"Ever since the beginning of my reign I have built so many temples, copied so many sacred books, and supported so many monks and nuns; what do you think my merit might be?"
"No merit whatever, sire!" Dharma bluntly replied.

"Why?" demanded the Emperor astonished.

"All these are inferior deeds," thus began Dharma's significant reply, "which would cause their author to be born in the heavens or on this earth again. They still show the traces of worldliness, they are like shadows following objects. Though they appear actually existing, they are no more than mere non-entities. As to a true meritorious deed, it is full of pure wisdom and is perfect and mysterious, and its real nature is beyond the grasp of human intelligence. Such as this is not to be sought after by any worldly achievement."

The Emperor Wu thereupon asked Bodhidharma again, "What is the first principle of the holy doctrine?"

"Vast emptiness, and there is nothing in it to be called holy, sire!" answered Dharma.

"Who is it then that is now confronting me?"

"I know not, sire!"

—Suzuki, *Essays in Zen Buddhism*, 189.

Page 37: *Ch'an is the Chinese version of the Sanskrit* . . . Ibid., 79.

Page 38: *With his "barebones Zen"* . . . The term *barebones Zen* is from Pine's introduction to *Zen Teachings of Bodhidharma*, xvii.

Zen and the Tea Masters of Japan

Page 40: *"This life of seventy years/Shout out!"* . . . As quoted in Hirota, *Wind in the Pines*, 120.

Page 41: *Emperor Shomu (701–56), himself a Buddhist* . . . Castile, *Way of Tea*, 37.

Page 43: *One such master was Murata Shuko* . . . Ibid., 43.

Page 45: *When Hideyoshi invited the emperor* . . . A modern reconstruction of this golden tearoom is displayed at the MOA Museum of Art in Atami, Japan.

Page 46: *The famous Taian Hut* . . . The Taian Hut is preserved at Myōkian Temple, Kyoto.

Page 46: *This meant that social hierarchies* . . . Castile, *Way of Tea*, 53.

Page 47: *The peak of Rikyū's public success* . . . Plutschow, *Historical Chanoyu*, 120.

Page 48: *"In less than ten years"* . . . Ibid., 150.

Page 48: *"When tea is made with water"* . . . Suzuki, *Zen and Japanese Culture*, 280.

Chanoyu

I owe many thanks to Rieko Miwa McMillan, a *chanoyu* instructor of the Urasenke school, for her patient explanations and demonstrations.

Page 49: *"I heard from the monks of Daitoku-ji"* . . . As quoted in Plutschow, *Historical Chanoyu*, 138.

Page 50: *"Proceeding along the roji-path"* . . . Ibid., 132.

Page 50: *In* The Book of Tea, *Okakura says* . . . Okakura, "The Tea Room," chap. 4 in *The Book of Tea*, 35.

Page 51: *The aim of both is to expand* . . . As described in Suzuki, *Zen and Japanese Culture*, 273.

Page 53 (image caption, additional credit line): *Philadelphia Museum of Art* . . . Purchased with funds contributed by the Otto Haas Charitable Trust, The Women's Committee of the Philadelphia Museum of Art, Maude de Schauensee, Theodore R. and Barbara B. Aronson, Edna and Stanley C. Tuttleman, The Hamilton Family Foundation, and Maxine and Howard H. Lewis in honor of the 125th anniversary of the Museum, 2000.

Page 56: *"Once a tea grower invited Rikyū"* . . . Sen, *Tea Life, Tea Mind*, 32–33.

Page 56: *"If asked/The nature of chanoyu"* . . . As quoted in Hirota, *Wind in the Pines*, 25.

Foreign Devils

Page 62: *"Trade was only the weaker alternative"* . . . Fitzgerald, *China*, 476.

Page 65: *Later, when tea became the main* . . . The description of tea as "that blasted vegetable" was used by Wood, *No Dogs and Not Many Chinese*, 23.

The Impertinent Novelty of the Century

Page 69: *"It must be a considerable"* . . . As quoted in Shalleck, *Tea*, 43.

Page 69: *"As to the virtues they attribute to it"* . . . As quoted in Ukers, *All About Tea*, 1:30.

Page 69: *Another critic, the Austrian* . . . Ibid., 1:33.

Page 70: *"One of our doctors"* . . . Ibid., 1:33.

Page 71: *"The best tea of the Celestial Empire"* and *"The Englishman is naturally lymphatic"* . . . As quoted in Shalleck, *Tea*, 51.

Page 72: *"To a pint of tea"* . . . As quoted in Ukers, *All About Tea*, 1:35.

Garway's Slightly Skewed View on Tea and the Resulting Broadside

In the 1700s, a broadside was a fairly large sheet of paper printed on one side only—usually with an official proclamation, a public controversy, an advertisement, or current news—that was distributed to the population.

Page 74: *An Exact Description of the Growth* . . . According to China scholar Joseph Needham, the list of tea benefits are derived from a Chinese Ming-era book on tea. The original Garway broadside is preserved at the British Museum. As quoted in Needham, *Science and Civilisation in China*, vol. 6, Sec. 40, p. 565.

The Penny Universities

Page 78: *"Man is a sociable creature"*. . . Colby, *Selections from the Sources of English History*, 211.

Page 79: *In his* History of England, *Thomas B. Macaulay* . . . Macaulay, *England in 1685*, 83.

Page 79: *"Dr. Tom Saffold at the Black Ball"* . . . As quoted in Ellis, *The Penny Universities*, 32.

Page 79: *"As you have a hodge-podge"*. . . Colby, *Selections from the Sources of English History*, 209.

Page 80: *"Whereas it is most apparent"* . . . As quoted in Ukers, *All About Tea*, 1:45.

The Revenge of the Fair Sex

The complete titles of the pamphlets quoted in this chapter are:

THE WOMEN'S PETITION AGAINST COFFEE REPRESENTING PUB-LICK CONSIDERATION THE Grand INCONVENIENCES accruing to their SEX from the Excessive Use of the Drying, Enfeebling LIQUOR. Presented to the Right Honorable the Keepers of the Liberty of *VENUS.—By a Well-willer, London*, Printed 1674.

The Mens Answer to the Womens Petitions AGAINST COFFEE: VINDI-CATING their own Performances, and the Vertues of their Liquor, from the Undeserved Aspersions lately Cast upon them, in their SCANDALOUS PAMPHLET—LONDON, Printed in the Year 1674.

WHIPPING-TOM: OR, A ROD FOR A PROUD LADY, Bundled up in FOUR Feeling DISCOURSES, Both serious and Merry. In order to touch The Fair SEX to the Quick.—LONDON: Printed for SAM. BRISCOE, at the *Bell-Savage* on *Ludgate-Hill;* also at the *Sun* against *John's* Coffee-House in *Swithin's-Alley, Cornhill*, 1722.

Page 85: *He was doing so well* . . . The shop is still in existence in the same location, at 216 Strand in the City of London.

Page 85: *Soon "great ladies flocked to Twining's house"* . . . Ukers, *All About Tea*, 1:46.

Page 86: *These were the same kinds of "real men" who* . . . The use of the fork at the table became a common practice in England during the eighteenth century.

Smuggling and Smouch

Many centuries before tea smuggling started in England, tea was an item of contraband and played an important role in the black market economy of T'ang and Sung China; there, too, the government held a monopoly on the trade. And tea smuggling is still an issue today among various tea-producing and -importing countries, such as China, India, Pakistan, Nepal, or Bangladesh, where the main purpose of smuggling is to avoid custom duties and trade tariffs.

Page 90: *The tax was soon converted* . . . According to Denys Forrest, this same tea tax was adjusted countless times and was not abolished until 1964. Forrest, *Tea for the British,* 34.

Page 91: *Legal imports of tea went* . . . Drummond and Wilbraham, *Englishman's Food,* 203.

Page 92: *"A quite peculiar elasticity"* . . . Shore, *Smuggling Days and Smuggling Ways,* 11.

Page 93: *"I like a smuggler. He is"* . . . As quoted in Repplier, *To Think of Tea!,* 37.

Page 94: *One of the most famous cases* . . . Shore, *Smuggling Days and Smuggling Ways,* 21–30.

Page 95: *"When the [ash tree] leaves are gathered"* . . . Twining, "Observations," 42.

Page 95: *Other accounts listed* . . . Forrest, *Tea for the British,* 71.

Page 96: *"Next to Charles II's attempt"* . . . and *"it was largely due"* . . . Ibid., 73–4.

Sugar, Anyone?

Page 100: *"The Butter and Tea which the Londoners"* . . . *A Tour to London,* M. Grosley, 1772, as quoted in Drummond and Wilbraham, *Englishman's Food,* 214.

Page 100: *In time, sugar became more affordable* . . . Statistics from Deerr, *History of Sugar,* 1:43.

Page 100: *The phenomenal success of the beverage* . . . The phrase "inseparable companions" with regards to tea and sugar was coined by Scottish jurist and theologian Duncan Forbes in 1744. See Mintz, *Sweetness and Power,* 114.

Page 101: *"Think but for one minute"* . . . and *"Sugar not made by Slaves"* . . . Deerr, *History of Sugar,* 2:296.

Page 102: *Before the century was over* . . . Mintz, *Sweetness and Power,* 143. And if anyone should think that ninety pounds of sugar a year is already an astounding amount of sugar: According to the USDA Economic Research Service, the 2003 yearly per capita sugar consumption in the United States was 141.7 pounds! The figure includes consumption of cane and beet sugar (61.1 pounds), corn sweeteners (79.2 pounds), edible syrups (.34 pounds), and honey (1.1 pounds). Yearly consumption has been decreasing from a 1999 high of 151.3 pounds.

Gin Lane, Tea Lane

Page 103: *"Wine, Beere, and Ale"* . . . As quoted in Drummond and Wilbraham, *Englishman's Food,* 112–3.

Page 103: *Samuel Pepys recorded serving* . . . Ibid., 106.

Page 104: *Colleges brewed their own beer* . . . Harrison, *Drink and the Victorians,* 37.

Page 105: *And things were not much different* . . . Quote in this sentence from *Lives of the Queens of England,* Agnes Strickland, 1882, as quoted in Ukers, *All About Tea,* 1:43.

Page 105: *Cheap, easily accessible, and deadly* . . . Some enterprising drinkers took it upon themselves to manufacture the brew at home, sometimes with abhorrent results. Recipes were exchanged quite openly, and here is one quoted by Drummond and Wilbraham, *Englishman's Food*, 198. In the authors' estimation, it is by no means the worst:

Oil of vitriol [sulphuric acid]
Oil of almonds
Oil of turpentine
Spirits of wine
Lump sugar
Lime water
Rose water
Alum
Salt of tartar

Page 106: *"The Chinese have an herb"* . . . *On the Causes of Greatness in Cities*, Giovanni Botero, 1589, as quoted in Ukers, *All About Tea*, 1: 25.

Page 106: *And so it was that tea became* . . . According to Denys Forrest, *Tea for the British*, 87.

Page 106: *Charles Dickens, that supreme chronicler* . . . Quotes in this sentence from Dickens, *Pickwick Papers*, 431. The financial benefits of selling tea at tea meetings are also not lost on Dickens who, in describing the monthly meeting of the Brick Lane Branch of the United Grand Junction Ebenezer Temperance Association, mentions the presence of "Mr. Jonas Mudge, chandler's shop-keeper, an enthusiastic and disinterested vessel, who sold tea to the members" and "a large wooden money box [that] was conspicuously placed upon the green baize cloth of the business table, behind which the secretary stood, and acknowledged, which a gracious smile, every addition to the rich vein of copper which lay concealed within."

Page 107: *"Gin-drinking is a great vice in England"* . . . Dickens, *Sketches by Boz*, 187.

Page 107: *Some of them, like social reformer* . . . Quote in this sentence from Cobbett, *Cottage Economy*, 23.

Page 108: *Feaster's morning Draught* . . . "The Family Oracle of Health," Vol. 1., 1824, as quoted in Drummond and Wilbraham, *Englishman's Food*, 338.

The Porcelain Secret

Page 112: *"They make in this country"* . . . As quoted in Ramusio, *Navigazioni et viaggi*, 320.

Page 112: *The Chinese had been producing* . . . In 2004 the city of Ching-te-chen, considered one of the most important porcelain centers in the world, celebrated one thousand years of porcelain making.

Page 115: *The company secretly discontinued* . . . Atterbury, *History of Porcelain*, 76.

A Large Cup of Tea for the Fishes

For information on tea in early America, the article Roth, "Tea Drinking in 18th-Century America," was very useful.

Page 122: *"Fain would I pause":* . . . Irving, "The Legend of Sleepy Hollow," 68–9.

Page 122: *"My health continues excellent"* . . . *Mémoires, ou Souvenirs et Anecdotes,* by M. le Comte de Ségur, Paris, 1843, as quoted in Roth, "Tea Drinking in 18th-century America," 70.

Page 123: *Onto this lively tea scene* . . . The term *Great Britain* as opposed to *England* is used here for the first time. Historically, the change took place on March 26, 1707, when the Acts of Union took effect and England and Scotland became the "United Kingdom of Great Britain."

Page 124: *And consume the Americans did* . . . Lawson, *A Taste for Empire and Glory,* 9.

Page 125: *"They divided us into three parties"* . . . Quotes in this paragraph are from Commager and Morris, *The Spirit of 'Seventy-Six,* 5–6.

Page 127: *In a matter of a few years* . . . The quote in this sentence is from Drake, *Tea Leaves,* 72.

The Opium Factor

I am indebted to historian Sanjay Subrahmanyam (Professor, Navin and Pratima Dashi Chair in Indian History at UCLA) for pointing me in the right direction in my opium research and for suggesting other historians knowledgeable in different areas.

Page 129: *"Strange and costly objects do not interest me"* . . . As quoted in Schurmann, *Imperial China,* 107.

Page 129: *But when the Dutch brought tobacco* . . . Wakeman, *The Fall of Imperial China,* 125.

Page 130: *"For it was opium which bought the tea"* . . . ibid, 127.

Page 132: *"The basic rule of foreign activity"* . . . Fairbank, *China Watch,* 15–16.

Page 133: *"During the first decade of"* . . . Wakeman, *Fall of Imperial China,* 126.

Page 133: *"Opium is not a necessity of life"* . . . As quoted in Booth, *Opium,* 111–2.

Page 134: *"It may be asked"* . . . Wright, *Chinese Empire—Historical and Descriptive,* 182.

Page 134: *"The limbs grow thin"* . . . As quoted in Booth, *Opium,* 128.

Page 136: *"It is true, I cannot prevent"* . . . Ibid.

China Pried Open

Page 138: *"Early this morning I sacrificed"* . . . As quoted in Waley, *Opium War Through Chinese Eyes,* 44. British sinologist Arthur Waley's commentary on the Opium War and his translations of Chinese texts in this book were valuable sources of information for this chapter.

Page 139: *His predecessor, Sir George Robinson* . . . The quote in this sentence is from Booth, *Opium*, 125.

Page 140: *"China was being viewed"* . . . Wakeman, *The Fall of Imperial China*, 132.

Page 141: *"Even though the barbarians"* . . . The letter in its entirety is quoted in Teng and Fairbank, *China's Response to the West*, 25.

Page 141: *"The plans for the campaign"* . . . Fairbank, *China Watch*, 14.

Page 142: *"Vessels of the opium fleet"* . . . Ibid.

Page 143: *Furthermore, China was to pay* . . . Ibid.

Page 143: *Jardine collected his opium* . . . The original paper documenting this transaction is preserved in the archives of Jardine, Matheson & Co., an active international corporation with bases in London and Hong Kong.

Page 144: *In* China Watch, *Fairbank defined the opium trade* . . . Fairbank, *China Watch*, 13.

The Tea Spy Who Came from the West

Much of the information for this chapter is from Robert Fortune's own books: *Two Visits to the Tea Countries of China* and *A Residence Among the Chinese*. I owe head librarian Roy Stone at the Los Angeles Public Library for going out of his way to find these books (along with several other rare ones,) for me. Chris Metro of the Los Angeles Public Library was also very helpful, as was Dottie Warren at the Young Research Library of the University of California in Los Angeles.

Page 146: *Tea was such an important item* . . . According to Hobhouse in *Seeds of Change*, 97.

Page 149: *"I suppose I must have been"* . . . Fortune, *Two Visits to the Tea Countries of China*, 2: 8.

Page 151: *"It seems perfectly ridiculous"* . . . and *"And yet, tell the drinkers . . ."* Ibid., 70–1.

The Wilds of Assam

Page 154: *A year later, an Englishman* . . . Ukers, *All About Tea*, 1: 134–35.

Page 155: *"It is with feelings of the highest satisfaction"* . . . As quoted in ibid., 1:139.

Page 156: *At the same time, the military-administrative* . . . According to Siddique, *Evolution of Land Grants*, 7 and on.

Page 156: *One rule required the applicant* . . . These rules, established in 1838, explain how, from the very beginning, the Indian tea industry was fundamentally different from the Chinese tea industry: while the latter was largely made up of small family plantations all across the country, Assam tea was from the very start a product of a large-scale corporate and capital-driven effort controlled from overseas.

Page 157: *Of the two imports—seeds and men* . . . The phrase "the curse of the India tea industry" is from H. H. Mann, "Early History of the Tea Industry in Northeast India," Calcutta, 1918, as quoted in Ukers, *All About Tea*, 1:138.

Page 157: *"This alone ought to point out"* . . . C. A. Bruce, "Report on the Manufacture of Tea, and on the Extent and Produce of the Tea Plantations in Assam," 1839, as quoted in Antrobus, *History of the Assam Company*, 466.

Page 158: *"Unless more labourers can be furnished"* . . . Ibid.

Page 159: *"Shoot away!" was the answer* . . . As reported in Ganguli, *Slavery in British Dominion*, 39.

Page 159: *Historian J. C. Jha, who studied* . . . As reported in Jha, *Aspects of Indentured Inland Emigration*, 145.

Page 159 *"I have seen dead and dying coolies"* . . . As quoted in Siddique, *Evolution of Land Grants*, 152.

Page 160: *By the turn of the century, almost 340,000 acres* . . . Ibid., 109.

Page 160: *In 1900 the north Indian plantations alone* . . . Encyclopedia Britannica 2003, S. V. "British imperial power, 1858–1947,—climax of the Raj, 1858–85—economic policy and development."

Page 160: *"Indeed the far flung Kingdom of India tea"* . . . Ukers, *All About Tea*, 1:133.

Tea Tom and Mr. Taylor

I owe much of the information for this chapter to Denys Forrest and his book *A Hundred Years of Ceylon Tea*, and particularly to Mr. Forrest's *trouvaille*—as he calls it in his preface—of James Taylor's precious correspondence.

Page 162: *In the beginning the results* . . . Ibid., 71 (footnote).

Page 164: *One writer of the time called him* . . . Ibid., 74.

Page 165: *"It is in no small measure due to"* . . . The quote is by R. W. Rayner, *World Crops*, 1960, quoted in Forrest, Ibid., 80.

Page 166: *Soon the general population* . . . Forrest, Ibid., 153.

Tea Clippers: A Race to the End

Page 171: *So when the shippers Howland and Aspinwall* . . . Whipple, *Clipper Ships*, 27.

Page 172: *"We must run a race"* . . . Paine, *Old Merchant Marine*, 160.

Page 174: *Today the* Cutty Sark *is dry-docked* . . . The *Cutty Sark*'s expected life span of 30 years has been extended to almost 140 years. She is a venerable old lady of the seas in dire need of restoration. The *Cutty Sark* Trust welcomes donations at: www.cuttysark.org.uk.

Page 175: *Third, its stockholders* . . . I owe Dr. Huw Bowen, British historian and expert on East India Company affairs, for the figures and explanations about the final years of the Company. Thank you also to the British Library for providing me with copies of the 1873 East India Company Stock Dividend Redemption Act.

Page 175: *"Let Her Majesty appreciate the gift"* . . . As quoted in Wilbur, *East India Company,* 421.

The Enigma of the Camellia

Page 186: *The tea tree, from which so many soaps* . . . I owe this explanation to David MacLaren, curator at the Huntington Botanical Gardens in California.

I Say High Tea, You Say Low Tea

Page 188: *Among the many details* . . . The quote in this sentence is from Ukers, *All About Tea,* 2:401.

Page 189: *The leisure classes of those times* . . . The quote in this sentence is from Drummond and Wilbraham, *Englishman's Food,* 213.

Page 190: *Ukers says that New Zealanders* . . . Ukers, *All About Tea,* 2:419.

Milk in First?

Page 191: *I was recently the guest* . . . Recounted by British writer and historian Cecil Roth, as quoted in Burgess, *Book of Tea,* 156.

Page 193: *Eric Arthur Blair, better known* . . . Quotes in this sentence are from Orwell, *The Collected Letters: Journalism and Essays of George Orwell,* 3:41–3. Orwell is indirectly connected to the story of tea through more than his knowledge of preparation techniques. He was born in the small village of Motihari in Bengal in 1903. His father, Richard Walmesley Blair, was employed there as a sub-agent of the Opium Department of the Indian Civil Service. His job was to supervise the poppy growers and maintain quality control of opium manufacture in a district that produced opium for export to China, where millions of addicts waited for the prized Bengali drug, the best on the market. More than fifty years after the end of the first Opium War, the empire was still heavily relying on opium production to secure income from the colonies, and continued to do so until 1917. Like many Victorian gentlemen of the time, Mr. Blair seems not to have had any moral qualms about his activities, which he considered part of his duties as a civil servant of the British Empire.

Page 193: *"Half the population of Britain"* . . . Maev Kennedy "How to Make a Perfect Cuppa: Put Milk in First," *The Guardian,* 25 June 2003.

Page 194: *"At the beginning of the Dinner"* . . . Johannes Nieuhof, *The Embassy of the Oriental Company of the United Provinces to the Emperor of China* (Amsterdam, 1665), as quoted in Ukers, *All About Tea,* 1:32.

The Accidental Inventors Part 2: Iced Tea

Page 198: *"Tea should be drunk when hot"* . . . Chia Ming, *Yin-shih hsü-chih*, a fourteenth-century Chinese work on dietetics, as quoted in Needham, *Science and Civilisation in China*, 6: 5 564.

Page 198: *Other food historians state* . . . For Lyndon N. Irwin, a professor at Missouri State University, the 1904 St. Louis World's Fair is a topic of special historical interest. His Web site has a reproduction of this newspaper article. Food historian Linda Stradley confirms Prof. Irwin's assumption on her Web site and quotes various iced tea and tea punch recipes from nineteenth-century cookbooks. For more information see www.lyndonirwin.com/1904%20Tea.htm and http://whatscookingamerica.net/History/IcedTeaHistory.htm.

Page 199: *Some commercial iced teas* . . . When it comes to sugar, reading labels carefully is an important and empowering act. Unfortunately, many of the commercial iced teas contain high fructose corn syrup, which is seen as one of the primary causes of the obesity epidemic in the United States.

What Color Is Your Tea?

I am indebted to David Lee Hoffman of Silk Road Teas in California for providing several of the explanations for this chapter and for acquainting me with the surprising variety and richness of Chinese teas. Each one I tasted had a story of its own to tell.

Page 200: *"Tea has countless forms"* . . . Owyoung, trans. of *Ch'a-ching*, by Lu Yü, vol. 1, pt. 3.

Page 204: *However, all* pu-erh *teas are aged* . . . David Hoffman once saw four baskets of aged *pu-erhs* be exchanged for a fifty-thousand-dollar car.

The Mystery of Acronyms

Manik Jayakumar of Qtrade International in California, one of the largest importers of fair trade organic tea in the United States, was very helpful in clarifying the mysteries of acronyms for me.

Page 209: *They represent about 31 percent* . . . Statistics according to the FAO, the Food and Agriculture Organization of the United Nations (e-mail from Kaison Chang).

The Tea Taster

I would like to thank tea taster Toby Fleming for pointing me in the right direction at the very beginning of my research on tea and for helping me make my first contacts in the tea world. Thank you also to the following people for their patient explanations and demonstrations with regards to the subtleties of tea tasting: David Lee Hoffman of Silk Road Teas in California; James Corfield, buyer at Fortnum & Mason, Mike Bunston, blender for Wilson, Smithett & Co.

Ltd., and presently chairman of the International Tea Committee, and Edward Bramah, director of the Bramah Museum of Tea and Coffee, all three in London; Joe Wertheim of Tea Importers in Connecticut; and Elizabeth Knight, author and tea sommelier at the St. Regis Hotel in New York.

Like Water for Tea

David Beeman, chairman of Cirqua Customized Water, Kelly Thompson of the Water Quality Association, and water quality specialists at the Los Angeles Department of Water and Power were all very helpful in clarifying water quality issues for this chapter.

Page 218: *"Of water, the water from the mountains is superior"* . . . Owyoung, trans. of *Ch'a-ching*, by Lu Yü, vol. 3, pt. 5.

Page 219: *The nun poured tea* . . . Tsao, *Dream of the Red Chamber,* 194.

Page 223: *"When bubbles appear like fish eyes"* . . . Owyoung, trans. of *Ch'a-ching*, by Lu Yü, vol. 3, pt. 5.

Tea Buzz

I owe explanations and clarifications for this chapter to: Anthony L. Almada, B.S.c. M.S.c., of IMAGINutrition in California; Julia Peterson, M.S., of the School of Nutrition Science and Policy at Tufts University; Prof. Dr. Ulrich H. Engelhardt of the Institut für Lebensmittelchemie in Germany; Douglas Balentine, Ph.D., of Unilever North America; and Mark A. Kantor, Ph.D., of the Department of Nutrition and Food Science at the University of Maryland.

Page 226: *Caffeine—the chemical term is* . . . In *All About Tea,* 1:553 and on. Ukers collected many quotes on the healthfulness of tea, many of which focus on the benefits of caffeine. Some are reasonable, some outlandish. One of the funniest ones is by a George Lloyd Magruder, a medical doctor and lecturer at Georgetown University in Washington, D.C. The quote appeared in the *New York Herald* in 1905:

> I cannot understand how there can be any discussion upon the effect of tea drinking and the result to the nervous system. In moderation tea helps the average person. A woman spends the day in hunting bargains, and gets home in the evening thoroughly worn out. She is in the condition known as "brain fag," and has resort to a cup of tea. Within a few minutes she feels refreshed and has a characteristic sense of well-being. That is the action of caffeine.

Page 228: *Studies of caffeine levels* . . . Lin, "Factors Affecting"; Khokhar, "Total Phenol"; Lakenbrink, "Flavonoids."

Page 228: *The opposite is true* . . . Santana-Rios, "Potent Antimutagenic Activity."

Page 229: *But, as a whole, tea suggests* . . . The FDA does not have recommended allowances for caffeine, and individual responses to caffeine vary widely. The average daily per capita caffeine consumption worldwide has been estimated at around 80 mg. In the United States the figure is 200 to 250 mg. For adults, the largest source of caffeine is coffee; for children it is soft drinks. Seventy percent of soft drinks contain 20 to 50 mg of caffeine, and the new "energy drinks," popular among dancing-through-the-night youth, have double that. For more information on caffeine, read the Johns Hopkins study at www.caffeinedependence .org/caffeine_dependence.html.

The 22,000 Virtues of Tea

Page 230: *"Tea has the blessing"* . . . As quoted in Plutschow, *Historical Chanoyu*, 42.

Page 231: *"If hot and thirsty"* . . . Owyoung, trans. of *Ch'a-ching*, by Lu Yü, vol. 1, pt. 1.

Page 231: *It is recorded in* Prescriptions from the Pillow . . . Ibid., vol. 2, pt. 7.

Page 231: *To cure small children of anxiety* . . . Ibid., vol. 2, pt. 7.

Page 231: *In another Chinese book* . . . Carpenter, back notes of *Classic of Tea*, by Lu Yü, 155.

Page 233: *According to a paper published* . . . For more information see lpi.oregon state.edu/infocenter/phytochemicals/tea.

Page 233: *A Boston University study.* . . . Widlansky et al., "Effects of Black Tea."

Page 233: *A recent University of Rochester study* . . . The study is based in part on the thesis of twenty-seven-year-old doctoral candidate Christine Palermo: Palermo et al., "Identification of Potential."

Page 234: *"I have found it advantageous"* . . . As quoted in Needham, *Science and Civilisation in China*, vol. 6, sec. 40, p. 563.

Page 234: *Research is ongoing* . . . McKay, et al., "The Role of Tea."

Page 235: *We are a long way from* . . . Martini quoted in Ukers, *All About Tea*, 1:33.

Two Leaves and a Bud

Page 239: *Worldwide tea acreage amounts to* . . . According to FAO Commodities and Trade, "Agricultural Commodities."

Page 239: *Today, the main players in tea* . . . Some facts and figures: India's yearly output is 820 million kg (around 1.8 billion pounds), while China's is 790 million kg, 75 percent of it green. In 2004, Kenya was the world's largest tea exporter (326 million kg), followed by Sri Lanka (290 million kg), then China (279 million kg), and India (183 million kg). Indonesia, Turkey, Vietnam, Japan, Argentina, and Bangladesh are also among the top ten tea producers. Although their individual production figures are much lower, together they export as much as Sri Lanka or Kenya and, as a whole, they represent serious competition for the established producers.

Page 240: *This is not surprising, since China* . . . OECD, "Economic Survey of China."

Page 240: *In 2004 world tea production* . . . FAO, "World Tea Production."

Page 242: *"A long line of women"* . . . David Crole, *Tea: A Textbook of Tea Planting and Manufacture*, as quoted in Leggett, *Tea Leaves*, 23.

Page 243: *Yet, where do they belong?* . . . I am grateful to E. Valentine Daniel, anthropologist and professor at Columbia University, who described this situation incisively to me over the phone but also in *Plantations, Peasants and Proletarians*, 278: "Yet most of those who 'returned' to their 'community' and 'homeland' discovered that they were not 'peasants' but only coolies who had given up their chance of becoming peasants again. They remained what they were: coolies. 'Sucked oranges' was the epithet given to the returned migrants from the Malaysian plantations in the villages of Tamil Nadu."

Page 244: *Aside from historical displacement and social marginalization* . . . For more specific information on tea and the working conditions of tea laborers, see Oxfam, "Tea Market," and ActionAid, "Tea Break."

Page 244: *To make matters worse* . . . In the belief that increasing market demand for tea would be a more successful strategy than limiting production to solve the overproduction problem, FAO launched a worldwide campaign encouraging tea consumption on the basis of its many health benefits. This has had good results, but the oversupply is still an issue. An additional effort is under way to solve the problem by gradually moving away from overproduction of low-quality cheap tea and concentrating instead on manufacturing smaller quantities of higher-grade tea.

Page 246: *Yet producing countries are squeezed out* . . . Some of these transnational companies have recognized the limits of extracting profits from plantations and are even beginning to sell them off. Given the oversupply of tea on the world market, they do not need to secure access to raw materials by owning their plantations anymore and can concentrate their efforts on the more lucrative end of business.

Page 246: *In some extreme cases* . . . A 2003 report on tea plantations in West Bengal describes abhorrent conditions of tea workers, abandoned to their fate, trying to survive by gathering whatever is edible from nearby forests and crushing stones for a few pennies a day. On one tea estate alone, twenty-two deaths by starvation were reported, principally among children under fifteen. Centre for Education and Communication, "Tea Plantations."

A Fair Cup

Thank you to fair trade producer Binod Mohan of Tea Promoters India for receiving me in Kolkata and for finding time in his busy schedule to explain the fair trade principles to me.

Page 249: *Today, the general fair trade movement* . . . Figures here and later are from conversations with Karimah Hudda at the Fairtrade Labelling Organizations International and documents by the Fairtrade Foundation, UK.

Page 250: *When we, as consumers* . . . More specifically, for a tea plantation to be fair trade certified, several conditions must be met. The company must have a democratic structure and transparent administrative practices. It must respect international standards in terms of nondiscrimination, health and safety of the workers, working hours, overtime, and sick or maternity leave. There must be no child or forced labor. Adequate housing, schooling, and health care must be provided as well as freedom of association and collective bargaining. Wages must meet or exceed regional averages and be paid regularly. Producers are also expected to make environmental protection an integral part of plantation management and to respect international standards regarding the use of pesticides and herbicides. If a tea plantation does not pass inspection, it is taken off the FLO roster and loses all the fair trade benefits.

Page 250: *They collect the fair trade premium* . . . This is the second phase of the process. Importers buy their tea from any of the FLO-registered tea plantations. They are required to pay the tea producer a negotiated price, which has to at least cover production costs, plus an additional 1 euro/kg ($1.20/2.2 pounds) for orthodox whole-leaf tea or 0.50 euro/kg ($0.60/2.2 pounds) for CTC tea. This last fee is called the fair trade premium. The importer also pays a fee to a national certification body in the consumer country in order to be a registered fair trade importer and to have the right to put the Fair Trade Certified logo on the product. In the United States, the certification agency is TransFair USA, based in the San Francisco Bay area, and the fee is $0.18 per pound of tea. TransFair USA also supervises the third stage of the process, retail sales. Through a rigorous auditing system of every link in the chain, it checks that the amount of fair trade tea sold around the country corresponds to the actual amount imported and approves every logo usage on packaging, thus ensuring that no one is using the fair trade label improperly. TransFair USA also maintains a list of fair trade retailers, searchable by product, city, or zip code. For more information visit www.transfairusa.org.

Page 250: *The priorities vary according to specific community needs* . . . Some of these examples were given by TransFair USA.

Page 251: *Time magazine deemed the issue* . . . To further confirm the growing publishing interest in fair trade: In 2005, Alex Nicholls, Ph.D., professor of Social Entrepreneurship at the University of Oxford, and Charlotte Opal, Rhodes Scholar and New Products Manager at TransFair USA, published a book entirely dedicated to fair trade: *Fair Trade—Market-Driven Ethical Consumption* (Sage Publications, 2005). The initial quote is lovely: "Let us spread the fragrance of fairness across all aspects of life."

Where the Birds Sing

Page 256: *For all this, Sir Albert is often referred to* . . . Sir Albert Howard's most notable contribution to organic farming is his 1940 book *An Agricultural Testament,* which contains knowledge and wisdom collected over a lifetime of research and observation.

Page 256: *"We in North America are wont to think"* . . . The preface was written by Liberty Hyde Bailey (1858–1954), renowned naturalist and horticulturist, rural sociologist, and dean of the College of Agriculture at Cornell University.

Page 258: *Certain trees, such as the native Indian neem tree* . . . The neem tree is such an important beneficial source that it is known as the "village pharmacy" in India. Recently, it was an object of a biopiracy (illicit appropriation of indigenous biomedical resources by corporations) attempt by a U.S. company trying to patent its antifungicidal properties. But the European Patent Office upheld a decision to permanently revoke the patent, setting a precedent for future cases. This has taken the value of the neem properties out of the hands of profit-driven corporations, restoring it as part of the traditional knowledge system accessible to all. The decision brought to a close a ten-year battle in the world's first legal challenge to a biopiracy patent.

Page 258: *Mulching, manuring, composting* . . . Vermicomposting is the process by which earthworms feed on organic decomposing material and convert it into worm castings, thereby producing a valuable, nutrient-rich soil amendment.

Page 258: *On the most advanced organic tea plantations* . . . The Austrian philosopher and educator Rudolf Steiner introduced the principles of biodynamics in 1924. Today biodynamic agriculture is a worldwide movement. For more information on biodynamics see www.biodynamics.com.

Page 260: *According to IFOAM* . . . IFOAM itself has grown tremendously since its inception in 1972 and now has under its umbrella 750 member organizations in 108 countries, dedicated to furthering the goals of organic principles in a variety of ways. IFOAM also notes that organic standards have been codified in the technical regulations of more than sixty governments.

Singpho Tea

Peggy Carswell deserves many thanks: for kindly and patiently making herself available to my incessant questions for the preparation of this chapter; for helping make my travels to Upper Assam useful and informative; and mostly, for turning my inquiries into Assam tea from mere research into a great human experience while getting to know her grower and farmer friends as well as all the wonderful volunteers of Fertile Ground. For anyone interested in Fertile Ground's work or to make a contribution, please visit http://www.civaid.org/fertileground/fertileground .htm or contact Fertile Ground, P.O. Box 179, Merville, B.C. V0R 2M0, Canada.

Rajesh Gudung (Singpho) and Pabitra Ningda also generously took time away from their work to answer my questions. Pabitra waited up for my late-night calls. Rajesh drove his motorcycle in the rain for twenty-five miles of very bumpy road to the Linkcentre in Margherita to answer my e-mails. I am deeply thankful for that. In Assam, Rajesh, the Ningda family, and Manjella showed me their plantations, and at Rajesh's house I was treated to a most unusual meal entirely prepared with jungle foods. Everywhere I went, I was offered *phalap*, and the sweet aftertaste of it remains in my memory along with the graciousness of Singpho hospitality.

I am indebted to Saunam Bhattacharjee of Assam Tea Company and the whole Bhattacharjee family for making sure that my travels in Assam were safe and for letting me visit their conventional and biodynamic tea gardens, Satrupa and Rani. Thank you also to Sudhir Prakash, chairman of the Tocklai Tea Research Association (TRA) in Jorhat, for facilitating my visit at TRA and setting up my tour of his tea estate, Khongea, in Upper Assam.

Page 264: *Amid such pervasive strife* . . . In India, the main Singpho villages—Dibang, Ketetong, Pangna, Ulup, Enthem, Mungbhon, Pangsun, Hasak, Katha, Bisa, Namo, and Kumsai—are located in the extreme northeastern part of Assam. Yet, ethnic Singpho predate modern international borders by many centuries. Although in Assam the Singpho population has dwindled to less than 15,000 from 50,000 only fifty years ago, the Singpho have a more substantial presence in Myanmar (around 300,000 to 400,000), where they are called Kachin, and in China (around 200,000), where they are known as Jing-po or Jingphaw.

Tea Meditation with Friends
Page 273: *"What is happening in the present"* . . . Thich Nhat Hanh, *Anger*, 45.
Page 273: *You can organize a tea meditation* . . . Ibid., 43–44.

Bibliography

Books

Allain, Yves-Marie. *Voyages et survie des plantes au temps de la voile*. Marly-le-Roi, France: Editions Champflour, 2000.

Antrobus, H. A. *A History of the Assam Company, 1839–1953*. Edinburgh: T. and A. Constable Ltd., 1957.

Audsley, George Ashdown, and James L. Bowes. *Keramic Art of Japan*. London: H. Sotheran & Co., 1881.

Atterbury, Paul, ed. *The History of Porcelain*. New York: Morrow, 1982.

Barnhart, Richard M., et al. *Three Thousand Years of Chinese Painting*. New Haven and London: Yale University Press, 1997.

Bibliothèque de l'Image and Mariage Frères. *Le voyage du thé—Album chinois du XVIIIe siècle*. Paris: Bibliothèque de l'Image, 2002.

Blofeld, John. *The Chinese Art of Tea*. Boston: Shambhala, 1997.

Blussé, Leonard, Willem Remmelink, and Ivo Smits, eds. *Bridging the Divide, 400 Years The Netherlands—Japan*. The Netherlands: Hotei Publishing, 2000.

Booth, Martin. *Opium, a History*. London: Simon & Schuster Ltd., 1997.

Burgess, Anthony, et al. *The Book of Tea*. Paris: Flammarion, 1992.

Campbell, George F. *China Tea Clippers*. New York: David McKay Company, 1974.

Carpenter, Francis Ross. *The Classic of Tea: Origins & Rituals*, by Lu Yü. Boston: Little, Brown & Co., 1974.

Castile, Rand. *The Way of Tea*. New York & Tokyo: Weatherhill, 1971.

Chaudhuri, K. N. *The Trading World of Asia and the English East India Company*. Cambridge: Cambridge University Press, 1978.

Cheng, François, ed. *In Love with the Way—Chinese Poems of the T'ang Dynasty*. Boston & London: Shambhala, 2002.

Cleary, Thomas, ed. and trans. *The Spirit of Tao*. Boston and London: Shambhala, 1993.

———, ed. and trans. *Vitality Energy Spirit, A Taoist Sourcebook*. Boston and London: Shambhala Dragon Editions, 1991.

Cobbett, William. *Cottage Economy*. London: Anne Cobbett, 137 Strand, 1838.

Collis, Maurice. *Foreign Mud*. New York: Alfred A. Knopf, 1947.

Colby, Charles W. *Selections from the Sources of English History, Being a Supplement to Text-books of English History—B.C. 55—A.D. 1832*. New York: Longmans, Green and Co., 1899.

Commager, Henry Steele, and Richard B. Morris. *The Spirit of 'Seventy-Six—The Story of the American Revolution as Told by Participants*. New York: Harper & Row, 1958.

Crole, David. *Tea: A Textbook of Manufacture and Planning*. London: Crosby, Lockwood and Sons, 1897.

Crossman, Carl L. *The Decorative Arts of the China Trade*. Woodbridge, Suffolk, UK: Antique Collectors' Club, 1991.

Daniel, E. Valentine, Henry Bernstein, and Tom Brass, eds. *Peasants and Proletarians in Colonial Asia*. London: Frank Cass & Co., 1992.

Deerr, Noel. *The History of Sugar*. 2 vols. London: Chapman and Hall, 1949.

Dickens, Charles. *The Pickwick Papers*, 1836. Reprint, New York: Bantam Books, 1983.

———. *Sketches by Boz*, 1833–6. Reprint, New York: Oxford University Press, 1987.

Drake, Francis S. *Tea Leaves: Being a Collection of Letters and Documents Relating to the Shipment of Tea to the American Colonies in the Year 1773, by the East India Tea Company*, 1884. Reprint, Detroit: Singing Tree Press, 1970.

Drummond, J. C., and Anne Wilbraham. *The Englishman's Food—A History of Five Centuries of English Diet*. London: Readers Union-Jonathan Cape, 1959.

Ellis, Aytoun. *The Penny Universities: A History of the Coffee-Houses*. London: Secker & Warburg, 1956.

Emmerson, Robin. *British Teapots and Tea Drinking 1700–1850.* London: HMSO, 1992.

Fairbank, John King. *China Watch.* Cambridge: Harvard University Press, 1987.

Fitzgerald, C. P. *China: A Short Cultural History.* 1935. Reprint, New York: Praeger Publishers, 1972.

Forrest, Denys. *A Hundred Years of Ceylon Tea—1867–1967.* London: Chatto & Windus, 1967.

———. *Tea for the British—The Social and Economic History of a Famous Trade.* London: Chatto & Windus, 1973.

Fortune, Robert. *A Residence Among the Chinese: Inland, on the Coast, and at Sea. Being a Narrative of Scenes and Adventures During a Third Visit to China from 1853 to 1856.* London: John Murray, 1857.

———. *Two Visits to the Tea Countries of China.* 2 vols. London: John Murray, 1853.

Ganguli, Dwarkanath. *Slavery in British Dominion.* First published as a series of articles in *The Bengalee* in 1886. Reprint, Calcutta: Jijnasa, 1972.

Gardella, Robert. *Harvesting Mountains: Fujian and the China Tea Trade, 1757–1937.* Berkeley: University of California Press, 1994.

Gokhale, Nitin A. *The Hot Brew—The Assam Tea Industry's Most Turbulent Decade (1987–1977).* Guwahati-Delhi: Spectrum Publications, 1998.

Goodrich, L. Carrington (preface), and Nigel Cameron (commentary). *The Face of China As Seen by Photographers & Travelers, 1860–1912.* New York: Aperture, 1978.

Harrison, Brian. *Drink and the Victorians—The Temperance Question in England 1815–1872.* Pittsburgh: University of Pittsburgh Press, 1971.

Hinton, David, trans. *Mountain Home—The Wilderness Poetry of Ancient China.* Washington, D.C. and New York: Counterpoint, 2002.

Hirota, Dennis. *Wind in the Pines—Classic Writings of the Way of Tea as a Buddhist Path.* Fremont, Calif.: Asian Humanities Press, 1995.

Hobhouse, Henry. *Seeds of Change: Six Plants That Transformed Mankind.* London: Macmillan, 1999.

Hodgson, Barbara. *In the Arms of Morpheus—The Tragic History of Laudanum, Morphine, and Patent Medicines.* Buffalo, N.Y.: Firefly Books, 2001.

Hosking, Richard. *At the Japanese Table (Images of Asia).* New York: Oxford University Press, 2000.

Huc, Evariste Régis. *Travels in Tartary, Thibet, and China, 1844–1846.* London: Harper & Brothers, 1928.

Hunter, William C. *The 'Fan Kwae' at Canton Before Treaty Days 1825–1844.* London: Kegan, Paul, Trench & Co., 1882.

Huxley, Gervas. *Talking of Tea.* Ivyland, Penna.: John Wagner & Sons, 1956.

Irving, Washington. *The Legend of Sleepy Hollow,* 1820. Reprint, New York: Random House Derrydale, 1998.

Jha, Jagdish Chandra. *Aspects of Indentured Inland Emigration to North-East India 1859–1918.* New Delhi: Indus Publishing Company, 1996.

Kämpfer, Engelbert *Geschichte und Beschreibung von Japan,* 1712. Reprint, Stuttgart: Brockhaus, 1964.

Keay, John. *The Honourable Company—A History of the English East India Company.* New York: Macmillan, 1994.

Keswick, Maggie, ed. *The Thistle and the Jade: A Celebration of 150 Years of Jardine, Matheson & Co.* London: Octopus Books, 1982.

King, Franklin Hiram. *Farmers of Forty Centuries—Permanent Agriculture in China, Korea, and Japan,* 1911. Reprint, Emmaus, Penn.: Rodale Press: 1973.

Kircher, Athanasius S. J. *China Illustrata with Sacred and Secular Monument, Various Spectacles of Nature and Art and Other Memorabilia.* Translated from Latin by Charles van Tuyl 1667. Reprint, Bloomington: Indiana University–Research Institute for Inner Asian Studies, 1987.

Lai, T. C. *At the Chinese Table (Images of Asia).* New York: Oxford University Press, 1984.

Lawson, Philip, *A Taste for Empire and Glory—Studies in British Overseas Expansion, 1660–1800.* Aldershot, Hampshire, UK: Variorum, 1997.

Leggett, Francis *Tea Leaves,* 1900. Reprint, New York: Francis H. Leggett & Co., 2004.

Levathes, Louise. *When China Ruled the Seas: The Treasure Fleet of the Dragon Throne, 1405–33.* New York: Simon & Schuster, 1994.

Lillywhite, Bryant. *London Coffee Houses.* London: George Allen and Unwin, 1963.

Macaulay, Thomas Babington. *England in 1685, Being Chapter III of the History of England.* Boston, Mass.: The Athenaeum Press, Ginn and Company, 1905.

Mackenzie, Donald Alexander. *China and Japan (Myths and Legends).* 1923. Reprint, New York: Avenel Books, 1986.

McClure Mudge, Jean. *Chinese Export Porcelain in North America.* New York: Clarkson Potter, 1986.

McCoy, Alfred W. *The Politics of Heroin.* Brooklyn: Laurence Hill Books, 1991.

Métailié, Georges. *Manger en Chine.* Vevey, Switzerland: Alimentarium, 1997.

Miller, Russell. *The East Indiamen.* Alexandria, Va.: Time-Life Books, 1980.

Mintz, Sidney W. *Sweetness and Power: The Place of Sugar in Modern History.* New York: Penguin Books, 1985.

Mitscher, Lester A., and Victoria Dolby. *The Green Tea Book.* Garden City Park, N.Y.: Avery Publishing Group, 1998.

Mosher, Stuart. *The Story of Money, as Told By the Knox Collection*. Buffalo, N.Y.: Buffalo Society of Natural Sciences, 1936.

Needham, Joseph. *Science and Civilisation in China*. Cambridge: Cambridge University Press, 1954.

————. *Science in Traditional China: A Comparative Perspective*. Taipei, Taiwan: Linking Publishing Co., 1982.

Nicholls, Alex, and Charlotte Opal. *Fair Trade—Market-Driven Ethical Consumption*. London: Sage Publications, 2005.

Okakura, Kakuzo. *The Book of Tea*. 1906. Reprint, New York: Dover Publications, 1964.

Orwell, George. *The Collected Essays, Journalism and Letters of George Orwell*. 4 vols. New York: Harcourt Brace, 1968.

Owyoung, Steven D. *A History of the Art of Chinese Tea and the Classic of Tea by Lu Yü (733–804 C.E.)*. Forthcoming.

Paine, Ralph D. *The Old Merchant Marine*. New Haven, Conn.: Yale University Press, 1921.

Pepys, Samuel. *The Diary of Samuel Pepys*. New York: Modern Library, 2001.

Pine, Red, trans. *The Zen Teachings of Bodhidharma*. San Francisco: North Point Press, 1989.

Plutschow, Herbert E. *Historical Chanoyu*, Tokyo: Japan Times, 1986.

Ramusio, Giovanni Battista. *Navigazioni et viaggi: Venice 1563–1606*, 1606. Reprint, Amsterdam: Theatrum Orbis Terrarum, 1967–70.

Repplier, Agnes. *To Think of Tea!* New York: Houghton Mifflin, 1932.

Sansom, G. B. *Japan: A Short Cultural History*. 1931. Reprint, New York: Appleton Century Crofts, 1943.

Schurmann, Franz and Orville Schell, *Imperial China: The Decline of the Last Dynasty and the Origins of Modern China, the 18th and 19th centuries (The China Reader)*. New York: Random House, 1967.

Scott, J.M. *The Great Tea Venture*. New York: E. P. Dutton & Co., 1965.

Sen, Soshitsu XV. *Tea Life, Tea Mind*, 1979. Reprint, New York: Weatherhill, 1997.

Seo, Audrey Yoshiko, with Stephen Addiss. *The Art of Twentieth Century Zen*. Boston & London: Shambhala, 2000.

Shalleck, Jamie. *Tea*. New York: Subsistence Press/Viking Press, 1971.

Shelden, Michael. *Orwell: The Authorized Biography*. New York: HarperCollins Publishers, 1991.

Shore, Henry N. *Smuggling Days and Smuggling Ways*. London: Philip Alan & Co., 1892.

Siddique, Muhammed Abu B. *Evolution of Land Grants and Labour Policy of Government—The Growth of the Tea Industry in Assam 1834–1940*. New Delhi: South Asian Publishers, 1990.

Siew, Lim Kean. *The Beauty of Chinese Yixing Teapots and the Finer Art of Tea Drinking*. Singapore: Times Editions, 2001.

Smith, Bradley, and Wan-go Weng. *China—A History in Art*. New York: Doubleday Windfall, n.d.

Smith, Woodruff D. *Consumption and the Making of Respectability, 1600–1800*. New York and London: Routledge, 2002.

Spence, Jonathan D., and Annping Chin. *The Chinese Century: A Photographic History of the Last Hundred Years*. New York: Random House, 1996.

————. *The Search for Modern China*. New York: W. W. Norton & Co., 1990.

Spongberg, Stephen A. *A Reunion of Trees: The Discovery of Exotic Plants and Their Introduction into North American and European Landscapes*. Cambridge: Harvard University Press, 1990.

Stevens, Keith. *Chinese Mythological Gods (Images of Asia)*. New York: Oxford University Press, 2001.

Suzuki, Daisetz T. *Essays in Zen Buddhism*. 1927. Reprint, New York: Grove Press, 1961.

————. *Zen and Japanese Culture*. Bollingen Series. Princeton, N.J.: Princeton University Press, 1970.

Temple, Robert. *The Genius of China—3,000 Years of Science, Discovery, and Invention*. New York: Simon and Schuster, 1986.

Teng Ssu-yü, and John K. Fairbank. *China's Response to the West*. Cambridge: Harvard University Press, 1954.

Thich Nhat Hanh. *Anger*. New York: Riverhead Books, 2001.

Thomson, John. *China and Its People in Early Photographs*. 1873. Reprint, New York: Dover Publications, 1982.

Tokunaga, Mutsuko. *New Tastes in Green Tea*. Tokyo: Kodansha International, 2004.

Trocki, Carl A. *Opium, Empire and the Global Political Economy—A Study of the Asian Opium Trade 1750–1950*. London and New York: Routledge, 1999.

Tsao Hsüeh-chin. *Dream of the Red Chamber*. (trans. by Chi-chen Wang), New York: Doubleday, 1989.

Twining, Stephen H. *The House of Twining 1706–1956*. London: Twining & Co., 1956.

Ukers, William H. *All About Tea*. 2 vols. New York: Tea and Coffee Trade Journal Co., 1935. Reprint, Hyperion Press, 1999.

Valfré, Patrice. *Yixing. Des théières pour l'Europe*. Poligny, France: Éditions Exotic Line, 1999.

Varley, Paul, and Kumakura Isao, eds. *Tea in Japan—Essays on the History of Chanoyu*. Honolulu: University of Hawaii Press, 1989.

Wakeman, Frederic Jr. *The Fall of Imperial China*. New York: The Free Press/Macmillan, 1975.

————. *Strangers at the Gate—Social Disorder in South China 1839–1861*. Berkeley: University of California Press, 1966.

Waley, Arthur, trans. *Chinese Poems*. 1946. Reprint, Minneola, N.Y.: Dover Publications, 2000.

————. *The Opium War Through Chinese Eyes*. Stanford, Calif.: Stanford University Press, 1958.

Warner, Jessica. *Craze: Gin and Debauchery in an Age of Reason*. New York: Four Walls Eight Windows, 2002.

Weinberger, Eliot, ed. *The New Directions Anthology of Classical Chinese Poetry*. New York: New Directions, 2003.

Werner, Edward and Theodore Chalmers. *A Dictionary of Chinese Mythology*, 1932. Reprint, New York: Julian Press, 1961.

————. *Myths and Legends of China*. 1922. Reprint, New York: Arno Press, 1976.

Whipple, A.B.C. *The Clipper Ships*. Alexandria, Va.: Time-Life Books, 1980.

Whittle, Tyler. *The Plant Hunters*. New York: PAJ Publications, 1970.

Wilbur, Marguerite Eyer. *The East India Company and the British Empire in the Far East*. New York: Richard R. Smith, 1945.

Williams, Samuel Wells. *The Middle Kingdom: A Survey of the Geography, Government, Education, Social Life, Arts, Religion of the Chinese Empire and its Inhabitants*. New York: John Wiley, 1859.

Wood, Frances. *No Dogs and Not Many Chinese, Treaty Port Life in China 1843–1943*. London: John Murray, 1998.

Wright, George Newenham. *The Chinese Empire—Historical and Descriptive*. London and New York: London Printing and Publishing Company, 1843.

Articles and Papers

ActionAid. "Tea Break: A Crisis Brewing in India." ActionAid, 2004. www.actionaid.org

Centre for Education and Communication. "Tea Plantations of West Bengal in Crisis." Centre for Education and Communication, New Delhi, 2003. www.cec-india.org

FAO Commodities and Trade Division. "Agricultural Commodities—Profiles and Relevant WTO Negotiating Issues." Food and Agriculture Organization of the United Nations (FAO), 2002. www.fao.org

Food and Agriculture Organization of the United Nations (FAO). "World Tea Production Reaches New Highs." FAO Newsroom. Written 14 July 2005. www.fao.org/newsroom/en/news/2005/105404/.

Khokhar, S., et al. "Total Phenol, Catechin, and Caffeine Contents of Teas Commonly Consumed in the United Kingdom." *Journal of Agricultural and Food Chemistry* 50 (2002): 565–70.

Lakenbrink, Christiane, et al. "Flavonoids and Other Polyphenols in Consumer Brews of Tea and Other Caffeinated Beverages." *Journal of Agricultural and Food Chemistry* 48 (2000): 2848–52.

McKay, Diane L., et al. "The Role of Tea in Human Health: An Update." *Journal of the American College of Nutrition* 21, no. 1 (2002): 1–13.

Lin Yung-sheng, et al. "Factors Affecting the Levels of Tea Polyphenols and Caffeine in Tea Leaves." *Journal of Agricultural and Food Chemistry* 51 (2003): 1864–73.

Organisation for Economic Cooperation and Development (OECD). "Economic Survey of China." Paris, 2005.

Owyoung, Steven D. "The Connoisseurship of Tea: A Translation and Commentary on the 'P'in-ch'a' Section of the Record of Superlative Things by Wen Chen-heng (1585–1645)." *Kaikodo Journal* Spring (2000): 27 25–50.

Oxfam. "The Tea Market: A Background Study." Oxfam, 2002. www.marketradefair.com

Palermo, C. M., et al. "Identification of Potential Aryl Hydrocarbon Receptor Antagonists in Green Tea." *Chemical Research in Toxicology* 16, no. 7 (2003): 865–72.

Roth, Rodris. "Tea Drinking in 18th-Century America: Its Etiquette and Equipage." Contributions from the Museum of History and Technology, Paper 14, Smithsonian Institution, Washington, D.C., 1961.

Santana-Rios, Gilberto, et al. "Potent Antimutagenic Activity of White Tea in Comparison with Green Tea in the Salmonella Assay." *Mutation Research* 495 (2001): 61–74.

Twining, Richard. "Observations on the Tea and Window Act, and on the Tea Trade." London, 1784.

Widlansky, M. E., et al. "Effects of Black Tea Consumption on Plasma Catechins and Markers of Oxidative Stress and Inflammation in Patients with Coronary Artery Disease." *Free Radical Biology and Medicine* 38, no. 4 (2005): 499–506.

Museum Publications

The Copeland Collection—Chinese and Japanese Ceramic Figures. The Peabody Museum of Salem, Salem, Mass., 1991.

Faulkner, Rupert, ed., *Tea: East and West.* Victoria and Albert Museum Publications, London, 2003.

Holland, Japan & De Liefde (Holland, Japan, and 'The Love')—The Netherlands and Japan: Four Hundred Years. Rijksmuseum voor Volkenkunde (National Museum of Ethnology), Leiden, The Netherlands, 2000.

Huang Shijian, and William Sargent, eds. *Customs and Conditions of Chinese City Streets in 19th Century—360 Professions in China.* Shanghai Classics Publishing House, China and Peabody Essex Museum, Salem, Mass., 1999.

Jackson, Anna, and Amin Jaffer, eds. *Encounters: The Meeting of Asia and Europe 1500–1800.* Victoria and Albert Museum Publications, London, 2004.

Surimono—Poetry and Image in Japanese Prints Hotei Publishing, Leiden and Rijiksmuseum, Amsterdam, 2000.

Views of the Pearl River Delta: Macau, Canton and Hong Kong. Urban Council of Hong Kong, Peabody Essex Museum, Hong Kong Museum of Art, 1996.

Worlds Revealed: The Dawn of Japanese and American Exchange. Peabody Essex Museum and Edo-Tokyo Museum, 1999.

Index

Index